WITHDRAWN
UTSA LIBRARIES

RENEWALS 458-4574

NEGOTIATING DEMANDS:
THE POLITICS OF SKID ROW POLICING IN EDINBURGH, SAN FRANCISCO, AND VANCOUVER

The relationship between policing and the governance of society is an important and complex one, especially as it relates to destitute areas. Through a comparative analysis of policing in skid row districts in three cities – Edinburgh, San Francisco, and Vancouver – *Negotiating Demands* offers an inside look at the influence of local political, moral, and economic issues on police practices within marginalized communities.

Through an analysis of various theoretical approaches and ethnographic field data, Laura Huey unveils a portrait of skid row policing as a political process. Police are regularly called upon to negotiate often-conflicting sets of demands, especially within the context of disadvantaged or troubled neighbourhoods. Examining a broad spectrum of police procedures and community responses, Huey offers a reconceptualization of the police as political actors who 'negotiate demands' of different constituencies. How the police meet these demands – through incident- and context-specific uses of law enforcement, peacekeeping, social work, and knowledge work – are shown to be a product of the civic environment in which they operate and of the 'moral-economic' forces that shape public discourse.

Negotiating Demands is an original and thought-provoking study that not only advances our knowledge of police organization and decision-making strategies but also refines our understanding of how processes of social inclusion and exclusion occur in different liberal regimes and how they can be addressed.

LAURA HUEY is an assistant professor in the Department of Sociology at Concordia University.

D0619764

WITHDRAWN
UTSA LIBRARIES

LAURA HUEY

Negotiating Demands

The Politics of Skid Row Policing in Edinburgh, San Francisco, and Vancouver

UNIVERSITY OF TORONTO PRESS
Toronto Buffalo London

Library
University of Texas
at San Antonio

© University of Toronto Press Incorporated 2007
Toronto Buffalo London
Printed in Canada

ISBN 978-0-8020-9290-8 (cloth)
ISBN 978-0-8020-9482-7 (paper)

∞

Printed on acid-free paper

Library and Archives Canada Cataloguing in Publication

Huey, Laura
    Negotiating demands : the politics of skid row policing in Edinburgh,
San Francisco and Vancouver / Laura Huey.

    Includes bibliographical references and index.
    ISBN 978-0-8020-9290-8 (bound)
    ISBN 978-0-8020-9482-7 (pbk.)

    1. Law enforcement – Political aspects – Cross-cultural studies.
    2. Police-community relations – Cross-cultural studies.   3. Skid
    row – Cross-cultural studies.   4. Police – Cross-cultural studies.
    5. Marginality, Social – Cross-Cultural studies.   I. Title.

    HV7936.P8H83 2007   363.2'3   C2006-906617-5

University of Toronto Press acknowledges the financial assistance to
its publishing program of the Canada Council for the Arts and the
Ontario Arts Council.

University of Toronto Press acknowledges the financial support for
its publishing activities of the Government of Canada through the
Book Publishing Industry Development Program (BPIDP).

Library
University of Texas
at San Antonio

Contents

Acknowledgments

This project would not have been possible without a lot of help and support. First, I would like to thank Richard Ericson, who supported this project from the beginning and who has been a kind and thoughtful mentor over the past six years. Thomas Kemple helped me work through my frustrations with this project and provided good humour and wise counsel. Simon Verdun-Jones has always been a source of support, and his many kindnesses throughout the years have always been greatly appreciated. Aaron Doyle generously served as an unofficial mentor. Kelsi Pradine served as a research assistant, spending long hours organizing my newspaper archives. I would also like to thank Mark and Debra Pradine for years of love and support. And finally, love and thanks to my husband Sandy McPherson.

Tables

Illustrations

NEGOTIATING DEMANDS

Introduction: Shooting Up on Adam Smith's Grave

The Canongate Kirk in Edinburgh is a beautiful old church: a classical Georgian design of grey stone, columns, and lovely red doors, nestled behind a paved stone entrance and majestic elms. The Kirk keeps celebrated company, as it sits between Edinburgh Castle at one end of the city's celebrated Royal Mile and the famous Holyrood Palace, once home to the rather unfortunate Mary, Queen of Scots. Surrounding this beautiful grey church is its Kirkyard, the present home of many of the city's former illustrious citizens. Within family crypts and behind upright stones, most weathered over centuries and some carved with skulls and other ghoulish reminders of their occupants' fate and the visitor's future, lie city officials, famous poets, war heroes, and other celebrated residents. One of these graves contains no less a figure of modern history than Adam Smith, the famed economist and father of classical liberal theory.

It is Smith who gave us the powerful metaphor of the 'invisible hand' silently guiding the workings of economies and thus of societies. It is to Smith and his belief in the positive power of unfettered capital that many present-day economists and political leaders have turned, launching a sea change in the structure of modern economics within the past thirty-odd years under the banner of neo-liberalism. Critics charge that these changes have resulted in massive accumulations of capital by some, economic instability and uncertainty for more, and loss of realized or potential hopes for far too many others. The results of this transformation have been nothing less than the creation of a devastating and perhaps un-crossable chasm between the haves and the have-nots. Further, it is Smith (1986 [1776]: 338) who argued that a primary purpose of government ought to be the preservation of this inequality – to 'maintain the rich in possession of their wealth against the violence and rapacity of the poor' – on the grounds that the economy provides for those who are willing to work. Everyone else is simply social detritus: the idle, the drunk, the undisciplined, the vagrant, and the criminal. Thus, it is with some irony that I note that Smith's current residence is also now a home of sorts to some of the city's indigent. At night the Kirkyard becomes a refuge and shooting gallery for addicts within the local street population, who spill over from the nearby skids: the Cowgate and Grassmarket. Their presence is clearly marked by orange needle caps, the tops of syringes used for injecting heroin, which litter the graves of Smith and other founding fathers.

That such a beautiful and historic spot should house, even temporarily, members of the city's addict population might seem odd to some observers. Most cities across Europe, Canada, and the United States, to varying degrees, seek to contain their 'problem populations' within highly segregated urban neighbourhoods, set apart from such beautiful public spaces and the people who utilize them. Attempts by the urban poor to move freely outside of their zones of containment are often met with harsh resistance from a larger society, which frequently prefers that 'social junk' (Spitzer 1975) remain out of sight. Cities now work to ensure that 'non-productive' elements remain socially and physically isolated through, among other tactics, the use of regressive housing policies, 'quality of life' bylaws, the concentration of poverty-related services, and aggressive policing – all practices that Smith would likely have approved of.

Such segregated neighbourhoods are heavily imbued with moral associations. The term ghetto, which refers to a racially and ethnically based segregated space, calls to mind stereotypical depictions of drug-dealing black gangsters, indiscriminately wielding weapons as they seduce kids into violence and addiction. Interestingly, images of the ghetto invoke the perception that the site is inherently criminogenic in that it is embedded within an urban subculture that serves to reproduce criminality. Skid row districts, another form of urban containment that houses the poor, similarly invoke a host of morally freighted images: from bloated old alcoholics whiling away the ends of their days in seedy barrooms, to scrawny addicts with needles hanging out of their arms, and to diseased and wasted prostitutes standing forlornly in dingy alleyways. However, unlike the ghetto, which is said to create its miscreants, skid row is a place where the morally lax who are produced elsewhere in society end up. The skids are 'the bottom of a downward path of social mobility' (Miller 1982: 2).

I use the term skid row to invoke a particular unique reality. Skid rows have historically been home to an overwhelmingly white male population comprising what Marx might term a surplus labour pool. Today, they are either predominantly white neighbourhoods or, as a consequence of immigration, ethnically diverse, and there are few if any jobs available for the people here. But what the skid rows of yesterday and today *do* share is that each stands as a living exemplar of decay – both moral and physical. Skid row is a permanent community that holds both transient and long-term residents, many, if not most, of whom are afflicted by problems that either cause or are caused by persistent poverty: addiction, mental illness, victimization through violence, physical or sexual exploitation, rampant disease, physical waste from lack of nutrition and/or medical and self-care, impermanent shelter and/or substandard housing, lack of economic opportunities, a decrepit physical environment, and, for many, a concomitant sense of hopelessness and despair. As a space, it embodies ultimate forms of social, political, economic, moral, and physical exclusion.

For sociologists and other social scientists, skid row has long been a place of immense interest because it provides a living laboratory for the study of social exclusion. Its social location – at the very margins of society – tells us not only about society's ideals with respect to culturally defined goals and norms but also about how those within the 'mainstream of society' view and act towards those who do not measure up to cultural standards. For this reason, in attempting to understand some of the strands of exclusivity that run within contemporary society, I looked to skid row and the treatment of its denizens as an appropriate starting point.

In order for excluded urban spaces such as skid row districts to exist, they have to be governed through policies and practices carried out by agents empowered to use exceptional powers and resources: local knowledge, physical force, surveillance, inter-institutional knowledge, resource networks, and so on. The public police as an institution is unique in both holding exceptional powers and, as part of a larger constellation of private and public regulatory institutions, having access to a wide range of resources. For these reasons the public police have long been viewed as a principal agency of exclusion.

It is too simple, however, to see skid row only in terms of exclusion and the police role as supportive of exclusion in these sites. It has also been the case, both historically and in the present era, that demands have been made of the police that fall outside the scope of simple area containment and/or law enforcement. These demands frequently arise from public expectations concerning the role of the police to provide assistance to those in need. Thus, the police often serve as a frontline response for situations requiring emergency shelter, detoxification, hospitalization, and so on. Also arising from these expectations are sets of demands placed upon the police by groups within and outside of skid rows to abandon enforcement of containment-oriented policies. In some cities, groups go further and call for police to actively participate in movements on the row that hold the possibility of increased inclusivity.

In the pages that follow I examine the political economy of contemporary policing by focusing on how demands ranging from total exclusion to total inclusion shape the nature of policing in skid row districts and how these demands further translate into policing styles and strategies. To this end, this work addresses one specific question: to what extent do structural conditions (i.e., political, social, and economic supports or constraints) lead to the willingness of public police to initiate or engage in inclusionary or exclusionary policing practices within skid row communities?

The observations I offer in the pages that follow centre on three claims. First, contrary to recent work in the exclusivity literature that suggests that Western societies are becoming uniformly more exclusionary as a consequence of a supposed rise in the American form of neo-liberalism (Young 1999), I argue that exclusion and inclusion are twin strategies for reproducing group solidarities that operate in culturally specific ways. We can find aspects of both inclusion and exclusion across a variety of contemporary Western societies – ranging from neo-liberal to Keynesian – and, more importantly, we can find these constants being played out in policies, programs, and practices of those who operate within the most excluded of sites: skid row districts. It is through this analysis that we come to see the influence of Adam Smith and the ways in which his views on economics, politics, and, most importantly, morality have come to shape contemporary economic forms, whether in support of aspects of his ideas (U.S. neo-liberalism and Ordoliberalism) or in opposition (Keynesian welfare economics).

Second, the political economy of crime shapes demands upon the policing institution. These demands range from increased exclusion to increased inclusion of marginalized groups, including skid row inhabitants. Demands are placed upon the institution as a whole and translate into administrative policies and frontline practices. One of the functions of the police, as a political institution, is to mediate these demands. Thus, we come to a new conception of the policing function on skid row:

the police as 'demand negotiators.' This conceptualization of the police offers a unique advantage over other models of policing in that it draws careful attention to the political economy of policing and the ways in which local policing policies and practices are shaped in response to public demands.

Third, contrary to Bittner's (1967) characterization of the police on skid row as unreflexive, the police as political actors are reflexive about both the nature of the roles they assume and the demands that they face from different segments of the public, demands that are often compet- ing and contradictory, ranging across a continuum of exclusivity– inclusivity. When police officers talk about their work on skid row and how they negotiate demands, aside from recognizing the political nature of their work, they also use terms that fall within and across multiple policing frameworks: law enforcement, peacekeeping, social work, and knowledge work. The police are revealed, at all levels of the institution, as political actors who broker the demands of various constituencies within the context of political economies.

This study is supported by research from a comparative analysis of policing within three skid row districts. Sites in Vancouver (the Down- town Eastside), San Francisco (the Tenderloin) and Edinburgh (Cowgate/ Grassmarket) were selected because of key similarities and differences with respect to policing styles and to the larger political landscape within which each institution is situated. These similarities and differences are fleshed out in the chapters that follow through analysis of my own empirical work in relation to each city's policing programs and practices – observations, interview data – as well as through analysis of other data sources collected for the purpose of siting each institution within a *civic* political framework. I emphasize the word civic specifically: although there is discussion within the pages that follow of larger political and economic shifts that have variously influenced each city's politics and in turn their respective police forces, I do not draw direct links between the macro-level theories discussed and the everyday world of frontline polic- ing. Rather, my focus is the ways in which civic-level politics (both from within and outside the institutions of governance) influence and shape the police institution and its response to service-related demands. To the extent that civic politics are forged within larger political discourses, it is relevant to address some of those discourses.

In the first chapter I discuss the theoretical context of this work through an exploration of the links between exclusion and inclusion, the moral economies of neo-liberal and welfarist systems, and the policing of skid row. In the second chapter I discuss the research methods employed, as well as some of the difficulties encountered in performing research and analysis of one of the most marginalized forms of community.

Chapters 2 through 7 function as paired chapters, with the first chapter in each pair serving as an introduction to the space studied and the chapter immediately following providing detailed analysis of the policing of that site. For example, the second chapter describes Edinburgh's Cowgate and Grassmarket, situating this site historically, socially, and politically. Chapter 3 describes the policing of Edinburgh's Cowgate and Grassmarket, examining the policing of this area in depth from the perspectives of police management, the frontline officer, and the community policed. Chapter 4 explores the geography, history, and politics of San Francisco's Tenderloin area, and chapter 5 details the policing styles and strategies present within this community. The focus of the sixth chapter is Vancouver's Downtown Eastside; an analysis of the policing of this site follows in Chapter 7.

The purpose of chapters 8 and 9 is to discuss the politics of policing that mould and direct practices and programs 'on the ground' in skid row. Therefore, these chapters represent a shift away from the core focus of much of the study – the empirical analysis of frontline policing – to attend to the nature of civic politics in each city that shapes the work of their respective police departments. In chapter 8, I examine some of the observations and other data discussed in previous chapters and introduce some new economic and statistical data for the purpose of systematically comparing the environments in which each of the three policing agencies operate, including the political and economic supports and constraints each faces. This comparison not only permits a broader analysis of each of the sites, but more importantly it allows me to delve more deeply into my contention that skid row policing is political and that the politics of the institution – its relative inclusiveness and/or exclusiveness – are largely dependent on political forces both within and external to the institution. The political process, I argue, casts police as 'demand negotiators' who are challenged to respond to varying sets of inclusionary-exclusionary demands within the framework of a civic system that limits the institution's choice of responses. Chapter 9 offers a comprehensive summary of the study's findings, situating these findings within larger political and economic shifts.

1 Inclusion, Exclusion, and the Policing of the Skids

Beggar in Edinburgh: It happened to me last week, a [man] he kicked my hat ...
It's really annoying when people kick your hat.
Interviewer: What's the reason for it?
Beggar: Because they can. They think we're alcoholics.

Street youth in Vancouver: Or if somebody offers you money for sex and stuff and
he won't leave you alone, if a couple people that we know – more street kids –
they'd be like 'what the hell are you doing?'
Second youth: Somebody just tried to do that. Tried to pay us twenty bucks.
First youth: Yeah. Twenty bucks. To have 'love' with him.
Second youth: Two animals.
Interviewer: Are people coming down here and trying to take advantage?
First youth: Yeah, totally. Just because we are ... [sentence left unfinished]

As the two preceding interview excerpts illustrate, exclusion and the
stigmatization that is carried with it are part of the daily reality of many
people. These are individuals who routinely experience verbal harassment, as well as mental, sexual, and physical threats and violence. This
abuse is directed at them from members of the so-called mainstream
society, who cling to the privilege of their social inclusion while abasing
those not similarly placed. In the first example, a street beggar in
Edinburgh describes a routine experience: having his begging hat – the
symbol of his exclusion – kicked [degraded] by members of the public.
In the second example, taken from an interview I conducted with three
teenaged girls panhandling on the streets of Vancouver, they are describing a form of degradation they had experienced at the hands of two men
visiting the area who sought to exploit their vulnerability for sexual gain.

Within the past few years, social exclusion, never completely out of vogue among social scientists, has re-emerged as a central concern within a body of work that attempts to cast exclusion as a deliberate byproduct of a shift from welfarism to neo-liberalism within Western societies (i.e., Young 1999; Bauman 1997). Much of this literature is theoretically oriented and is not rooted in empirical research and description. Thus, we have little understanding of the scope and nature of how exclusion is experienced on the ground. Further, inclusion merits little attention, although exclusion can and does generate resistance; as was noted by the young female beggars above, they actively resist attempts by those outside their social network to exploit their situation. Further, those moments of resistance are often supported by the larger community of excluded youth who, in protecting their vulnerable members, demand that those in the larger society treat them respectfully. Resistance against what Ruddick (2002) terms the 'social death' suffered by the excluded can also spur larger political activity, including the formation of resistance-oriented groups, the development of social networks to foster community activism aimed at engendering inclusion, the laying of legal claims based on citizenship rights, and the creation of media campaigns and public protests to provoke public sympathy and garner support (see also Allen 2000).

A further problem with analyses of 'the new exclusionary society' arises as a consequence of the treatment of forms of neo-liberal governance and policy: all too often 'neo-liberalisms' are presented as almost a unitary, unstoppable, monolithic force rather than as a permeable phenomenon embodying differences and degrees. Cultural, political, and historical variations between countries are glossed over in order to preserve accounts that depict a 'West' whose members are seen as increasingly cold, calculating, and selfish. For example, Bauman (2000), following Giddens (1994), claims that economic and social 'precarization' produced by Western neo-liberal economic policies has led to a weakening of human bonds and a widespread view of the world and its inhabitants as 'disposable objects.' This coldness is said to be particularly manifest in social policies and practices that further exclude those on the margins of society.

This study represents an attempt at fleshing out aspects of how both exclusivity and inclusivity are expressed in contemporary societies. In the following pages, I look at a primary means by which the state governs on society's margins: through the public policing of skid row districts. This work rests on the belief that the treatment of skid row inhabitants reflects the values, cultural aspirations, and fears of the larger society, which articulate the style of policing that is exhibited there. I am not alone in this view, as Herbert (2001a: 445) explains: 'The police are the most visible and symbolically potent form of governance in the modern city.' Yet, with the exception of Bittner's seminal study (1967), the role of the public police on skid row – a site where this institution perhaps most perfectly represents the 'thin blue' line – has remained largely unexplored. This deficit is remedied in the present work through an exploration of skid row policing within three very different urban contexts representing unique political and cultural configurations.

In order to provide some context for this study, in the sections below I explore aspects of the literatures on exclusivity, neo-liberal and welfare systems, and skid row policing. My purpose is to begin the process of linking the production of exclusionary, inclusionary, and coercively inclusive demands to different socio-political-economic configurations at the civic level. Further, I link these demands to the workings of a unique institution – the public police – which I depict as being tasked with responding to these demands.

Rethinking the *Exclusive Society* Thesis

Much has been written on the perceived increase in exclusivity in Western cultures as a consequence of the rise of U.S.-style neo-liberal policies (i.e., Bauman 1997, 1999; Jordan 1996; Gray 1999). However, I am particularly interested in a recent thesis offered by Jock Young in *The Exclusive Society* (1999) because it encapsulates many of the problems that we find within contemporary thinking on the connections between neo-liberalism and exclusiveness (as manifest through criminal justice policies). Young begins his thesis by contrasting the neo-liberal political mood today with the period following the Second World War. The post-war period is said to be a time of heightened social inclusion as evidenced by an emergent focus on rights discourse, increases in the social safety net, and the beginnings of rehabilitative efforts directed at reforming 'deviants' from the norm. Young makes much of these social goals, arguing that they signal a desire on the part of Western societies to treat marginalized 'others' as potential citizens who are simply misguided individuals needing help to return to the fold: 'the deviant "other" is ... subject to the goal of assimilation and inclusion. The discourses both penal and therapeutic are, therefore, of integration' (ibid.: 6).

Young then sketches out the transition from this post-war welfare liberalism to neo-liberalism. The increasing shift towards neo-liberalism within Western societies is said to be evident in a collection of social policies aimed at dismantling the welfare state (ibid.). Other effects of neo-liberalism include heightened market insecurity due to deregulation and the re-creation of individuals as responsible, reflexive risk-takers and risk-managers for a wide range of risks from personal health to local crime prevention. Each of these activities is said to result in a heightened insecurity among individuals as they begin to realize their precarious social and economic positions within the new order. According to Young, relative deprivation has become not merely a look upward to see one's place relative to a desired target group, but also a look downward to reassure one's self that there *are* people below. The realization that economic gaps between the middle and lower classes are no longer as significant as the former would hope is seen as a driving force behind increased intolerance of the chronically poor (ibid.; see also Jordan 1996).

This intolerance is said to be manifest in the shift away from viewing outsiders as 'deviants' from the norm who can be 'restored' to society through rehabilitation; now they are cast as dangerous parasites who benefit at the expense of 'honest folk' through crime and weak public policies (see, for example, Murray 1999). These beliefs are reflected in an increasing array of forms of social protection aimed at excluding the potential risks that the newly dangerous outsiders represent. Protection ranges from prison mega-complexes to gated communities, private security, surveillance cameras, and other physical and spatial barriers.

Young's thesis – that Western societies are shifting away from a Keynesian welfarism towards neo-liberalism and thus becoming increasingly exclusive – is founded upon two faulty premises. First, as O'Malley and Palmer (1996: 141) note, Keynesianism 'never was ensconced firmly and evenly throughout the social domain.' The United States stands as an excellent example: while various post-war governments in the United States flirted with aspects of Keynesian economic thought,[1] intervention into the economy was, for the most part, limited to the establishment of regulatory controls (Yergin and Stanislaw 2002). Similarly, inclusivity was neither universal, nor the dominant social value in the West.[2] Indeed, the continuing existence of skid rows offers a different historical reality from that which Young paints. Rights discourse, rehabilitation, post-war economic boom, and other indicators of the 'golden age' had little impact upon these sites. In his study of New York's Bowery district, Giamo offers the following relevant observation:

From the 1940s on, skid row responded by becoming less a direct consequence of capricious labor market forces wrought by an unregulated system
of industrialization. Yet the homeless were still prevalent on the Bowery and
in other skid rows throughout the country, lending substance to an abiding
state of disenfranchisement in the midst of national prosperity ... Though
the extent of homelessness had diminished, the intensity of its condition
had not. (1989: 28–9)

While Young is correct in noting that the post-war period saw the
beginning of government-sponsored rehabilitation and reform initiatives directed at skid row inhabitants, rehabilitation did not signal a
desire on the part of the larger society to openly integrate the row's
'deviants' back into the fold. Quite the reverse is true; this was the
beginning of the concentration of social services on skid row, efforts that
reinforced skid row's exclusion from the mainstream by attempting to
reform the skid rower within his or her own milieu. If the poor and the
addicted needed assistance, they would have to stay on the row to
receive it.

A headline from a 1953 Vancouver newspaper on the city's skid row
district reads: 'Salvation Army's "Harbour Light" Brings New Hope to
Outcasts' (Tryon 1953). The use of the term 'outcasts' to describe
people on skid row hardly conjures an image of inclusivity. I also find it
telling that it is the Salvation Army and not a state agency that is bringing
hope to the skid rower. This headline resonates with both historical and
contemporary research (see Wiseman 1970; Giamo 1989) in suggesting
that the importance of government support of rehabilitation programs
in the 'golden age' has been somewhat over-inflated, at least with respect
to those inhabiting the extreme margins of society. Certainly in skid row
and many other marginalized communities, the voluntary sector has
historically been a major, if not the major, provider of rehabilitation
programs and social assistance (outside of welfare cheques and food
stamps). Organizations such as the Salvation Army and the Catholic
Missions established soup kitchens, emergency shelters, half-way homes
for parolees, detox centres, and longer-term residences for the poor and
addicted (Giamo 1989). Thus, when Young cites government funding of
social services as an indicator of the inclusive society, what he fails to
note is the significant degree to which such services were privately
organized and funded. In some cases, private services were substantially
more important to the survival of the skid rower than public services, as
they were often more readily accessible and generally not subject to

'means testing.' For example, during Britain's 'golden age' of welfare, three types of benefits received by some two million people were subject to 'means testing,' even after enactment of the *National Insurance Bill* (1946), which was supposed to have eliminated the practice (Bauman 1997).

Much of Young's analysis of neo-liberalism is taken up with quantifying contemporary forms of exclusivity. For example, he looks to the rise in imprisonment rates across Western nations over the past thirty or so years. Given that the poor generally, Aboriginals, African-Americans, and other often excluded groups are traditionally over-represented in incarceration statistics, this is not unjustified. However, another way in which exclusivity is counted is problematic. Young attempts to demonstrate the exclusive society by pointing to what he perceives to be an increasing number of groups being socially stigmatized – such as welfare recipients, prisoners, and single mothers. However, it is not all that clear that these are groups newly perceived as socially dangerous. Certainly, public hysteria around teenage mothers pre-dates the rise of neo-liberalism. Another problem with this particular method of counting is that every individual member of each excluded group is treated as though he or she occupied the same social location. While it is the case that each group identified is stigmatized, and has been historically to greater or lesser extents, they are accorded different treatment based on their overall status and have differential access to opportunities. For instance, where the unwed teenage mother in suburbia may have access to subsidized daycare to attend schooling in her home district, the skid row mother is likely to be battling social services for custody of her children by virtue of the fact of where she lives.

To be clear, I do not mean to suggest that aspects of how exclusion is played out have not changed at all over the past thirty years. As Ellickson (1996) notes, whereas in the 1950s and 1960s skid rowers had been the focus of institutional regulation by the police, salvation-oriented missions, and welfare agencies, they did not draw significant attention from a larger society that preferred that they simply keep to their place.[3] This is no longer the case for two main reasons. First, the numbers of those on the row have grown significantly as a result of American-style neo-liberal policies. Aside from cutbacks to social spending, increasingly deregulated Western markets have resulted in economic changes leading to unemployment and chronic underemployment (Bauman 1999; Gray 1999; Kaplan 1997).[4] Globalization and harmful trade agreements are clearly implicated in job losses, as is the largely unfettered ability of corporations to deskill the labour force and to create substandard jobs and wages. Further, barriers to the receipt of social services and/or collective insurance benefits, through 'means testing' or residency requirements, have increased tremendously in a number of jurisdictions. Second, physical changes to the urban environment have a profound impact on those on the row. The push to 'reclaim' space through gentrification forces skid rowers out of their home into new areas. Similarly, 'densification' in the urban centre – a process of luring people into living, working, and playing in the city – has increased pedestrian traffic of individuals with income. Densification thus also increases exposure to the skid rower, who can subsidize meagre welfare cheques with money made through panhandling and other activities (Ruddick 2002; Wardhaugh 1996). This exposure, coupled with an urban mythology focused on crime and disorder, awakens collective fears concerning the stranger, fears that were supposed to have been contained with the formation of excluded spaces (Davis 1992).

Contrary to what Young's 'exclusive society' thesis seems to suggest, the exclusive society remains an inclusive one, although this is often expressed in the form of what I term 'coercive inclusion.' For example, rehabilitation of the 'troublesome' has continued to the present; if anything, rehabilitation rhetoric has increased as part of neo-liberal discourse (both American and European variants) that focuses on individual responsibility. To illustrate this point, we only need to look to most Western states' welfare systems. Today, the focus of welfare agencies tends to be on rehabilitating the individual in a way that was not historically the case. Welfare-to-work measures, welfare time limits, the redesignation of the unemployed as 'jobseekers,' the redesigning of welfare offices to make them look more like employment centres, and the rhetoric centring on welfare as temporary aid rather than as lifestyle, are all indicators of a new resurgent interest in rehabilitation and/or reform of the 'non-contributing' outsider (Rose 1999; Wilson 1996). The inclusive aspect arises from the desire to incorporate 'outsiders' into the mainstream of society as productive, self-governing individuals. The coercive element is expressed through the provision of limited and limiting choices offered to the individual that involve the threat of punitive action. Ultimatums are issued: attend job training or be cut off welfare; attend alcohol treatment or go to jail.

Further, to the extent that both coercive inclusion and exclusion generate resistance both from within the mainstream society and along the margins, we also find strands of inclusiveness that are demanded from many sides. These strands can be seen in protests against welfare cuts, demands for improved healthcare access for the poor, calls for institutional reforms of those agencies that are seen as mistreating the poor, and a variety of other measures. As I illustrate in later chapters, the degree of popular support for inclusion of the marginalized is, like support for exclusionary and/or coercively inclusive measures, relative to characteristics of each political-economic-cultural environment.

Thus far, I have identified at least two significant problems contained within Young's thesis: the misrepresentation of the historical welfare state as an ideal form of inclusive Keynesianism and the lack of attention paid to the continuing existence of inclusion in the present day, albeit often in a coercively inclusive form. A further problem of some significance is Young's conflation of different models of neo-liberalism. There are multiple regimes of power that we classify as neo-liberal despite their often distinct features (Dean 1999). What these regimes share is a central philosophical premise: the belief that the market is the best means of ensuring the health of a democracy. Health, under this articulation of liberal ideals, is a form of collective security that arises through the exercise of rational individual liberty (free choice and healthy competition among equals in the market). The extent to which this liberty is maximized within a given society is contingent upon the model of neo-liberalism discussed. Further, the extent to which there is a punitive drive manifest within a particular social system is dependent on that system's moral-economic foundations (in the 'ideal type') as well as the historical and cultural forces that give it shape and meaning on the ground.

Political Economies as 'Ideal Types'

In chapters 2, 4, and 6, I sketch out some of the historical, social, and other background considerations that have given shape to the different political-economic forms present in each of the cities examined. As I argue in these chapters, each city represents some key aspects of what we would term neo-liberal governance. However, while there are similarities in styles of governance between Edinburgh, San Francisco, and Vancouver, there are also significant differences that can be attributed in part to the adoption and modification of different political models.

In order to clarify the ways in which the schools of neo-liberalism identified with Edinburgh, San Francisco, and Vancouver are reproduced, combined, and/or deviated from in the daily practices of local governance, the purpose of this section is to briefly introduce the three major economic models relevant to situating the politics of each site: Ordoliberalism, the Chicago School model of neo-liberalism, and Keynesian welfarism. Each model is discussed as an 'ideal type,' that is, as a purely theoretical model apart from its actual empirical manifestations or historical configurations. Further, in keeping with one of my central concerns – the ways in which exclusion and inclusion play out in urban space and through urban politics – we will primarily be looking at these models in terms of the underlying moral-economic imperatives they create, particularly in relation to the treatment of the poor.

At this point, I return to Adam Smith gathering dust in his home in the Canongate Kirkyard. I return to Smith because his work gave birth to two different schools of neo-liberal thought, as well as shaping the formation of Keynesianism, if often only in response to the practice of neo-liberal tenets on the ground. Aside from his *The Theory of Moral Sentiments* (1759), his writings on jurisprudence and his economic work in *The Wealth of Nations* (1766) – the most influential text for latter-day laissez-faire economists – each reveals a moral philosophy rooted in tenets found within both stoicism and Scottish Calvinism (Clarke 2000). Smith extols the perfect meritocracy, one in which the acquisition of wisdom and virtue are manifested through prudence and diligent work. Under such a system, social stratification is deemed to be necessary to the healthy functioning of society in that it provides a reward system for the virtuous and something for the less than perfectly virtuous to strive for. Essentially, what Smith prescribes is a version of a Calvinist normative system, one that would later be captured by Weber (1991 [1904]) in his conception of the 'Protestant ethic' of hard work and its doctrine of predestination and in the related concepts of the deserving and undeserving poor.

Some scholars have pointed to Smith's sympathy principle (1986 [1759]) as an example of the possibilities of a compassionate side to classical liberalism and latterly American neo-liberalism (Zweig 1979). In doing so, such writers conveniently ignore two central facts contained within Smith's work: he explicitly privileges the normative social hierarchy over the compassionate treatment of the poor, thus firmly placing individualism over any form of collectivist action, including poor relief; and he affirms the moral binary of 'deserving' and 'undeserving':

> The distinction of ranks, the peace and order of society, are, in a great measure, founded upon the respect which we naturally conceive for the

[rich and the powerful]. The relief and consolation of human misery
depend altogether upon our compassion for the [poor and the wretched].
The peace and order of society, is of more importance than even the relief
of the miserable ... nature has wisely judged that the distinction of ranks, the
peace and order of society, would rest more securely upon the plan and
palpable difference of birth and fortune, than upon the invisible and often
uncertain difference of wisdom and virtue. (Smith 1986 [1759]: 136)

For Smith, nature (God) has removed the need for humans to exercise
subtle judgments as to each other's relative wisdom and virtue, substitut-
ing instead a plain marker: birth and fortune. However, such a plan does
permit distinctions to be made based on accidents of fortune: widows,
orphans, cripples, and the sick may become destitute through no fault of
their own. Others – the wastrel, the criminal, the drunkard, the vaga-
bond, and generally anyone who fails to ascribe to the virtues of work,
enterprise, prudence, sobriety, and general piousness – are seen as
deserving of their fate and undeserving of compassion and charity. They
serve as little more than exemplars of the consequences of living profli-
gate lives.

While the lives of the 'undeserving' poor have some social utility in
that they symbolize the pitfalls of waste, this use is offset by the potential
danger that each represents to the orderly functioning of the good
society. As Buchan (2002: 203) explains of early liberal thought:

Criminality was perceived as consisting of forms of conduct that threatened
the security of citizens, the health of the economy, and the wealth of civil
society; namely property crimes, vagabondage, masterlessness, begging and
idleness ... For this reason, one can detect in the work of a range of political
thinkers in the early-modern period, a consistent effort to define the nature
of government in terms of the management of opinion and conduct in
order to create harmonious, peaceful, law-abiding, and productive civil
societies.

In his work on 'governmentality,' Foucault teases out this thread that
runs through the work of several early thinkers (Smith, Hume, Locke,
Hobbes), as he traces the rise of civil society as a disciplinary society. For
Foucault (1991), classical liberalism is inherently linked to processes of
rationalization that have as their end the advancement of the various
economies (family, community, nation). The liberal state thus serves the
public through creating conditions upon which these economies can be

maximized: order maintenance. Order maintenance is to be achieved through techniques of self-regulation (Smith's diligent worker) or, conversely, through the identification and segregation of those who cannot or will not conform to the normative order.

The moral vision of political economy articulated within classical liberalism is today found within the form of neo-liberalism developed by economists Friedrich von Hayek, Milton Friedman, Gary Becker, and others who were based at the University of Chicago following the Second World War. Hayek was trained in classical liberal economics; thus the primary tenets of the Chicago School model can be traced back to Smithian foundations. These tenets were also developed largely out of Hayek's experience of totalitarianism in the 1930s and 1940s. His seminal treatise, *The Road to Serfdom* (1969 [1944]), can be read as an impassioned libertarian response to the planned economies and totalitarian regimes of the period, mainly Nazism and socialism (Stalinism).

For Hayek, the perfect liberal society is a meritocracy in which enterprise, skill, prudence, and risk-taking are rewarded:

> The economic freedom which is the prerequisite of any other freedom cannot be the freedom from economic care which the socialists promise us and which can be obtained only by relieving the individual at the same time of the necessity and of the power of choice; it must be the freedom of our economic activity which, with the right of choice, inevitably also carries the risk and the responsibility of that right. (Hayek 1969 [1944]: 100)

In the ideal form of the true market economy, a populace is not dependent upon the 'inefficient' state to intervene in the market on its behalf, but is instead individually 'responsibilized' into becoming educated participants who look after their own self-interests (Ericson, Barry, and Doyle 2000; O'Malley and Palmer 1996; O'Malley 1992).

The relationship between the individual and the state espoused by Chicago School theorists rests on libertarian values clearly rooted in the Puritan ethic, so famously described by Weber. In particular, there is an espousal of the notion of the 'American dream' – the belief that 'work ethic' is the primary determinant of social success. In relation to our central concern here – the treatment of the most marginalized of the urban poor – it is important to note that the corollary of the meritocratic belief in hard work as determinative of social placement has led to the creation of two categories of the poor who are subjected to differential treatment. The first category is that of the morally deserving: those who are physically unable to work are deemed worthy of private (not public) charity. The second category is composed of the morally undeserving: those who are viewed as able to work but demonstrate insufficient work ethic (variously depicted as lazy do-nothings who seek to live off the sweat of others). It is this latter group who are principally associated with skid row, a fact often reflected in society's treatment of skid row denizens.

Although aspects of Adam Smith's views on moral economy were to play a major role in the formation of the Chicago School model, some of the inconsistencies and contradictions within his work were to lead other scholars into very different directions. For example, whereas Smith viewed capitalism as a system of 'natural liberty' (1986 [1776]), he also recognized that it was an imperfect system with the potential to produce socially and economically undesirable effects. In *Wealth of Nations* (1986 [1776]), Smith describes the monopolistic tendencies of the unfettered market, which operate against the interests of the consumer, produce a decline of the martial spirit and what Marx (1966 [1844]) would later term the 'alienation' of workers through the growing specialization of labour. The aspect of Smith's views which emphasized morality as a precondition to the successful working of the economy gave rise to a second school of neo-liberalism: the *Ordoliberalen*.

The *Ordoliberalen* is a German style of liberalism that emerged in the late 1920s out of the writings of intellectuals of the Freiburg School (notable members include Alexander Rüstow, Alfred Müller-Armack, and Franz Böhm). The Ordoliberals reading Smith, as well as Weber and Marx, sought to reduce some of the irrationalities of capital first identified by Smith while retaining as a central premise a belief in the market as the best means of providing personal freedom and economic well-being (see, for example, Rustow 1980; Ropke 1987). In contrast to the laissez-faire economics that *The Wealth of Nations* influenced elsewhere, it led to the creation of a social market model, in a post-war Germany reeling from the effects of totalitarianism, that recognizes not only the inherent potential for inequality that an unfettered market produces but the fact that inequality undermines the order good governance is intended to produce. The irrationality of capital is to be compensated for by a different set of ethical principles than those that inform the American model of neo-liberalism: 'We also well know that if we seek a pure free market economy based on competition, it cannot float freely in a social, political and moral vacuum, but must be maintained and protected by a strong social, political and moral framework' (Wilhelm Ropke cited in Yergin and Stanislaw 2002: 16).

What we see under the *Ordoliberalen* model is a very different form of 'moral economy,' one that explicitly rejects the extreme individualism promoted within other economic schools:

> The striking failure of economic liberalism [in the late nineteenth century] is to be explained as a problem in the history of religious doctrine. Eighteenth-century deism, which was itself based on a stoic tradition and which stood as godfather to economic liberalism, was permeated with the religious belief that the laws of the market are effluences of divine world reason, and that it would be sinful arrogance to interfere in such a divinely given order with mere human measures. This optimistic, absolutist belief in subtheological rationalism led to what I have termed a 'sociologic blindness' for the political and social conditions under which alone the laws of the market operate beneficently. (Rustow 1980: 455)

The social market is an attempt at promoting not only economic growth and individual freedom, but moreover the aims of social justice. The latter is to be accomplished through a reduction of class conflicts with the recognition of points of mutual interest, public provision of social security measures, and the establishment of a variety of private, public, and private–public partnerships to foster public well-being. In contrast to the planned economies of interventionism, each solution proffered must operate cooperatively with the market. The tempering of individual freedom with cultural norms stressing ethical treatment of others, and increased capital ownership throughout civil society, results in a society that is more likely to embody a broader, more inclusionary set of ethics than what we find under contemporary Puritan-based regimes. In short, the Ordo model is hardly consonant with the image of American exclusionary neo-liberalism.

Like the Ordo model, the welfare state similarly sought to compensate for the 'irrationalities' of capital. Its economic prescriptions rest on the work of its principal founder, John Maynard Keynes, who was substantially influenced by the works of Rousseau and Marx. Rousseau, in particular, is to be credited with developing the first significant critique of the 'selfish' individualism of laissez-faire. For Rousseau, egalitarianism – freedom from want and from class exploitation – was the central guarantor of liberty. The proper role of the state is to redistribute wealth to ensure collective happiness. Marx expanded upon these concerns in his analysis of the pernicious effects of the capitalist class system. Marx's writings subsequently spurred the socialist aims of labour groups, which found expression in welfare-oriented laws that offered protections to labourers. Other influences on welfare-oriented economists were Dewey and Hobhouse, who argued that self-interest should be harnessed to the public good on the grounds that individuals are products of a social system (see also Simmel 1971 [1903]).

The Keynesian welfare state thus represents yet another form of 'moral economy,' one that rejects extreme individualism in favour of a more collectivist approach. For welfare-state economists, the laissez-faire of classical liberal economics is objectionable on two primary grounds. First, as Keynes notes in *The End of Laissez-Faire* (1927), the belief that an unfettered market produces bountiful social benefits is predicated on the erroneous assumption that certain ideal conditions are always present, thus ignoring such fundamental problems as knowledge gaps, the production of monopolies, and long adjustment periods. In relation to the central thesis of this work, the unchecked marketplace is also objectionable on humanitarian grounds: the structured inequities produced by the unregulated market worsen social conditions, particularly disadvantaging the most vulnerable segments of society (ibid.). The answer provided by Keynes is 'interventionism': to reduce capital's irrationalities through fiscal policies and regulatory measures introduced and overseen by the state. Keynes's prescription is thus the planned economy that scholars working in the Chicago and *Ordoliberalen* traditions have found so objectionable.

Skid Row and Its Control

Each of the political economies described above, both in their ideal forms and as hybridized versions on the ground, embodies aspects of exclusion and inclusion, although all too often the latter find expression in the form of coercively inclusive demands. Both sets of demands, ultimately, are intended to regulate the economy through the social and political enforcement of cultural norms aimed at conforming behaviour. Those who are deemed able and potentially willing to conform are subject to coercive inclusion in the form of welfare limits, welfare-to-work programs, and cultural shaming mechanisms such as those employed against 'welfare queens' and 'deadbeat dads.' Those who are viewed by society as intransigent 'delinquents' are conversely subjected to exclusion in its many forms. Skid row is a form of exclusion written in physical and social space.

Despite the long history of 'skid row'[5] as an object of social-scientific inquiry and disciplinary knowledge, a central problem located within the vast array of literature available is the fact that little attention has been paid to defining 'skid row' as an analytical concept. More often it has been invoked as a descriptive term used to identify a slum-like area of an inner city used to house alcoholics and other indigents. To be clear though, skid row is not a slum: whereas the inhabitants of the slum may be poor and disenfranchised like the denizens of the row, the former do not attach the same degree of moral stigma and blame as the latter because the circumstances of the slum dweller may occur through misfortune, but the 'lifestyle' of the skid rower is conceived of as one of choice and thus moral fault. In the present work skid row is conceptualized as a civic space defined through the real or perceived moral delinquency of its residents.

To clear up another common misconception, in some parts of the United States and Canada where the composition of the local skid row population contains a large number of people of colour, skid row is sometimes mistaken for the ghetto. Like the ghetto, skid row is a social and physical space composed of four constitutive elements: stigma, constraint, spatial confinement, and institutional encasement (Wacquant 2002, 2003). It too stands as an exclusionary device used to isolate groups from the dominant society, checking the possibility of association and thus of contamination. However, skid row differs from the ghetto in the composition of its population: whereas the ghetto is an ethnically homogeneous space that physically embodies ethnoracial domination, skid row is the physical embodiment of the moral dimensions of the relations of ruling. Rather than serving as a mechanism for the voluntary or involuntary enclosure of distinct ethnic and racial groups (as Wacquant [2003] notes, throughout history ghettos have served as both), historically skid row served as a holding pen for the white male population who made up the surplus labour force for the growing industrial economy. Throughout much of its history it was a racially segregated space where whiteness was preserved through discriminatory policies and practices aimed at keeping people of colour off the row (for a discussion of the racially exclusionary practices on skid row see Blumberg, Shipley, and Shandler 1973). Today, skid row is an ethnically heterogeneous space that serves two important functions.

On one level, skid row exists as a distinct and often inclusive community for the marginalized poor and other social outcasts. Residents here share a common bond: they are frequently, if not daily, made aware of their outcast status, being subjected by the larger society to treatment as forms of social detritus. Inclusion is expressed within the community in a variety of ways, including the use of unique social codes and rituals of the street. For example, the word 'six' in Vancouver's Downtown Eastside – meaning 'watch your back' – serves to warn people on the street of the presence of a police officer or other outsider who might represent a potential threat. The dangers of street life sometimes require a different prioritizing of normative values because of the premium placed on personal safety in a frequently chaotic and violent space (the more friends one has within the community, the more support may be available to call upon during critical times). Thus, behaviours and attitudes that would often fail to be understood in other neighbourhoods – such as remaining friends with someone who stole your money the day before – are accepted within skid row society.

While much of skid row operates through inclusionary mechanisms, skid row is a community like others in that exclusionary attitudes and behaviours cut across community lines. We see this in the creation of distinct subgroup identities (such as alcoholics, addicts, and 'straights') and even more exclusive networks within subgroups (such as drug and/or alcohol sharing systems – e.g., 'bottle gangs' or 'needle buddies'). Whereas sharing groups may exclude individuals from participation in their networks for a variety of reasons, larger subgroups may be at odds due to competition over spaces or resources, as well as over behaviour deemed problematic. For instance, in each of the skid row communities studied, alcoholics and addicts were heard to demand that the 'troublesome' other be moved either elsewhere within the community or outside it. As I note in the following chapters, heroin addicts in Vancouver complain about the 'intolerable' behaviour of crack addicts, whereas street drunks in the Cowgate and Grassmarket want heroin addicts pushed out of their neighbourhood.

While I have been focusing on the local community thus far, we can also see that on another level skid row principally serves the exclusionary goals of the larger society through its use as a site of containment for the urban poor who, for reasons of mental illness, drug and alcohol addiction, and/or other delinquent status are excluded from the formal economy. This is the surplus labour population of yesterday that has come to increasingly constitute the bulk of today's prison population: beggars, addicts, prostitutes, petty thieves, the homeless, and the transgendered and others who escape from decreed gender norms. As Wacquant (2002) depicts the ghetto as an ethnoracial prison outside the gates of the penitentiary, so too we might cast skid row as a dungeon for those whose present 'lifestyle' is deemed morally delinquent and thus dangerous by the larger society.

Skid row is thus properly viewed as the naked manifestation of the exercise of power in society, the power to control and punish through social, political, and economic exclusion. This power is exercised through the creation of a group of individuals as a defined community – written in physical and social space – that is at once both criminal and criminalized: a community of moral delinquents that stands at the heart of the law, 'or at least in the midst of those mechanisms that transfer the individual imperceptibly from discipline to the law, from deviation to offence' (Foucault 1979: 301). The delinquent community serves society on multiple levels. It provides a means of quarantining problematic social types who might 'infect' members of the larger public with their morally lax lifestyles and/or politically dangerous views. This containment space also provides the 'police' – that is, the larger constellation of institutions that supervise and control the lives of the indigent, the mad, and the criminal – with a means of identifying their target population and renders members of this population subject to easy surveillance and infiltration in order to assess and minimize the risk that they represent to the larger community (Foucault ibid.; Rose 1999). Further, such spaces function as living moral exemplars of the dangers that befall those who do not embrace the benefits of industry and moral correctness. And, as Foucault suggests, by marginalizing real and/or potential threats to the orderliness of society within excluded spaces, 'it is possible to divert [their] self-absorbed delinquency to forms of illegality that are less dangerous: maintained by the pressure of controls on the fringes of society, reduced to precarious conditions of existence, lacking links with the population that would be able to sustain it' (ibid.: 278).

Punishment of delinquents beyond the limits of legal incarceration is normalized: the power to punish becomes 'natural and legitimate,' as society's tolerance for the delinquent's 'bad lifestyle' decreases (Foucault 1979: 301). This punitive drive finds expression along two registers: the legal register of justice and the extra-legal register of discipline (ibid.). With respect to the present study, the legal register is seen to constitute those laws and registers that increasingly trap and imprison the delinquent skid rower within a vicious circle of penality – for example, anti-urination and defecation bylaws imposed in sites with limited toilet facilities for the poor, or narcotics laws that imprison addicts for failing to rehabilitate themselves in treatment beds that do not exist. The register of discipline constitutes those normalizing institutions that serve to organize and co-govern skid row populations. These institutions support the legal register by attempting to discipline those who are governable and by securing information on the ungovernable that can be fed into and utilized by the legal system. I see neighbourhood patrol programs as a particularly illuminating example of the latter register and its work in supporting processes of discipline and exclusion. Neighbourhood patrols use their presence as a reminder to 'disorderly elements' that there is a morally correct way of behaving: those who do not embrace the 'moral lifestyle' are subject to surveillance by other residents – their photographs will be taken and information about their personal activities will be passed on to the police. The intention of such law-abiding citizens is not, however, merely to provide support for the legal machinery but to initiate its workings in order to reform an area's delinquents and, failing that, to punish those who resist rehabilitation.

In order to better understand how individuals are 'policed' on skid row, I utilize a multi-dimensional conception of policing that is grounded in a view of policing as a set of processes that ultimately form a broader framework of security/regulation that is organized both by and under the state. The origins of this framework are most clearly articulated by Foucault in *Discipline and Punish* (1995 [1977]) and in his later studies of 'governmentality' in which he describes the replacement of traditional forms of overt state regulation with sophisticated coordinate systems of micro-disciplinary techniques diffused throughout the social body. According to this perspective, the public police are merely one apparatus of social control in a much larger scheme, not only involving the government as an interested party in the normalization of captive populations but also incorporating various other normalizing institutions throughout civil society. As Foucault (1994: 195) explains, '"police" is not an institution or mechanism functioning within the state but a governmental technology peculiar to the state – domains, techniques, targets where the state intervenes.'

In relation to the governance of deviant populations, the task of managing what Rose (1999: 262) terms 'enduringly problematic persons in the name of community security' requires the knowledge, expertise, and powers of the public police as well as those of social workers, probation officers, education and health experts, and often the resources of private agencies. Thus, a portion of the present study is concerned with the inter-institutional relations that constitute 'policing' – 'policing' as both a broader discipline-oriented framework and, more narrowly, as an institution (the public police). With respect to the latter, this conception incorporates four models of public policing that, as I demonstrate throughout, operate simultaneously on the row: police as law enforcers, peacekeepers, social workers, and knowledge workers.

Law Enforcers

In 1967, Egon Bittner published an ethnographic study of the policing of skid row districts by two American police forces. Drawing on work by Banton (1964), he explored two distinct types of police roles and their function on skid row. The first of these is the police as 'law enforcers' – that is, as individuals whose functions are principally oriented towards processing cases through the criminal justice system. Their practice primarily consists of arrests and arrest-related procedures such as information taking, locating witnesses, filing or advising charges, testifying, and other activities that expedite criminal justice processing.

For many scholars, law enforcement is the primary role that defines the policing function, and it is held to be unique to this institution:

> The policeman shares with others a wide variety of resources that can be used in dealing with a problem. However, these resources exist within the context of those resources (law enforcement and force), which he does not share with others and that are, in effect, unique characteristics of his role. (Shearing and Leon 1992: 218–19)

The power to invoke the law through a range of sanctions from issuing tickets to effecting an arrest – a form of coercion in and of itself – coupled with the ability to use force in effecting a resolution, is said to define the police institution and separate its practitioners from others who are similarly tasked with dealing with society's problems. As Bittner notes, we implicitly accept and recognize these exceptional powers when we choose to handle a problem by 'calling the cops.'

However, as most policing scholars recognize, while these powers are central to the policing function, officers typically spend very little of their time in actual law enforcement pursuits. And when police do so, as Wilson (1968: 19) points out, the patrol officer's function is often largely a clerical one: 'he asks routine questions, inspects the premises and fills out a form.' Traditionally, the average patrol officer spends much more of his or her time on simple order maintenance tasks which do not result in the direct invocation of the law – that is, in a ticket, a summons, or in an arrest. More recently though we have seen the rise of a policing model that prioritizes law enforcement as a core strategy for dealing with crime and disorder: the 'broken windows' model.

This model is based on a hypothesis that suggests that crime can be reduced through surveillance and the reduction of environmental cues that are seen as inherently criminogenic – such as broken windows, graffiti, and other signs of urban decay, which are said to signal to would-be offenders that a space is 'undefended' (Wilson and Kelling 1982; Kelling and Coles 1996). The role of the public police under this model is to proactively enforce all laws, but particularly minor offences, which are seen as escalators to more serious offences – that is, to 'repair the broken window' (Kelling and Coles 1996).

As Harcourt (2001) suggests, police practitioners frequently misunderstand the broken windows model as a form of order-maintenance policing. However, with its emphasis on law enforcement as the primary means for addressing crime and disorder, broken windows cannot be understood as anything but a law enforcement model. Order maintenance, which is described in further detail in the next section, involves the use of police discretion to deal with minor offences. Broken windows replaces that discretion with policies that mandate the aggressive policing of all offences but particularly lower-level criminal offences and/or municipal infractions (ibid.).

Peacekeepers

The second role that Bittner assigns to the police is 'peacekeeping,' which is also frequently referred to as 'order maintenance.' This practice encompasses informal extra-legal activities designed to minimize disorder and to reduce tensions that could lead to crimes or disturbances, such as settling personal disputes and/or issuing warnings to those who are or might be doing wrong.

According to Bittner, the style of policing in skid row reflects structural demands placed upon the police. Of paramount importance to police decision making is the fact that such spaces serve to concentrate 'certain types of persons' (1967: 714). The role of the police officer within this community is to contain the space and its inhabitants. The means by which this containment is effected is of minimal interest to the institution; police managers simply assign officers to the district, on a more or less permanent basis, and leave it to officers' individual discretion as to how best to maintain order in the site. The space is seen to lend itself to the use of informal proactive techniques. Police operate under the premise that, given the nature of the population and the potential for trouble that inhabitants represent, allowing simple disputes or offences to go unchecked may lead to an escalation to more serious offences. Thus, informal preventative action rather than reaction becomes the norm. Bittner sets out five types of lesser demands, or 'demand conditions,' that are placed upon the police in this district that increase the likelihood of extra-legal measures. These are:

1. the need to supervise licensed premises and the regulation of traffic;
2. situations involving minor offences where discretion can be invoked;
3. situations involving non-criminal matters where police authority can be invoked;
4. crowd control; and
5. duties with respect to individuals who require special assistance such as youth and the mentally ill.

Bittner notes that in responding to these conditions, police officers utilize three strategies: a 'richly particularized knowledge of people and places in the area,' discretion, and coercion (1967: 707). Knowledge of the site and its inhabitants assists the officer in formulating the best response for reducing the potential for trouble on the row. Decision making that centres on whether to invoke the law or to use discretion is a fundamental aspect of the police role. Such decisions are not based on individual culpability but instead reflect the need to 'solve certain pressing practical problems in keeping the peace' (ibid.: 710). As Giffen (1966: 156) suggests, the power of arrest is frequently exercised by police as 'the easiest means of keeping down the number of [drunks] in circulation.' Drunks are generally arrested in situations where they are creating a public disturbance or posing a danger to themselves or others (Giffen 1966; Blumberg et al. 1973; Gammadge, Jorgensen, and Jorgenson 1972). The use of coercion is thus often aligned with the need to keep peace; its use is 'determined mainly by exigencies of situations and with little regard for possible long range effects on individual persons' (Bittner 1967: 707).

Social Workers

Some of the literature that followed Bittner's skid row study began to draw out more fully implications arising from his observation that the police frequently serve non–law enforcement purposes. A picture of the police as social service providers began to be built up from this and similar work that depicted skid row police officers providing various forms of assistance to the skid rower and/or acting from motives not directly related to law enforcement or peacekeeping. Blumberg et al. (1973) looked at the use of arrest for public intoxication and noted that officers invoked this power in situations where they perceived that the person arrested may have placed him or herself in 'danger.' Examples of 'danger' include the threat of overdose, threat of victimization (being 'rolled'), and over-exposure to the elements (ibid.). Wallace notes that 'Police say they arrest more drunks in the wintertime because they can easily pass out in an alley and freeze to death before anyone finds them' (1965: 95; see also Blumberg et al. 1973; McSheehy 1979). Wiseman (1970: 67) describes the skid row police officer as social worker when she states that one of the functions these officers serve is to provide assistance to inhabitants 'in the manner of the parent who disciplines a child for his own good.'

The social work model also arose from studies that looked at the reasons why police are mobilized to respond to service calls generally (Skogan 1990). As one of the few state agencies providing public services twenty-four hours a day, seven days a week, police are frequently called upon to address non-policing matters. Other scholars note that it is also the authority and resources of this institution that lead members of the public to seek police assistance and advice for a variety of non-criminal matters (Waddington 1993).

The social work model was extended in the 1990s with the rise of community policing and problem-oriented policing, two approaches which, theoretically, emphasize the social work aspect of policing through a recasting of the police role as proactive 'problem solvers' within local communities. This recasting, as Trojanowicz, Kappeler, Gaines, and Bucqueroux (1998: 19) argue, is not antithetical to traditional under-standings of the police role, as some critics of community policing have suggested, because 'the fact is, social work has always been an important element of police work.'

As community policing is ostensibly the model under which each of the forces studied is operating, I want to briefly review the principles of this model and two major concerns that arise from its use in the field. Although community policing has been aptly described as 'a remarkably amorphous term' (Herbert 2001a: 448), it is generally understood as a set of policies and programs aimed at increasing interaction between the police and community for the purpose of fostering joint ownership of and responsibility for a defined set of community problems arising from local crime and disorder. A wide range of programs operate under this model, including community police stations, neighbourhood foot patrols, local watch groups, police outreach programs, community–police meetings, and so on (ibid.). Community policing is informed by a democratic ethos: its underlying philosophy is that the police are accountable to the community. The community is no longer the passive recipient of police services or the creators of policing problems, as was often understood under the professional model of policing, but rather an active participant, *with the police*, in the solution of local problems (Trojanowicz et al. 1998). The result is the creation of programs, such as those noted above, which place the police within the community rather than operating above it.

A variety of criticisms have been directed against the community policing model. I shall limit myself to two concerns raised within the literature that are most relevant to the present study. The first arises from a set of criticisms that suggest that community policing is more appropriately viewed as a 'rhetorical strategy' used for political purposes rather than as a legitimate mode of policing (Loader 1999; Lyons 1999). This view is based on studies of the model in the field, such as Saunders's (1999) examination of a community policing project in Boston which found that a significant gap existed between the model's promises and its practice. In the case of the Boston program, the police failed to implement mechanisms for determining community needs or for solving local problems. The program also failed to address the community's belief that the police lacked public accountability. These failures led Saunders to dismiss community policing as little more than a means of reproducing inequities under the guise of egalitarianism. However, O'Malley and Palmer (1996: 145) note that while there 'is little doubt' that the police–public relationship as idealized in the community policing model is 'often an illusion at the level of practice,' such dismissals neglect the fact that the rhetorical imagery invoked by the community policing model 'is powerful.' The public is no longer a passive recipient of state services but rather active consumers of a 'market-modeled service' with all of the market-based rights and responsibilities that the consumer–service provider relationship implies (ibid.: 145; see also Loader 1999).

The second relevant concern arises from the frequent conflation of community policing and 'broken windows' (Herbert 2001a; Kleinig 1993). This conflation is problematic because, whereas community policing stresses the community and the police as equal actors responsible for crime and disorder in a neighbourhood, 'broken windows' stresses the dominant role of the police as facilitators for crime reduction and provides a significantly reduced role for the community (Herbert 2001a). As Herbert explains, under 'the broken windows approach, this active role for the citizenry [as envisioned by the community policing model] is eclipsed by the dominant power asserted by the police, primarily through their practices of intimidation and arrest' (ibid.: 446). The result has been that cities that employ aggressive policing tactics against minor offenders, notably enforcing 'status offences' against the visibly poor, claim that, in enforcing the desires of businesses and some community residents, they are representing 'the community' and are thus engaged in community policing (Kleinig 1993). Often this claim rests on tenuous grounds.

Knowledge Workers

Bittner's work focuses on police decision making as an informal process framed by local knowledge and the exigencies and context of a given situation. A deserved criticism of this approach has been that it obscured the institutional and structural underpinnings of decision making. The work of scholars such as Ericson (1982) and Manning (1977) reveals a picture of police work as embedded in institutional rules and communication systems. The police officer 'negotiates order' 'variously employing strategies of coercion, manipulation, and negotiation ... with respect to legal rules, administrative rules, and "recipe" rules of the occupational culture of line officers' (Ericson 1982: 9).

In the 1990s, the communications-oriented focus on policing led to another reconceptualization of the police role, this time as knowledge workers who gather information into formats that can be readily utilized by other institutions to achieve governance (Ericson and Haggerty 1997). The basis for this theoretical insight was twofold: ethnographic data that revealed changes in the volume and style of police information gathering and its uses, and new work arising from the sociology of knowledge. According to Ericson and Haggerty (1997: 41), 'policing is not just a matter of repressive, punitive, deterrent measures to control those who are morally wrong. It is also a matter of surveillance, of producing knowledge of populations that is useful for administering them.' Thus, whereas Bittner and others have emphasized the police use of force or, alternatively, peacekeeping or problem-oriented measures to resolve situations, Ericson and Haggerty point out the degree to which the police dispose of cases by means of diverting individuals to other institutions. A driving force behind much police information gathering directed at regulating conduct is the insurance industry and the law of contracts. Police have learned that it is more expedient to have property crimes involving theft, fraud, or vandalism dealt with by insurers who can and will invest resources in both proactive enforcement (i.e., through supporting private security programs for particular types of theft and, more commonly, through contracts that require policy holder vigilance) and reactive efforts (fraud detection programs, raising deductibles). While these authors mainly document the offloading of police responsibilities in relation to upper and middle concerns, this process also has significant impacts on poorer communities. For example, in and around some skid row districts, public police officers actively work with private security, with the latter becoming increasingly responsible for lower-level crime prevention and response duties (see Huey, Ericson, and Haggerty 2005). Such cooperative networks also serve to enhance the ability of the public police to acquire street-level information for their own uses and to share information with the private sector to increase surveillance of row residents (ibid.).

Of the four policing models, the knowledge worker conception is the one that is invoked most commonly in discussions of neo-liberal governance and the treatment of crime. This is not altogether surprising given that a central concern within neo-liberal regimes has been risk management and that police systems frequently serve risk management goals. In relation to skid row, policies of dispersal and containment are frequently effected through the use of 'risk' rationales (see Castel 1991; Ericson and Haggerty 1997). Identified 'risks' to segments within society – the skid rower as criminal, addict, and/or mentally ill person – are variously identified, monitored, controlled, and contained in order to minimize or to advert perceived or real dangers that they represent (Ericson and Haggerty 1997). This process largely occurs through technical policing solutions, such as computerized mapping systems, databases, CCTV cameras, each of which generates data in formats that are transferable to other institutions for legal and extra-legal regulatory purposes.

The present study utilizes each of the policing models discussed in an attempt to understand the dynamics of policing skid row districts. Focusing on policing within and across each framework is necessary for two important reasons. First, as I demonstrate throughout this study, police work at both management and street levels utilizes these frameworks as strategies in support of their primary mandate: controlling territory. Thus, we need to situate different activities according to the model that provides the most explanatory power. Focusing on police as law enforcers does not adequately account for those times in which they perform what is clearly recognized as social work. Second, a multi-dimensional view of policing is necessary to the task of more fully articulating and understanding the complexities of an occupation that requires both fixed rules and a dynamic approach to a multitude of situations. As I also attempt to demonstrate throughout this work, police officers utilize strategies that can serve multiple purposes simultaneously. This fact alone necessitates a move away from unidimensional frameworks.

Some readers may question the wisdom of putting together four apparently very different models of policing. I first became aware of how these frameworks function together through reviewing the differences between the Bittner and the Ericson and Haggerty conceptions of policing. In doing so, I noted that the seeds of Ericson and Haggerty's *Policing the Risk Society* can be seen in Bittner's work, although Bittner left them unexploited. These seeds are found in a brief section in the conclusion of 'Police on Skid Row' (1967: 714):

> Peacekeeping procedure on skid-row consists of three elements. Patrolmen seek to acquire a rich body of concrete knowledge about people by cultivating personal acquaintance with as many residents as possible. They tend to proceed against persons mainly on the basis of perceived risk, rather than on the basis of culpability. And they are more interested in reducing the aggregate total of troubles in the area than in evaluating individual cases according to merit.

There are, of course, significant differences between the two perspectives that need to be acknowledged; however, these are largely differences of degree rather than of kind. For example, we can locate a difference in relation to Bittner's 'knowing' and Ericson and Haggerty's conception of knowledge work – that is, the scale and techniques of 'knowing' individuals and groups within a territory and the uses that knowing now takes. Bittner's skid row community of 1967 no longer exists, and the skid rows of today – the populations of which have grown and changed considerably over the past thirty years – can no longer be managed solely through personal relations between the police and the policed. While much of the policing that occurs on skid row today is about informal regulation, it is also about managing populations utilizing institutionally embedded knowledge networks.

Another difference I note between the Bittner and the Ericson and Haggerty models is found in relation to how police process cases. Again, this difference is not as significant as it might appear at first glance. Bittner describes one of the roles police adopt on the row as 'law enforcers' – that is, working to secure convictions. And yet, Ericson and Haggerty depict police as frequently seeking to dispose of cases by offloading them onto other institutions. However, in the majority of cases, Bittner's police actually do the same thing, although this is not made entirely explicit in his study. As he notes, row officers use informal peacekeeping techniques as a means of extinguishing potential problems. This technique is used to avoid formal processing and has one of two possible consequences: it defers problems for the police to another day or displaces them onto other institutions for corrective action. Finally, Ericson and Haggerty also acknowledge that the police continue to maintain their traditional law enforcement role; officers continue to process cases under their model, just not as frequently as the public might believe.

Like other researchers, I note that the seeds of the police-as-social-workers framework can also be located within Bittner's conception of peacekeeping (Toch and Grant 1991). Patrol officers then as now 'help people to obtain meals, lodging, employment, that they direct [row denizens] to welfare and health services and that they aid them in various other ways' (Bittner 1967: 709). A police officer in Kentucky who picks up a local alcoholic for transport to the hospital offers the following as his rationale: 'I'm taking him to the emergency room for alcohol poisoning ... It's for his own good, otherwise he might get run over by a car' (Decker 2002).

Wiseman (1970) asks how it is that the police, with minimal resources, are able to contain the social misfits who make up skid row. In looking at the answers that she provides, we can see again an overlap between the various models. Wiseman suggests that two factors are involved: a well-defined understanding of when and where it is appropriate to apply formal and informal means of coercion, and knowledge of the area which is used to pre-plan deployment of patrols and supporting machinery. At the time of Wiseman's writing, knowledge of the space was used to project when and where crimes would occur in order to ensure sufficient police coverage. This projection was rather roughly done, and the supporting machinery consisted primarily of paddy wagons that were used to pick up 'nuisance' drunks. Today, the local knowledge of the skid row officer is fed into the institution, which similarly calculates out police shift coverage. But the supporting apparatus is incredibly more complex and is increasingly geared towards managing the space through targeting and governing troublesome populations. The police in Wiseman's time did not have geographic information systems (GIS) that could pinpoint, with finer degrees, criminal 'hot' spots by target space or population. If you ask the police today where to find, for example, territory on skid row controlled by drug dealers of a particular race or ethnic type, this information can be supplied on demand and is used to formulate department policies and actions. In some cases, sweeps based on this information are acted on jointly with agents from other institutions, such as Immigration and Corrections (parole or probation services). Thus, while we still have the individual patrol officer walking the beat on the row and gathering local knowledge, the volume and uses for this information have increased dramatically.

Conclusion

In this chapter I have provided a theoretical context for the study that follows. This was done, firstly, through a critical examination of recent theoretical work that explores the purported movement towards more exclusive societies, which has been explained as a consequence of the rise of neo-liberalism in the West. What this analysis revealed was that exclusion, inclusion, and coercive inclusion are social constants. As we saw, even during the 'golden age' of welfarism, exclusion and coercive inclusion were present, manifest through formal and informal policies that relegated individuals to socially, economically, and politically isolated communities such as skid row districts.

I then addressed the claim that neo-liberal models of governance are inherently exclusive by fleshing out the origins of the two major schools: the *Ordoliberalen* model and the Chicago School. Further, I looked at the rise of welfarism as a practical response to the vagaries of life under systems of unfettered capitalism. From this analysis, we saw that each political form has a uniquely different moral perspective that influences the development of public policy with respect to the treatment of social and economic inequality. However, again, under each system we find present forms of exclusion, inclusion, and coercive inclusion directed at or located within marginal communities.

As the focus of the present work is skid row and its policing, I offered an analytical definition of skid row as a social and physical location, before similarly defining my use of the terms 'police' and 'policing.' From this, I moved into a discussion of the four theoretical policing frameworks that inform the present study and the ways in which these frameworks necessarily operate together as a set of responses to the demands that the policing of skid row generates.

2 Alkies, Smackheads, and *Ordos*: Skid Row under Ordoliberalism

In this chapter and the next, I analyse Edinburgh's political economy as representative of key characteristics of the *Ordoliberalen* model. The first section outlines the political, historical, geographical, and social dimensions of the Cowgate/Grassmarket in order to provide a context for understanding the present study and the dynamics of inclusion and exclusion that are played out 'on the ground' in this community. To this end, aside from discussing the site's history and geography, I also describe its current inhabitants, attempting, if only modestly, to illuminate aspects of their world for the reader. Following this, I provide a brief discussion of the politics of Edinburgh's skid row, highlighting the range of inclusionary-exclusionary demands that the site produces. I then explore the larger political environment that gives shape to the production of these demands.

Edinburgh's Skid Row: The Cowgate and Grassmarket

The city of Edinburgh is divided into two sections that are referred to as Old Town and New Town. Old Town is the southern part of the city and is the site of many historic landmarks dating to the Middle Ages, including the Holyrood Palace, Edinburgh Castle, and the Royal Mile. It is also the site of three streets – West Port, Cowgate, and Grassmarket – that join, running west to east. West Port, at the westernmost section of the area, is in the process of being 'gentrified,' although it retains many of the characteristic hallmarks of the skid row district: shelters, hostels, and other services for the urban poor; a decreasing number of vacant buildings; downmarket pubs promising live girls and pole dances; and the unmistakable presence of drunks.

Illustration 2.1 Grassmarket memorial (foreground) (author's photo).

To the east, West Port is joined to Grassmarket. 'The Grass' is remark-able in the fact that is a well-populated road filled with brightly painted restaurants, clothing stores, coffeehouses, clubs, and pubs. Populating this pretty landscape, however, are individuals, shabbily dressed, sleeping on benches next to a car park or drinking cider next to a memorial in the area's centre.

Further east, Grassmarket merges into Cowgate, the landscape becom-ing visibly more bleak and empty, consisting largely of vacant and boarded buildings. South Bridge, connecting Old Town to New Town, crosses over Cowgate, giving the atmosphere a particularly subterranean feel. Moving eastward towards Holyrood, Cowgate becomes populated again, although the street continues to convey a feeling of vacancy. This empti-ness is hardly surprising given that the population of the entire Edinburgh area known as 'Old Town' – which includes Cowgate and the Grass-market – is only some eight thousand residents (Edinburgh Old Town 2003). For the past few decades, many area residents had been poor and/or addicted to drugs and alcohol. However, new housing develop-ments in the area that contain a mix of properties have led to both a small population increase and some socio-economic diversification.

The history of the Cowgate/Grassmarket area is about six hundred years old. Cowgate's name derives from its historical use: it was the Cow-gait, or path, through which farm animals were taken from St Cuthbert's Meadows to the St Leonard's pastures. From 1460 until the late 1700s, the area around Cowgate evolved into a wealthy neighbourhood, distin-guished by well-appointed homes for the upper classes (Dick 2003).

Illustration 2.2 View of Cowgate (author's photo).

Grassmarket was a central marketplace within the city that existed from the 1400s to the early 1900s. Grassmarket continued as both a market and as a place of execution. By the mid-1800s, however, both sites had become one large slum housing the city's urban poor, many of whom were Irish immigrants who settled there from the 1830s to the 1850s (Daiches 1978). Endemic poverty, crowded tenements, crime,[1] and disease were rampant, earning the site its reputation as one of Europe's worst slums.[2] Robert Louis Stevenson described the Cowgate of the mid-nineteenth century as follows:

> In one house, perhaps, two score families gather together; and, perhaps, not one of them is wholly out of the reach of want. The great hotel is given over to discomfort from the foundation to chimney-tops; everywhere a pinching, narrow habit, scanty meals, and an air of sluttishness and dirt ... social inequality is nowhere more ostentatious than at Edinburgh ... to look over the South Bridge and see the Cowgate below full of crying hawkers, is to view one rank of society from another in the twinkling of an eye. (cited in Daiches 1978: 225)

The first half of the twentieth century saw the development of council housing as a means of reducing the concentration effect of the slums by dispersing the urban poor to flats in the outer areas of the city (Anderson, Kinsey, Loader, and Smith 1994). However, the hostels in Cowgate/ Grassmarket remained. Lloyd (2001) states that the area's poor 'would drape themselves over clothes lines to catch a wink of sleep in the infamous hostels of Edinburgh's Grassmarket.'

Other forms of urban redevelopment had an impact on the area. For example, a round of redevelopment on Grassmarket in the last century resulted in several properties being refurbished in a small pocket of the street – including historic taverns, cafés, and shops – creating a small but bustling retail and tourist destination. Thus, the one thing that immediately strikes the visitor to the Grassmarket is the mix of money and poverty. Money is represented in the form of the trendy cafés and deluxe tourist accommodations, but poverty is also present in the hostels and missions and in the outdoor spaces that provide temporary shelter for 'rough sleepers'[3] – the term used in Britain to describe those without shelter. Further, despite advancing gentrification, the 'Grass' not only continues to house many of the city's poor but also serves as a principal social venue for street-entrenched individuals from throughout the city.

At the turn of the 1900s, attempts at redevelopment, including the opening of the upmarket department store J&R Allan, were intended to bring people into the Cowgate. This store closed in 1976, likely because Cowgate had fallen increasingly into disuse and disrepair (Dick 2003). Cowgate remained largely ignored by the city and developers until a faulty fuse box in one of the elevator shafts in the abandoned J&R Allan building sparked a fire in December 2002 that devastated Cowgate, destroying several historic properties (Davidson and Ferguson 2003).

Cowgate remains at present largely underdeveloped. There are some low-budget student hostels, but the majority of buildings appear, at first glance, to be abandoned or nearly vacant. I say at first glance because several of these apparently discarded buildings house discreet facilities that cater to the area's number one industry: drink tourism. The influx of tourists from other parts of the British Isles, who come to enjoy cheap bachelor and bachelorette parties, lost weekends, and other party experiences, are serviced by an over-concentration of liquor licence seats within this small neighbourhood, leading to its local renown as Piss Alley.[4] Piss Alley causes significant problems for local residents, businesses, and police in the form of large groups of drunken revellers generating noise, vandalism, violence, and, prior to the mandatory road closing from 10 P.M. to 5 A.M. each night, incidents of drunken pedestrians being struck by cars.

The Cowgate and Grassmarket also house many of the city's urban poor. Although the poor who live in this site can be viewed in a variety of ways, I want to draw two separate distinctions. The first follows from the views of residents of the streets, who distinguish among themselves between alcoholics ('alkies' or 'street drinkers') and addicts ('smackheads' or 'junkie-bes'). Street drinkers tend to be older males who live in or near the area; however, this group is not exclusively male – I did meet two female street drinkers and service providers (social workers/providers of social services) offered descriptions of others. Nor were street drinkers uniformly older; one of the female drinkers I met was likely under thirty, as were a couple of the males. Of the older males, who make up the majority, many live in the area, sleeping rough, using shelter beds or lodging in permanent residences. A 'wet' hostel in Gilmer's Close caters specifically to the needs of alcoholics, offering beds for active drinkers.

The Cowgate and Grassmarket are also home to a number of street-entrenched drug addicts. As is the case with street drinkers, the numbers of addicts to be found in the area are unknown. Some service providers in the Cowgate estimate that there are fewer addicts than street drinkers, suggesting that addicts are more likely to be found in the low-income housing tracts outside the city centre, in places such as Wester Hailes. Others suggest that the number of addicts in the Cowgate/Grassmarket area is relatively higher: one hostel worker estimated that 80 per cent of service users at his facility were addicts, with the majority being injection heroin users.

Unlike the situation in many North American cities, the bulk of Edinburgh's street addicts use heroin rather than crack cocaine or crystal methamphetamine. As one police source advised, groups associated with crack have attempted to make inroads into the Edinburgh drug market, but to the extent that heroin remains relatively inexpensive, it is the primary drug of choice on the streets.

Drug dealing is a relatively discreet business; in the Cowgate and Grassmarket you have to be part of the street scene or know someone who is in order to score drugs. As one young addict explained, 'it's only the junkies who ken [know] the dealers.' Some addicts set up on their own as dealers of small quantities of drugs to people they know as a means of keeping themselves supplied. However, more often than not, addicts work directly for dealers as 'runners,' holding money and/or drugs and negotiating sales for the dealers. A significant amount of drug dealing takes place not in the street but through area shelters and missions. As a local addict explains, 'Most of the homeless places [shelters, hostels, missions] you can get hash, smack, you can get anything.' This is well known not only within the street community but also by hostel workers and other service providers, as a hostel worker advised:

> There's small-time dealers who come around this area. We've had eight that we know about who run for bigger dealers. [The bigger dealers] try and find someone who'll do running for them ... And how we check, we check who was not popular previously and has suddenly become popular. And it's a constant game and dealers change and ... if somebody's excluded from dealing you'll find that somebody else [is involved]. It's organized.

Service providers must remain vigilant against drug sales on their premises. In Britain, service providers who knowingly allow drug activity to take place within their facilities can be charged with an offence – something which several service providers told me caused them significant concern, particularly as a local shelter had been raided by Edinburgh's Lothian and Borders (L&B) regional police force narcotics squad a few months previously.[5] Despite this vigilance, discreet drug dealing on premises that provide services to the street crowd continues, and, when caught, dealers and addicts are informally disciplined by agency staff, who use the threat of ejection to keep order.

The second significant distinction to be made among those in Edinburgh's skid row arose during discussions with area service providers who deal with clients who are either 'sheltered' in some fashion – in spaces ranging from temporary to permanent accommodations – or who 'sleep rough.' Individuals whom I met represented both groups. Some had housing elsewhere in the city but came to the Cowgate and Grassmarket to socialize with their friends, to score or sell drugs, to access services or meals, or to participate in 'treating' networks, an informal system through which participants take turns pooling and sharing resources such as alcohol, cigarettes, money, or drugs. Some locals are 'housed' in beds provided by one of the area missions, such as the Salvation Army or the Cowgate Centre.

Under new legislation, Edinburgh City Council is obligated to secure housing for all individuals upon request. As of 2003, there were 248 shelter beds available for an estimated population of 103 homeless individuals (Rough Sleepers Initiative 2003; Edinburgh Evening News

2003b). Choice of accommodation depends on what is currently available and the needs of the requester. Some individuals do not accept council accommodation, opting instead to 'sleep rough.' While this may be considered a personal 'choice,' this choice is framed by the realities of the street. There are people who 'sleep rough' for reasons of personal security: it is commonly known on the street that hostels house individuals who victimize others, particularly the most vulnerable (see also Fitzpatrick and Kennedy 2001). One elderly street drinker I met, suffering from cancer, had his money repeatedly stolen from him while staying in a local hostel. The thefts only stopped when a friend began operating as his 'banker.'

People who 'sleep rough' find spaces in private and public areas that they see as providing them with some privacy and a measure of safety from both the elements and from humans (particularly from youths and/or drunken revellers who may prey on them when they are asleep). A tour of the historic cemetery in Greyfriar's Kirkyard in Cowgate provides ample evidence of its use as a place to 'skipper' – a site used for sleeping rough. Many of the graves are covered with cans and broken glass; one family vault revealed recent evidence of human defecation. Ordinarily, these pieces of 'material culture' could be equally attributed as the work of local youth; however, on walking through the Kirkyard on several occasions, I saw street drinkers openly eating on and sleeping among graves and, on one occasion, with a tent pitched in a family vault. Vaults in particular offer the best 'skippering' because they are rarely locked, provide a roof of sorts, and, because they are situated at the edges of the cemetery, are less exposed to view. In Greyfriar's I looked for, but did not find, evidence of its use by addicts; Canongate Kirkyard is a place more commonly used by addicts.

Although the population of Cowgate and Grassmarket tends to distinguish among themselves based on their drug of choice, a third group who fits within and across both of these groups is the mentally ill. It is difficult to estimate their numbers within the Edinburgh street population generally, as no figures appear to exist on this subject. However, a local mental health outreach worker estimates that at least one-quarter of the street population is mentally ill and that the number is likely higher among the addicts population. The latter estimation represents the fact that here, as elsewhere, a lack of facilities and services for the mentally ill has resulted in people in skid row districts having what is termed a 'dual-diagnosis': mentally ill and 'self-medicating' with alcohol and non-prescription drugs.

Although the common perception in Britain and elsewhere is that street-entrenched individuals, whether in skid row districts or elsewhere, are *a* if not *the* criminal element, as is all too often the case, street-based residents of the Cowgate and Grassmarket tend to be frequent victims of crime. Their victimization occurs both inter-class and intra-class. Instances of the former often involve intoxicated individuals who have come to Piss Alley for a night on the town and who decide to physically abuse area residents.[6] A few of the 'beggars' I spoke with recounted stories of being on the receiving end of threats and physical abuse by drunken louts. As a local service provider explains,

> Most of the crime [in this neighbourhood] would be related to the clubs and the nightclubs. Especially [on] the weekends ... which then affects our clients, because if they're trying to beg they quite often get beaten up or robbed by night clubbers, groups of young folk out for a good time, been drinking. 'Well here's somebody, let's have some fun.' You get the good money from folk coming out of nightclubs because they're drunk. So [the beggars] get the money, but you also get the [other clubbers] who become violent and aggressive.

Crimes that occur intra-class involve offences ranging from petty thefts, to harassment and intimidation, to serious assaults and murder. Violent offences often involve the use of a knife. One service provider estimated that some four-fifths of his client group carry concealed knives. 'Taxing' is a common problem on the street, particularly for the older alcoholics, who tend to be victims. This is a form of extortion, often practised by younger addicts, that involves intimidating a weaker individual into cashing a welfare cheque – a 'GIRO' – and turning over money in order to avoid physical abuse:

> If I'm bigger than you and more ruthless than you, I accompany you to the post office with your GIRO and I have a knife, then you'll give me a percentage of your GIRO, and that's very, very common. The level of intimidation and violence is really quite high.

Because of the use of harassment and intimidation by the addicts, the alcoholics prefer to remain separate from them. In response to a question on how the police could reduce crime in the area, one former street drinker told me that the best solution would be to 'get rid of the smackheads [heroin users].' Given that both groups experience exclusion on a daily basis, it is with some irony that I note that there are exclusionary desires produced within the community itself directed at those whom some (the alcoholics) perceive to be 'troublesome' (the addicts).

The Politics of Edinburgh's Skid Row

The nature of excluded spaces is that they frequently serve as the site for demands that range from the fully exclusionary, to the coercively inclusive, to the completely inclusionary, and variations thereof. In this section, I discuss in fuller detail the nature of the demands that are made by, or on behalf of, those who inhabit Edinburgh's skid row. Doing so permits an opportunity to see not only the nature and popularity of certain types of demands but also to begin to see how the larger political environment shapes these demands.

In the first chapter I stated that skid row is a manifestation of exclusion in society. It is typically the product of moral codes, expressed in retrograde zoning regulations, civic ordinances, and criminal laws that create the poor, the mentally ill, the addicted, and other unfortunates as 'deviants' to be socially, politically, geographically, and economically isolated from the rest of society. In Edinburgh, addicts and derelicts live on skid row, but they are not contained or constrained through public policies. Instead, the site represents the leftovers of a historic home for the poor. This is not to suggest that the site does not produce exclusionary demands; rather, the demands articulated do not often have a public voice and are seldom, if ever, expressed in public policies. They are, instead, smaller-scale in nature, involving localized problems and/or incidents in which a resident or merchant calls the police to demand the expulsion of a skid row inhabitant from an area on the grounds that he or she is being a nuisance and/or interfering with business. The preferred solution for all parties – the police, the merchant, and the inhabitant – is for the individual to be 'moved along,' that is, sent packing back to the skids or at least to somewhere else (other than jail).

While exclusionary demands are localized and their proponents typically do not seek and/or receive popular support, coercively inclusive demands centred on the control of the Cowgate and Grassmarket population have recently begun to increase and to find support from city councillors and business and resident groups. In 2003, for example, business and resident groups in the city's Old Town became vocal critics of the begging and other behaviours of the local homeless population,

demanding that the Edinburgh Council institute proposed local ordinances tackling public drunkenness and anti-social behaviour on the
grounds that the presence of drunken beggars was disrupting business
and harming local tourism (Mather 2003). Their demands can be placed
within the context of a larger trend in both Scotland and the United
Kingdom: councils elsewhere had begun enacting bylaws prohibiting
various forms of 'nuisance' behaviour, such as public drinking, public
loitering, and begging near cash machines, and, at the national level, a
proposed bill to tackle anti-social behaviour before the Scottish Executive. Although the demands of merchant groups in the Old Town were
centred on controlling the behaviour of the local homeless (and excluding the uncontrollable through the use of punitive measures), not all
anti-social efforts are aimed exclusively at the homeless. Other individuals and groups associated with 'uncivil' behaviour have also become
targets, including youth, certain forms of criminal elements, partiers,
people who play their music too loud, and so on. One source advised
there was even some discussion in Edinburgh about regulating the noise
levels of the nighttime ghost tours through the Old Town centre.

The civic code of behaviour that the Traders' Association, a local
merchants' organization, and local resident groups had called upon City
Council to enact had in fact been proposed two years earlier but had
failed to go anywhere. As a representative of the city explained, 'we've
been looking at that and ... just when we get to the last stages and we pass
it over to the legal department, after years they just shelved it. Too many
problems, they just quietly shelved it.' With demands for a civic code
seemingly on the increase, and with similar codes being discussed and/
or passed elsewhere, discussion of a code has been revived; however, as
of the time of writing, no civic code has been enacted.

After I had spoken with representatives of the city, as well as police and
local homeless agencies, it became clear that, despite the vocal demands
of a number of merchants, with support from some council members,
there was no significant appetite for the enactment of a local code. City
officials I spoke with suggested that the problem of public drunkenness
associated with the homeless could easily be responded to through the
provision of 'wet hostels,' that is, private spaces where alcoholics could
drink out of the sight of tourists. Police officials interviewed felt that
public bans on behaviour were unnecessary – they have the means to
address issues with the existing offence of a 'breach of the peace' – and
represented retrograde attempts at using the law to deal with complex
social issues. Further, both police and city officials agreed that measures

to move public drinking or drug use by the homeless away from 'problem areas' – local shops, high school yards, and so on – were preferable. Indeed, it seems that not all local merchants supported the crackdown on town drunks proposed by their merchants' association. I met one business owner from the area who expressed sympathy for the area's alcoholics and felt that a more appropriate target for regulation was the drink tourism in the area that leads to vandalism, debris (human and other), noise, and other problems.

Demands for exclusion, or, as in this case, coercive inclusion with the threat of exclusion, often generate inclusionary demands in response from those targeted and/or from the groups that serve them. In response to the merchants' demands, a representative from a major homeless agency issued such a counter-demand by arguing that alcoholism and drug addiction 'need to be solved rather than punished' and that 'there needs to be adequate support for these people, and a need to understand the problems that homeless people face in order to help them properly' (cited in Mather 2003). Other groups, both publicly and in interviews, expressed similar views.

The coercively inclusive demands of those who wanted to have enforceable behaviour codes are not simply met with countering inclusionary demands, resulting in a series of nonproductive exchanges that typically occur elsewhere. Rather, the Ark Trust, a major provider of services to the area's homeless, and the Old Town Business Association met in order to find common ground. The result was that the two organizations put together a project involving a series of training workshops for area merchants on issues related to homelessness as a means of alleviating some of the tensions between groups (Ferguson 2003c). Council agreed to fund the workshops; political and other support for the project came from the police and council housing staff and social workers who agreed to participate. The workshops, which are also intended to be open to residents, included face-to-face meetings between workshop participants and homeless individuals in order to 'break down mistrust and barriers' on both sides, and a survey of area residents' perceptions on crime related to homelessness (ibid.).

The Larger Political Context: Edinburgh as *Ordo*

Provision for homeless people in Edinburgh is very good. [It] passes the rest of Britain, the rest of Scotland (Shelter worker, Edinburgh)

The demands produced of and within Edinburgh's skid row are a direct reflection of the city's politics and those of the larger Scottish political and social culture. Although attempts have been made to use coercive inclusionary tactics to regulate the conduct of the row's inhabitants, such attempts have been met with inclusionary demands that have led to significant exchanges between groups, exchanges that emphasize a commitment to social inclusion. Throughout this section, I will discuss in further detail the commitment to social inclusion as part of the larger political context, which distinctly represents some aspects of an *Ordoliberalen* approach to the economic and social spheres.

In order to address problems of social exclusion within Edinburgh, the city's council funded an independent commission chaired by Edinburgh's Lord Provost to identify, study, and offer recommendations aimed at fostering social inclusion throughout the city. In June 2000 the Commission delivered the One City report, which contained analyses of various identified problems – unemployment; low pay; limited skills; poor housing; poor educational experience; high crime levels; bad health; disability and family breakdown; age, gender, and racial discrimination – and a list of eighty-seven recommendations to address these issues. Council accepted the report and developed it into a multi-agency project funded by the city and through grants secured from the Scottish Executive and the European Community.

The project centres on recommendations that fall within six themes. These themes include: (1) achieving civil rights and social justice; (2) reducing income inequalities; (3) fostering citizen communication and information and the development of (4) preventative agencies; (5) multi-agency, cross-sector partnerships; and (6) resources for inclusion. A working group sponsored by Council – the Edinburgh Partnership Group – supervises the implementation and monitoring of recommendations and reports on successes and challenges that have been encountered in the implementation process. Individual recommendations have been assigned to council departments with responsibilities in areas covered by the report. Each department is tasked with either implementing a recommendation directly, creating a multi-agency partnership to effect implementation, and/or sponsoring public or private agencies in the implementation of the specific recommendation.

Since the program was begun in 2000, One City has met with both successes and stumbling blocks. Since many of the recommendations covered by the report, such as those concerning the need to facilitate care of the elderly, are outside the scope of this study, I would like to review some results that have a more direct bearing on the issues and problems encountered by inhabitants of Cowgate/Grassmarket. For example, in 2001, through the Rough Sleepers Initiative, a 'wet hostel' with ten permanent and three temporary flats was funded that can admit practising addicts with severe addiction problems (One City 2003). Several steps have also been taken to ensure that those without means can receive public access to government and other information. These steps include Internet facilities, which have been installed in all public libraries, service outlets to provide information and advice on housing issues, and a Welfare Rights Service to provide assistance to individuals in securing benefits claims that they are eligible to receive (ibid.). Funding has also been provided to community food programs, café facilities for the homeless, and school snack programs (ibid.).

Some of the tasks associated with the One City recommendations are significantly more ambitious than those implemented thus far. For example, to address income inequality, the report proposes a 'wide ranging review of benefits policies with people who depend on them, to ensure that they are effective and consistent with social inclusion policy. This [review] should give consideration to a basic income scheme' (One City ibid.). However, neither Edinburgh City Council nor the Scottish Parliament can implement this recommendation, as income support programs remain a function of the United Kingdom government.[7] At best, Council can lobby the United Kingdom government for changes to income support. I do note, however, that the willingness of Council to offer support for such redistributive schemes, and in many cases to actively lobby and work in support of the aims that underlie such schemes, is indicative of the depth of civic voters' commitment to public welfare in their city.

The city's current efforts at dealing with its homeless population are supported by Scotland's Parliamentary Executive. Since 1998, the Executive has developed a variety of initiatives aimed at alleviating the effects of poverty and social exclusion, including the establishment of a Homelessness Task Force that has made a series of recommendations incorporated into a Homelessness Bill; a Rough Sleepers' Initiative that has provided £36 million in funding for shelter, health care, and other services for the homeless; the Empty Homes Initiative, which provided £24 million to local councils for use in converting vacant properties into living spaces for the homeless; and the recently passed Homelessness Act. This act could be characterized as fairly progressive because, among other changes, tests that had formerly denied and delayed assistance and services to the homeless have been removed. Further, the act also places a mandate upon the various levels of government to provide accommodation and services for all homeless.[8]

Whereas Scotland's powers to establish laws and regulations with respect to housing and accommodation have recently devolved, the funding and administration of income support programs remains the province of the United Kingdom government. This has resulted in a situation whereby the homeless and other urban poor in Edinburgh receive accommodation and services from their local council funded by the Scottish Parliament, with income support received separately. Income support in the U.K. is a means-tested benefit available to those who fall below a standard fixed income level[9] and who are not eligible for their unemployment benefit (jobseeker's allowance). Aside from government income, qualified recipients also automatically receive free school meals, prescriptions, dental care, eyeglass coverage, housing benefits, council tax benefits, and free milk and vitamins for expectant mothers and children under the age of five.

Political and social attitudes of those in the United Kingdom have historically been 'left of centre' in contrast to the United States or parts of Europe[10] (Paterson et al. 2001). This orientation is said to be particularly true of Scotland in relation to the rest of the U.K.: 'the finding has generally been that Scotland tends to be more in favour of state action to overcome inequalities of wealth, and more supportive of state provision in key parts of the welfare state such as health and education' (ibid.: 121). Paterson et al. (ibid.: 124–5) base their support for this contention on data drawn from the Scottish Parliamentary Election Study (National Centre for Social Research 1999), among other sources, which suggest that

> large majorities [of Scottish voters] believe that the government is responsible for dealing with some of the central social problems that have always been the preoccupation of the welfare state – the effects of ill-health, retirement, disability, unemployment and old age. There is fairly clear support for more public spending to cope with these matters, even if that meant taxes rising.

Given that Scotland has traditionally been seen as supportive of the welfare state (see also Hearn 2002), it is something of a paradox that, until devolution, Scotland was part of a constitutional union in which successive voter majorities, from 1979 to 1997, elected Conservative governments running on a distinctly American-style neo-liberal political platform. Clearly, it is beyond the scope of this study to neatly resolve this paradox; however, Denver, Mitchell, Pattie, and Bochel's study (2000) of various Scottish voter and public opinion surveys and Paterson et al.'s analysis of the Scottish Parliamentary Election Survey of 1999 (ibid.), shed some insight.

Based on examinations of public opinion surveys on the issue of devolution, Denver et al. state that support for a Scottish Parliament was, for many voters, tied to support for public welfare policies (ibid.).[11] The authors further suggest that this finding 'is not surprising as devolution came to be seen as a way of avoiding or opposing the imposition of "Thatcherite" policies on Scotland' (ibid.: 200). They add:

> The association between the two was confirmed in the referendum. Conservatives and those of a right-wing disposition were least likely to support a Scottish Parliament while those favouring state intervention, identifying with the working class and left-leaning political parties were most likely to do so. In essence, support for a Scottish Parliament went hand in hand with support for more left-inclined policies (ibid.).

Another indication of the feelings of Scottish voters towards the neo-liberal agenda of the Tory ruling party of the 1980s and early 1990s can be gleaned from Monaghan's (1997: 22) contention that 'the Conservative vote in Scotland went into consistent decline throughout this decade and their power base was dramatically reduced north of the border; they did not control any regional councils and only a handful of small district councils.' Rather than embracing Thatcher's neo-liberalism – a form that approximated the prescriptions of Hayek and the Chicago School – the majority of voters in Scotland explicitly rejected it in favour of an orientation that encompasses social justice aims, a choice that was repeatedly expressed through a variety of political forums ranging from local council votes to the referendum on devolution (Monaghan 1997; Denver et al. 2000). However, in retracting from the neo-liberal agenda presented, voters did not call for a return to the earlier Keynesian model of government planning.[12] Rather, by demanding the inclusion of social justice aims within a market-based economy, they sought a form of social market economy not entirely dissimilar from the model advocated by the *Ordoliberalen*.

I should also note another important influence on the decision of

Scottish citizens to adopt a version of the Ordo model: Scotland's participation within the European Union (EU). EU policy is clearly predicated
on some of the major principles of Ordoliberalism. We see this most
clearly in the adoption of social inclusion as an EU policy goal and the
methods selected for advancing inclusion. The EU supports inclusionary
programs through a funding mechanism called the European Structural
Funds. Two EU programs are most relevant to this discussion: the European Regional Development Fund (ERDF) and the European Social
Fund (ESF). The purpose of the ERDF is to improve economic prosperity and social inclusion by investing in projects to promote diversified
development. The ESF promotes inclusion through funding training,
human resources, and equal opportunities schemes that promote employment. In short, both programs attempt to address social exclusion as
defined in terms of labour market participation. That is, exclusion is
seen as tied to market performance and conditions, and remedies thus
lie in inclusionary markets and market expansion. The mechanism for
accomplishing these goals, as mandated by the EU, is private–public
partnerships (Scottish Executive 2004).

Scotland's allocation from the Structural Funds for the period of 2000
to 2006 is over £950 million (Scottish Executive 2004)). Following from
the principles contained within the EU's provisions, inclusionary inter-
ventions in Edinburgh take place in cooperation with the market – that
is, they are aligned with market needs and dictates and represent the
amount of inclusion that it is believed the market can bear. To ensure
that market needs are represented, the bulk of inclusionary work is
undertaken by private–public partnerships. The participation of the
business sector in facilitating socially beneficial work aims to encourage
social responsibility towards the public while reducing the potential for
group conflicts to emerge.

The policy framework for Scottish economic development is set out in
The Way Forward (Scottish Executive 2000), a report of the Scottish
Executive. In this report, we see most clearly the shift from Thatcherite
neo-liberalism towards the *Ordoliberalen* approach. For example, the Scottish Executive describes their policy framework as an attempt to establish
an 'overarching vision ... of the kind of society that we would like to see
in 5 to 10 years time and the kind of economy in Scotland that would
best serve that purpose' (ibid.: xii). No longer does the social sphere
serve the economy, but rather the emphasis is on the improvement of
society and the economy as a tool to further that goal. Further, the
framework redefines the roles of the state and the markets in a manner

that is characteristic of the Ordo model: 'private enterprises [are to] be the key driver of the new economy' (ibid.: viii), whereas the government's function is to create public policies that promote both economic equity and efficiency. The government will perform this task through 'the provision of legal and regulatory systems that maintain the interests of society without imposing inordinate burdens on enterprises' (ibid.: 28–9). Finally, implicit in this document is both a rejection of Keynesianism – 'private sector and economic markets are generally better able to make efficient decisions about the conduct of economic activity than the public sector' (ibid.: 28) – and a rejection of American neo-liberal ideology – 'markets may fail to deliver the allocation of resources and the level of activity that are socially desirable' (ibid.: 29).

Are the Scottish voters' aims of a social market founded on economic increase and social inclusion to be realized? The result of devolution was a set of high expectations among the voting public concerning the ability of the Scottish Parliament to improve public welfare in Scotland (Denver et al. ibid.). These expectations have been met with a growing awareness of the limits of Scotland's parliamentary powers (Paterson et al. ibid.). To the extent that taxation in Scotland remains a United Kingdom power, the ability of the Scottish Parliament to engage in wider redistributive schemes, such as increased social benefits, is limited (Denver et al. ibid.; Paterson et al. ibid.). This limitation, serious as it is, has not however impeded successive Scottish Executives from effecting policies and programs aimed at increasing both public welfare (through both new and traditional redistributive schemes – e.g., the Homeless Bill) and the inclusion of a variety of traditionally marginalized groups.

It could be argued, though, that the introduction of an Anti-Social Behaviour Bill in October 2003 by the Scottish First Minister is hardly an example of social inclusion in that it would lead to the problematization, indeed the criminalization, of certain forms of 'uncivil conduct' (that this conduct has class-based dimensions has certainly not escaped those critics who represent the individuals most likely to be affected by the bill's provisions). In contrast to the Homelessness Act, which was popularly supported, various provisions of this bill have met with widespread criticism from a variety of public and private individuals and organizations, including not only homeless advocates such as Shelter Scotland, but also academics, the Association of Chief Police Officers of Scotland, the Law Society of Scotland, the Scottish Police Federation, the Scottish Federation of Housing Associations, the Scottish Children's Reporter Administration, and the Scottish Legal Aid Board (Denholm 2004).

While some of these organizations have expressed concern about a lack of clarity in some of the bill's provisions and others have cited concerns about inadequate funding for the increased services that would be required to meet the bill's goals, in interviews with senior police staff I was repeatedly advised that anti-social behaviour codes, which create new offences and give police enhanced powers, were both unnecessary and socially undesirable. As of this writing, the bill has not been enacted.

Conclusion

In this chapter, I explored Edinburgh's skid row district through an examination of aspects of its geographical, historical, and social dimensions. This was followed by a discussion of the politics of the site and the demands made of and by its inhabitants. This discussion revealed that the discourse surrounding the Cowgate and Grassmarket is predominately inclusive. Inclusionary discourse consists of both demands that inhabitants be embraced by the larger society as citizens who need assistance and understanding as well as coercively inclusive demands that denizens conform to normative codes under the threat of punishment (expulsion to jail).

The discussion of the site's politics was followed by an examination of the larger Scottish political and social culture that gives rise to the nature of demands produced within and in response to skid row. This analysis provided a context for understanding the influence of the *Ordoliberalen* model in shaping a cultural commitment to social inclusion within the city of Edinburgh and in its institutions.

3 Community Policing as Knowledge Work

The primary purpose of this chapter is to explore the conception of police as 'demand negotiators' through an examination of the ways in which the Lothian and Borders (L&B) regional police force in Edinburgh respond to inclusionary and exclusionary demands directed at Edinburgh's skid row residents. I argue throughout that the style of policing used here is reflective of the larger institutional environment: it is one that is mainly consonant with elements of the *Ordoliberalen* political model, significant aspects of which are found within the larger political culture. However, while the L&B model privileges inclusionary work through the use of private–public partnerships, exclusionary attitudes and behaviour towards those on skid row continue to operate on an individual level on the frontlines.

I begin this chapter by providing a brief overview of the structure of the Lothian and Borders regional police force. I then offer an institutional analysis of Edinburgh policing, as it relates to the Cowgate and Grassmarket, through an examination of major policing programs and their effects on this neighbourhood. This analysis reveals the ways in which knowledge work is privileged within the institution – within the framework of a community policing model – and how this privileging can be interpreted as a response to demands for increased police service with minimal resource increases. From this, the analysis turns to street-level policing, and I explore questions relating to how frontline officers in Edinburgh's skid row district understand and perform their roles and functions 'on the street' within the four policing frameworks discussed earlier. Here we see how frontline police officers utilize these frameworks to understand and negotiate the sets of demands that are placed upon them from different local constituencies. Officers' perceptions are compared with those of the residents policed in order to explore key similarities and differences. Finally, through a discussion of police willingness to effect positive social change in the neighbourhood they serve, we see how police officers at all levels of the institution understand themselves as political actors within a larger politicized environment.

The Lothian and Borders (L&B) Police

The city of Edinburgh is policed by the Lothian and Borders (L&B) Police, a regional force that covers the city of Edinburgh, East Lothian, West Lothian, Midlothian, and the Scottish Borders. The force was founded in 1975 from an amalgam of the Edinburgh City Police, the Berwick, Roxburgh and Selkirk Constabulary, and the Lothian and Peebles Constabulary. Approximately 2600 police officers and 1100 civilian staff members comprise the L&B's six divisions. The force's annual budget for the fiscal year of 2002–3 was approximately £164,000,000, with funding being received jointly from the Scottish Executive (Lothian and Borders Police 2003b). The Scottish Executive funds 51 per cent of the police budget and the regional Police Board funds 49 per cent, which includes of a support grant from the Executive and local taxes.

The city of Edinburgh comprises the L&B's 'A' Division. In April 2003, this division was reorganized through the implementation of 'Operation Capital,' a plan aimed at fostering community policing and increasing resource efficiencies. Prior to the reorganization, Edinburgh had fourteen police stations within three policing divisions: City Centre, West End, and Leith. These divisions are now merged into one central division, headed by a chief superintendent and headquartered at the St Leonard's Police Station. The organization's emphasis on community policing is now manifest within the structure of the division itself. Aside from the operation of specialized units, Division A is policed through a combination of relief (patrol response) and sector (community-based) policing strategies, with the number of assigned community policing positions exceeding that of regular patrol officers by a ratio of 60 to 40 per cent.

Car patrol and immediate-response functions are performed by officers on one of four response teams deployed from the Craigmillar, Drylaw, St Leonard's, and Corstorphine stations. The response teams are composed of a minimum of twenty-one patrol cars that are responsible for responding to calls on a city-wide basis. These cars handle calls for police attendance for serious offences that are prioritized as call grades one (immediate police response) and two (requiring police attendance in less than one hour). Patrol cars are not specifically assigned to work within the Cowgate and the Grassmarket but do respond to calls in this neighbourhood, patrolling these and other areas when not responding to calls for service ('down times').

Community policing functions in Edinburgh are performed by community beat officers (CBOs) working within one of six local policing areas (LPAs). The six LPAs are South (Howdenhall, Morningside, Newington), East (Portobello, Craigmillar), North and Leith (Drylaw, Leith), West (Queensferry, Corstorphine, Edinburgh Airport), Pentlands (Balerno, Oxgangs, Wester Hailes), and Central (Murrayfield, Gayfield, Southside, Tollcross, which covers the Cowgate and Grassmarket). Each LPA contains 'sectors' consisting of 'beats' patrolled by CBOs on foot. The new police beats and sectors are conterminous with electoral ward boundaries in order to provide police, city councillors, and local members of the Scottish Parliament (MSPs) with one point of contact for constituency-related problems. The Cowgate and Grassmarket are each part of the Central LPA, headquartered at the Gayfield Police Station. Cowgate forms part of the beat assigned to approximately twenty CBOs and five sergeants, who are assigned to five teams reporting to the Southside sector inspector (Central LPA; officers for this LPA are deployed from the Gayfield police station). This beat corresponds directly to the city electoral wards of Southside and Holyrood, representing a geographically large and socio-economically diverse site. Grassmarket is part of the Tollcross sector, which corresponds to the city electoral wards of Tollcross, Dalry, and Fountainbridge. This sector is similarly staffed by a sector inspector, who is assigned a roughly equivalent complement of sergeants[1] and CBOs. CBOs in these sites perform routine beat functions, perform community liaison work, and respond to grade three (response within four hours) and four (response within a day) calls. Grades five and six do not require a police presence and are handled by the police call centre.

The work of the CBOs, which is discussed in further detail in later sections, is supplemented by that of the Community Safety Branch, which is staffed by specialist officers known as crime prevention officers (CPOs). CPOs function as official liaisons between the police and various communities, offering police educational services and working with other agencies and groups on local policing-related community problems.

Policing Cowgate/Grassmarket: The Organizational Perspective

In multiple interviews with police and other sources, it became clear that Edinburgh's police and populace do not draw sharp distinctions between the Cowgate and Grassmarket and the rest of the city. Further support for this contention can be drawn from the fact that, despite being what I term a skid row district with a sizable street-based population, the Cowgate and Grassmarket do not receive special police attention. There is no saturation policing, nor are there police programs specific to the area to combat its perceived ills. Rather, policing levels and service are generally the same within this community as they are throughout the city. In the remainder of this section, I discuss the nature of this service and its impacts on both the city as a whole and on the Cowgate and Grassmarket.

The new community policing model implemented by the L&B force is built on two key components of community policing programs generally: community partnering and public consultation (O'Malley and Palmer 1996; Trojanowicz et al. 1998). Community partnering is formalized in policies and programs that fall under the umbrella of what the force terms 'partnership working.' Partnership working serves two major functions for the organization: it fosters resource efficiencies and it feeds demands for institutional knowledge that are produced from within and outside.

It has been argued that implicit within community policing programs is a recognition by police managers that resource efficiencies can be gained by 'offloading' responsibility for crime prevention or response through redefining criminal or disorderly behaviour as social problems with causes more appropriately addressed by other institutions (Ericson 1994). In discussing the new model, senior police management acknowledge as a central concern the need to improve resource efficiencies within the organization, particularly at a time of increasing demands and limited resources. Further, they acknowledge that partnership working permits opportunities to 'responsibilize' through sharing or offloading responsibilities onto other agencies (Garland 1996). Partnership working is thus justified in light of both the system capacity limits of the organization and the restrictions placed on the institution's powers and mandate. The following comment from a senior police manager exemplifies the organization's focus on rationalization, efficiency, and responsibility shifting:

Over time, particularly in this part of the country, we recognized that there are a lot of other resources and a lot of other expert players in their fields ... We're terrible, one of our weaknesses as an organization is that we get sucked into the vacuum, and we end up doing jobs that we didn't do before, and shouldn't do. We end up doing non-police jobs, things like social care jobs. And we see active partnership working as being a way of making sure that we get the best out of everybody, and others have to take the responsibility.

Concern with institutional cost-effectiveness is part of a recent trend within the public sector towards 'public managerialism' (O'Malley and Palmer 1996; Rose 1999; McLaughlin and Murji 2001). Public managerialism is based on the belief that governments can and should be run like private enterprise. Thus, police managers and other public sector heads are expected to implement policies and procedures that emphasize fiscal responsibility, accountability, standardization of processes, performance measures, and competitiveness. Whereas in the private sector each of these corporate values supports profit as the bottom line, in the public sector the bottom line is good service, which is defined largely as service that is inexpensively and efficiently provided. L&B management has adopted the 'new public management' approach. This is evident from the words of a high-ranking police official who advised: 'We see the ability to harness energies of different agencies effectively as being a key to success and a key performance indicator.' However, as I discuss later, management's concern with 'efficiencies' does not preclude the organization from attempting to further social justice aims.

Thus far, I have been focusing on how the new model promotes responsibility sharing across agency networks. However, 'responsibilization strategies' (Garland 1996) initiated by the L&B also commonly target individuals. A prime example of this is the force's drug education work, where CPOs work with community groups and schools to educate young people on drug use and its effects. This crime prevention activity could be explained as a traditional social work function of the police; however it is justified within the organization in light of its ability to produce resource efficiencies. This justification is found in the words of a CPO in the field: 'The more effective we are at working with people in prevention work and safety work, then the less we have to do the enforcement side.' Crime prevention creates resource efficiencies through teaching individuals techniques of self-governance. This officer further adds: 'It's massively more cost effective from a business perspective to try and approach [the drug issue through crime prevention] rather than from an enforcement angle.' What we see in this officer's words is the institutional privileging of knowledge work over law enforcement on the grounds that the latter is ineffective, both in terms of costs and resources.

'Partnership working,' and the new community policing model that supports it, has entailed a shift within the working culture of the L&B force. As an occupation that utilizes authority to achieve objectives, the police have come to be seen, and to see themselves, as 'experts' on a much wider variety of issues than the new model permits them. Officers are now encouraged to acknowledge, both openly and privately, that they 'don't have all the answers' and that it is 'okay to say that we can't do something' (senior officer). As a frontline supervisor explained, a process had to be put into place whereby 'the more astute sergeants [had] to accept this [new attitude] and work with the street level officers to accept this.' The process of garnering acceptance of this shift through the ranks is furthered by the willingness of senior police management to publicly adopt the same attitude. As one high-ranking official stated, 'We are a law enforcement agency. We do not have the answers to all of society's problems.'

Acceptance of 'partnership working' has also been made easier by the recasting of frontline officers' roles. Patrol officers no longer have to assume responsibility for less serious calls, which have traditionally been disparaged as being 'not real police work' (Van Maanen 1978a; Chan, Devery, and Doran 2003). These calls are instead routed at source to community beat officers. And while the CBOs are now tasked with responding to lower-level calls from residents and businesses concerning safety and crime issues, work formerly looked down upon, their role has been reconceived as a 'specialist' position within the organization. They are now 'security experts' who operate within security networks, advising individuals, groups, and other agencies on how to prevent and respond to crime (Ericson 1994; O'Malley and Palmer 1996; Ericson and Haggerty 1997). With partnership working, CBOs have become 'knowledge brokers' who are tasked with negotiating outcomes with other agencies through the use of the organization's knowledge of security-related issues. This knowledge is built up primarily through the work of both sets of frontline officers – patrol and CBOs/CPOs – who each feed the system through their respective modes of intelligence gathering. The CBO position is seen as particularly useful in this regard by senior management. This was made clear by a senior officer who acknowledged that the organization accepted that the use of CBOs would likely not have a direct effect on reducing area crime rates. However, these positions provide benefits to the organization through knowledge production, as this senior officer explained: 'The CBOs ... have the opportunity to get to know their public ... they're speaking to people ... they start getting low-level intelligence coming back and it's fed into the system ... the greater picture: overall intelligence for the city.'

Prior to the reorganization of the Edinburgh divisions, the L&B held extensive public consultations in order to develop a model of policing that would garner widespread support. Again, such efforts are identified with community policing programs in other jurisdictions, which have similarly looked to public input as a means of not only designing systems and programs but also re-legitimating police service in light of increasing public exposure of system limitations (O'Malley and Palmer 1996; Garland 1996). One significant result of the consultation process in Edinburgh has been the return of the 'beat bobby.'

As Shearing and Stenning (1984) have observed, an increasing feature of urban life is the embedding of security and control functions within structures and forms that are represented as fun, friendly, helpful, and/ or non-coercive, rendering such control consensual. This is no less the case in Edinburgh, where the security functions served through the knowledge work of the CBOs are obscured through an institutional representation of these police actors as 'beat bobbies.' The 'beat bobby' is the immensely popular old-style Scottish police officer who walked a designated beat within a community and took ownership of that beat through the cultivation of personal relations with area residents. Residents, community groups, and service providers, in a variety of forums ranging from personal interviews to community meetings and letters to the editor in local newspapers, repeatedly expressed a preference for a community-oriented approach built on the back of the 'beat bobby.' The power of the 'beat bobby' mythology is understood and used by the police to make control of communities a consensual phenomenon – indeed, as a phenomenon that is dictated by the public: 'When I joined it was beats ... and we're trying to get back to that because, again, it's trying to meet public demands' (senior officer). What remains only obliquely acknowledged is the extent to which this new form of 'beat bobby,' heralded as a symbol of 'community,' actually serves extra-local and extra-institutional security purposes. We see these purposes most clearly in the previously cited comments of the senior officer who noted that local intelligence gathered by CBOs is expected to have little direct effect on communities but would assist in creating a knowledge base for city-wide intelligence.

Although a good portion of community policing now rests on the frontline work of specialist positions such as the CBOs and CPOs, community policing requires police visibility not only in the street but also through other media (O'Malley and Palmer 1996). To this end, the L&B produces communications for external consumption. Annual newsletters containing information on force clearance rates and police initiatives raise public awareness while simultaneously attempting to satisfy demand for public accountability. Force-produced fact-sheets on such issues as 'personal safety' and 'pedal cycle security' similarly serve dual purposes: they garner positive public relations for the police while providing a means by which the police can educate the populace to accept responsibility for crime prevention.

Organizational goals of police visibility, public consultation, and public accountability are served through police attendance at community meetings. Although significant emphasis is placed on police attendance at community meetings generally, for some positions – CBOs, CPOs, and, depending on the nature of the meeting, inspectors and divisional commanders – such attendance is a mandatory job requirement. During my time in Edinburgh, I attended a Local Community Development (LCD) meeting for the Central City District (which includes Cowgate and the Grassmarket). An LCD meeting is a smaller-scale version of a city hall meeting at which councillors, police, city hall workers, community groups, and residents of a local area attend to discuss local issues. Representing the police were the superintendent of Central Edinburgh Division and the chief inspector for the City Centre, who were present to field questions directly from the audience of residents. What was interesting to note was the degree of professionalism with which the officers responded to questions from the audience of residents, some of whom were overtly critical or inquired about matters irrelevant to police concerns. The force requires officers who attend public meetings to receive training in working effectively in those situations, and this training was apparent in the adept handling of resident queries.

Whereas in some cities a police presence is not welcomed by groups that work with extremely marginalized residents, each of the service providers interviewed sought cooperative relations with the police and desired to foster positive interactions between police and their clients. Some service providers actively maintain friendships and/or effective working relationships with police personnel; others make a point of inviting CBOs to come to their facilities for coffee and a chance to meet clients. As a consequence of staffing shortages following the implementation of Operation Capital, shortages that are discussed more fully in chapter 8, the Cowgate, Grassmarket, and other areas of the city were without a full complement of CBOs on the street during the research period. This fact was lamented by service providers, who depicted this gap in service as representing, for their clients, a loss of opportunities for building relationships. For many service providers, 'partnership working' is seen as preferable to the traditional law enforcement approach prevalent in many skid row communities because it represents a move away from exclusion-oriented policing towards a form that offers the potential for increased inclusivity.

The juxtaposition of these two approaches and service providers' feelings about each are seen most noticeably in relation to discussion of how calls for police service have been handled during the post-Capital police 'resource crunch.' Service providers noted that altercations on their premises that escalated beyond what could be informally resolved – perhaps involving violence or threats – are designated by police call-takers as priority one or two offences to be responded to by a city-wide patrol team. It is felt by service providers that patrol officers who respond to such calls are only interested in effecting a summary resolution, usually through the medium of arrest. However, the resort to law enforcement (arrest) is seen as a failure of the community policing model, with its emphasis on greater inclusion. Some service providers believed that summary arrests are indicative of discriminatory attitudes held towards their clients: '[These officers] got no sense of community ... They take them away to Mayfield and Dalkeith [jails]. I don't say it's a form of positive policing.' The majority felt that such arrests represent an undesirable form of exclusion-oriented policing that hampers the social work goals of the service provider.

In relation to CBOs, service providers were of the view that these officers were much less likely to resort to law enforcement. As one outreach worker stated of the CBOs, 'I get the impression that the police to an extent ... they don't want to be arresting people if they can avoid it.' Unsurprisingly then, given the belief that law enforcement impedes social work goals, service providers expressed a preference for having calls for service responded to by CBOs rather than by patrol officers. It was felt that social programming would be facilitated by having CBOs accessible because they not only have detailed knowledge of the street milieu but are perceived as being more likely to have an empathetic understanding of street life. To be clear: service providers do not require the police to be social workers themselves but rather to assist the social work process through providing knowledge of the local population, expertise on security issues, and, occasionally, the threat of resort to authority or force (arrest) in effecting social work outcomes with recalcitrant individuals. In short, area service workers favour inclusionary policing that is occasionally coercively inclusive, but only under exceptional circumstances. To the extent that CBOs, as the social worker cited above suggests, do not appear to be actively engaging in exclusionary policing (such as arresting individuals for status offences), the situation suits both institutions.

Thus far I have been focusing on the new community model. The discussion has revealed a picture of pragmatic police managers who are concerned with increasing efficiencies, gathering intelligence, and legitimating their service in the eyes of the community. This however is only a partial picture of the agency studied, and I must also include some discussion of a recent police management initiative that shows the organization's support for what I term 'pro-social policing' – inclusionary policing that advances the cause of social justice.

Marginalized communities typically have fairly low crime reporting rates for a variety of reasons, including a fear of being discriminated against by the criminal justice system and a lack of trust in the police. This is hardly surprising for members of the homeless community, particularly those well entrenched in street life and/or living in skid row communities, who are likely to view the police negatively because their contact with this organization has been limited to being treated by its agents either as criminals or potential criminals (Black 1980). And yet, as senior police within the L&B acknowledge, the problem of 'hidden crime' also tends to be higher within marginalized communities. This is certainly the case with the homeless who experience harassment, intimidation, and violence from within and outside their communities. And, to the extent that some crimes are committed intra-class in Edinburgh as in other cities, the 'hidden crime' problem is compounded as a result of group codes that prohibit 'grassing' (the Scottish term for reporting offences to the police committed by others in the group).

To address victimization experienced by those on the street, the homelessness distance reporting program was initiated in July 2003 following the release of a private report by the Ark Trust. The Ark, a service provider for the homeless community, explored the issue of barriers to crime reporting by young homeless people, producing a set of recommendations to foster better police–homeless community relations. These recommendations were, in essence, demands for improved police service for this marginalized community. In response, a senior police official began working with local service agencies to set up a distance (or remote) reporting scheme. The program was intended to permit homeless people to anonymously file complaints with service providers, who would, in turn, forward complaints to a designated police inspector. The inspector, the service provider, and the complainants work together to determine how to proceed on a complaint.

What I find particularly interesting about this initiative is that it involves actively encouraging people to report to the police – that is, to consume police services. Given that a primary focus of the L&B organization appears to be on increasing resource efficiencies through reallocating social problems to other agencies or through responsibilizing citizens to deal with their own problems, this process of working within marginalized communities to increase reporting of 'hidden' offences seems to be at odds with current management philosophy, and yet it is supported and encouraged within the organization. During the course of interviews with at least two high-ranking officers, when the name of the leading proponent of the distance-reporting program was raised, he was spoken of in positive terms because of his ability to 'not take a traditional approach' (senior officer) – that is, to respond positively to the demands of a given community within the existing institutional framework. I see such programs as indicative of the L&B's willingness to mirror itself on the larger political environment in Edinburgh by attempting, in *Ordoliberalen* fashion, to marry social justice goals with 'enterprise' concerns.

Policing Cowgate/Grassmarket: The Frontline Perspective

I conducted interviews with frontline officers who represented various positions within the organization. These interviews generally began with a fairly broad question: 'What do you do?' One officer explains his work in the following terms:

> A great deal of our job is patrolling. If you're not involved in inquiries, you're patrolling. On patrol downtime, when you're not going to a job – that's an inquiry or a particular incident – if you're not going to an incident, you're patrolling. Looking for things happening on the street. That's how we do it. If we're not doing incidents, we're also doing inquiries, follow-up inquiries.

Another describes his function as follows:

> We work with numerous agencies and partner agencies with common goals themselves. And there's a lot of sense in going along to meet with them and trying to see what we can do with these agencies. It's difficult to say a certain percentage, but we do attend a fair number of meetings [and are] asked to represent the service.

A third explains her perception of 'the job':

> I'm a community beat officer and my function is to respond to grade three and four calls ... I'm also supposed to be on the beat, walking the beat, meeting with people, and dealing with issues that go on in my beat. And, also, anything else I'm supposed to do [laughs]. Quite often we cover ... ourselves, we cover the high courts, superior court, the court of appeal, prison escorts that are required to go to the Royal Infirmary ... palace details, football details ... you name it, we do it.
> Q: You're a general dogsbody? [laughs]
> A: Yeah. [laughs]

As this exchange illustrates, a recurring theme in interviews with frontline officers and their supervisors was the frustration lower ranks experience in being 'abstracted' away from duties on the street to attend to tasks that are perceived as being either time-wasting and/or 'not real police work.' In response to a question asking whether beat officers were able to build up police knowledge of local drug activity, an officer complained, 'A lot of the time recently you've got abstractions, a lack of resources. You're not on your beat enough. You're not getting allowed to build up a picture because as officers you're doing other things.'

I also asked officers to what extent they saw themselves and the role they serve on the streets as fitting into one of four frameworks identified: as law enforcers, peacekeepers, social workers, and knowledge workers. Officers, both frontline and management, tended to prioritize and emphasize their roles as knowledge workers above the other role categories. One officer stated that she saw herself as 'more of the information worker, because everybody's got to work together, to get involved.' Another officer, who also saw himself primarily in terms of knowledge work, explains how this approach translates on the street:

> We try and do that [knowledge work]. Some officers more than others. Hopefully now that things have settled down a bit with Operation Capital

that we will somehow have time to pop out to Cowgate day centre. 'How are
things going? Who's been off the drugs? Who's been harassing?'

The prioritizing of knowledge work over other roles by individual officers appears as an obvious product of the working culture of the force,
with its emphasis on the importance of 'partnership working.'

The reciprocal nature of knowledge work has been explored in the
literature within the context of inter-institution partnerships (Ericson
and Haggerty 1997); however, knowledge sharing at street level is critical
to effective police work on skid row (Bittner 1967). An officer reveals
how this relationship often works in the Cowgate and Grassmarket:

> What's been happening is ... a guy and a girl going about trying to rob
> homeless people, so if we can get the word out on the street. If you treat
> them right, you can use them as information as well. We try to find out the
> word on the street from the homeless, the beggars, from the staff at the
> Cowgate Centre and the skin clinic [a bathing facility for area residents].

Although a good portion of the knowledge work that occurs on skid
row involves little more than routine conversations through which information is gathered and/or shared, the knowledge worker role is significantly more complex as a consequence of the fact that the police
institution is organized around formats, rules, and technologies that
demand standardized knowledge production (Ericson 1994; Ericson
and Haggerty 1997). The frontline officer is therefore required to translate the variables of human nature as it exists on skid row into formats
that can be processed both for her own knowledge – the basis upon
which to make local decisions – and for the decision-making purposes of
those linked into the larger system. The most frequently occurring
example of how this plays out on the street is the warrant-checking
process. Both observations and interviews confirm that it is standard
procedure for officers to demand identification for the purpose of
checking for warrants in situations where it appears that one or more of
the individuals they are in contact with may be of the 'criminal element.'
Warrants are checked and sometimes individuals searched, regardless of
whether an individual is a victim, witness, or perpetrator. My first exposure to this process occurred when I witnessed patrol officers attend a
domestic dispute call in a public street outside of the Cowgate and
Grassmarket. Both the alleged male perpetrator and the female victim
were searched and checked for warrants. I subsequently asked a police

officer about this process, particularly as it is one that is seen as discriminatory by service providers and some area residents:

> There's several reasons to what we are doing ... Officer safety is an issue. In a
> situation that I don't know, I'm going to check out ... is that person wanted
> on warrants? ... duty, duty to the person, duty to the law. And, another one,
> has that person committed a crime? Is there a pattern here?

Scrutiny of the reasons offered by the officer reveals the mix of local
and extra-local decision-making factors that are involved in the warrant-
checking process. Local concerns involve officer safety and the need for
knowledge to assist in expediting resolution of the instant case. Extra-
local factors, which are described by him as 'duty to the law,' include the
need to provide knowledge and bodies to the larger criminal justice
system, of which the police form only one part. The issue of whether the
individual checked has committed an act or actions that form a pattern
is necessary for both the resolution of the instant case and, depending
on the nature of the activities involved, may be information necessary to
the police system and to other public and private agencies (insurance
companies, social service agencies, private security, and so on). The warrant-checking process can thus be seen as a means by which the frontlines
satisfy extra-institutional demands for the production of knowledge.

While the rationales in support of the warrant-checking process are
clearly justifiable, it is also apparent that warrant checking is exercised in
a discretionary fashion, largely context-specific, and can be applied in a
discriminatory way, as some service providers suggest. In response to the
charge of discriminatory police, one officer states: 'We're not targeting
homeless people ... If a homeless person's a victim of an assault in the
streets, I don't need to check him out.' However, another frontline
officer contradicts this statement: 'Quite often if you know [someone's]
a beggar, you'll check them out for arrest warrants. They get checked out
all the time.' Further, street residents whom I spoke with advised that
police will periodically come through an area – such as Hunter's Square –
and do systematic criminal records checks of the residents sitting there. I
was curious to know whether such checks are performed as part of a
process for pushing residents out of a particular area, but street drinkers
whom I spoke with advised that police simply come through and 'ask
your name and your details. Got any warrants out?' Street drinkers who
might feel pressure to leave an area, particularly during the city's Fringe
Festival, advised that if asked to leave they would simply refuse and that

police 'don't do anything because I've got my civil rights.' Thus, we see that law and local mores not only check potentially exclusionary actions but also permit resistance to such activities.

Officers interviewed also acknowledged the importance of their role as law enforcers. As is the case with police forces in other jurisdictions, 'real police work' – police work associated with arrests – is venerated by the organization and rewarded by supervisors (Manning 1978; Chan et al. 2003). This is the case regardless of whether officers are in patrol or in one of the community-based branches. For example, in describing how collecting knowledge through the use of observation, rumour gathering, and so on, facilitates the policing of drug activity, a CBO emphasized the importance of making arrests: 'At the end of the day, you've got a possible drugs seizure, drugs capture. That always looks good. Senior officer says, "That's well done."' However, the ability to effect arrests and 'look good' for management is constrained by the organization's demands for knowledge as expressed through policies and procedures that require information to be passed up the hierarchy. Police officers who are unable to effect an immediate arrest based on their information cannot hoard knowledge without incurring sanctions: 'We get information; if we can't deal with it, it's passed on. It's got to be passed on. It's duty, procedures' (police officer).

Another officer, who saw herself in terms of both her law enforcement and knowledge work roles, stated that the attraction of the job is lack of ambiguity: things are 'black and white,' because 'the law's the law ... and I always maintain that.' In balancing a variety of demands made of her from varying sources, such as other institutions or local constituencies, this officer could rely on 'the law' as both an interpretive guide to decision making and as a bulwark upon which to justify decisions. In this fashion, the officer attempts to sidestep the thorny issue of taking personal responsibility for negotiating demands on the row, relying instead on 'the law' as both a justification and as a shield from public criticism.

When questioned about her use of police discretion, though, this frontline officer also acknowledged a willingness to see policing as involving 'a big fuzzy haze, if you like.' Whereas she generally maintained a view of police work as law enforcement – 'black and white' – she was willing to allow that some hazier situations exist in which she would be willing to use her discretion. However, these situations were very few and typically involved what are perceived to be low-level infractions or offences (traffic violations by tourists and/or cases involving a small quantity of marijuana).

Such a formalized approach to the law enforcement role does not lend itself well to the peacekeeping aspect of the role, which involves informal use of authority and discretion to maintain order (Bittner 1967; Punch 1979). However, there are peacekeeping aspects built into the police function on skid row as a consequence of the demands officers deal with, the limited amount of resources they can bring to bear on a situation, and their own personal feelings, which are often expressed in a willingness to exercise authority and/or discretion. The police officer as peacekeeper can be seen in the steps taken by individual officers to negotiate complaints and thus tensions between residents, tourists, local businesses, and street beggars. As one officer explained, 'You might see [a homeless person] begging next to a bank or a cash line [automated teller] machine. People are put off. They don't want to use the cash line machine. So we'll have a word with the person and tell them to move on.' Although such actions are viewed as discriminatory by many area residents, for the individual officer this is a question of balancing the rights of people to use facilities, against the right of the street person to beg – that is, a question of negotiating conflicting demands. These demands are negotiated through the informal mechanism of asking the beggar to move on or to refrain from some certain behaviours in order to resolve the conflict. For senior officers whom I spoke with, resort to such informal modes of regulating behaviour is viewed as preferable to resort to exclusion through legal processes.

Social work aspects of the job are not typically valued by L&B officers nor viewed as a significant part of their street duties. As one officer explained, '[I place] less emphasis on the social work, because there are social workers to do social work.' One police action that has traditionally been viewed as social work within the literature is the arresting of intoxicated individuals 'for their own safety' (Blumberg, Shipley, and Barsky 1973; McSheehy 1979). In Edinburgh, police similarly effect arrests of individuals who are considered 'drunk and incapable.' As a senior officer explains, 'A lot of [alcoholics], they drink so much they pass out and then we get involved with them. And they're arrested – in inverted commas – simply because we want them taken off the streets for their own safety.' However, a frontline officer who spoke about such arrests makes it clear that he does not view this process as an attempt at providing assistance but rather as a legal duty that must be performed irrespective of his personal wishes:

It's more time consuming than anything. I could do other things. But it's part and parcel, and if the police won't do it, who will? The buck stops with me, so I've got to do something. It's a dirty job ... If they're quite badly drunk there's new procedures in force that we've got to take them to the hospital rather than the cells. So again time spent taking to the hospital, which is in southern Edinburgh ... it's a time-consuming exercise when we're so hard up resources-wise, and there's lots of other things that you could be attending.

What this officer does not appear to recognize is that such procedures are part of a larger move towards a harm-reduction approach to the treatment of addiction. The cell is replaced with a hospital bed, indicating also the replacement of a punitive, exclusion-oriented treatment of the inebriated (under the guise of 'protection') with a more inclusionary view of addiction and its consequences as conditions necessitating medical treatment. That such a transition should also work to the advantage of the police in their quest for increasing efficiencies – through shifting the burden of monitoring drunks from police jailors to the medical professions – is hardly surprising. Rather, it is a further example of the unique way in which the L&B utilize other agencies to decrease internal resource inefficiencies while fostering inclusionary aims.

In the comment above, the officer refers to the fact that oftentimes police on the street are called upon to do 'dirty work' (Hughes 1962; Von Maanen 1978a). This is an important part of skid row policing and thus deserves some attention. In dealing with the denizens of the Cowgate and Grassmarket, police officers may be required to touch, search, physically arrest, and/or transport individuals who are unwashed; wearing filthy clothes; covered in urine, feces, or vomit; have open sores or wounds; are carrying used needles ('sharps'); and/or are behaving violently or strangely. The police officer's job requires that they have physical contact with such people, and this presents concerns over 'contamination' not only from filth and muck but also from HIV, hepatitis C, and other infectious diseases:

> The issues from that arise from lots of people who're smoking and jagging – injecting. So we have to watch out as there's sharps on them. If you're searching them or lifting them into the back, that's another thought process that's going through your mind. You hope you don't get [poked] ... or if there's scabies or some skin infection ... so it's a dirty hands-on job. We have quite a bad problem with both alcoholics and drug users. (police officer)

One of the questions that I explored with frontline officers was how they viewed the people they police on skid row. I did not ask this question outright, feeling that I would gain a better sense of officer attitudes through what was revealed to me through discussion of other topics. Their responses to a variety of questions reveal a mix of both inclusionary and exclusionary attitudes among frontline officers. For example, while discussing public attitudes towards those from the Cowgate and Grassmarket who earn money through panhandling, a frontline officer advised: 'A lot of police do think [public drunkenness and panhandling] is an eyesore in the city.' The following is an excerpt from an interview with a CBO who similarly reveals the negative attitudes with which some frontline officers approach the Cowgate/Grassmarket community. The quote is taken from a portion of an interview during which I was asking an officer about his negotiation of demands on skid row:

> Q: Some of your time is spent balancing demands because, on the one side, you've got people saying 'I don't want to see [public drunkenness]' and on the other side, this is a community. So in terms of being a CBO you have to be a resource for [the skid row community] as well.
> A: Yeah, I have to tolerate them.

The use of the word 'tolerate' is indicative of how this officer feels about having to honour claims made by addicts, street drinkers, and/or panhandlers, who have the legal right to sit in public spaces and consume beverages, socialize, and/or ask for spare change. It is something that he is legally obliged to do but has negative feelings about because their status and behaviour are offensive to him. Other officers also revealed negative attitudes towards the local street population through stories depicting panhandlers as wealthy imposters or as 'aggressive.' Further, whereas officers told stories about helping non-street-entrenched community groups and residents, no similar stories were told of providing assistance to skid row residents.

The same approach was taken with L&B police managers, who were also not asked any direct questions concerning their own attitudes towards skid row residents in order to avoid eliciting falsely positive responses. I include the results of those interviews in order to contrast views expressed by managers with those of frontline officers and their supervisors. Police managers, while stressing the dysfunctions of the community, expressed views that were significantly less negative towards Cowgate and Grassmarket denizens than their frontline officers. One manager depicted efforts at instituting an anti-panhandling bylaw as attempts at 'criminalizing people because of their lifestyle.' He further added:

There's rarely a week goes by that the papers don't say something about aggressive begging. The discourse is very negative. The reality is that most of the beggars in the city centre – I can't speak for any other city – sit very quietly in a very broad city ... I would love to meet somebody who makes thirty thousand pounds a year ... I don't think that living on the street and committing crime to stay alive on the streets would be anybody's first lifestyle choice.

This manager made it clear that these were his personal views, not to be interpreted as those of the organization. However, other managers also expressed concern over demands that issues associated with homelessness and poverty should be treated as criminal law problems. For example, in discussing the repeal of legislation that formerly provided the police with broad powers to arrest people for public obstruction and begging, one police manager said, 'We lost a lot of effective police powers, but we moved on as an organization. I wouldn't like to see that return because that doesn't serve the long-term issues associated with people protecting homeless or beggars.'

Differences with respect to how street-level officers and managers viewed skid row residents reflect different orientations towards 'the job': policing as operating in areas that are 'black and white' or 'shades of grey.' The adoption of one of these perspectives over the other may be best explained as a function of one or more of three variables. The first variable is the officer's individual views and experiences. For instance, one police manager who exhibits both understanding and a compassionate attitude towards marginalized street communities advised that his views have been shaped, in part, by a family connection to alcoholism. Second, as I have discussed previously, the organizational culture in which officers perform their tasks can be influential in shaping attitudes. Certainly, the effects of the L&B's working culture upon individual actors is easily seen with respect to the willingness of frontline officers, CBOs, and CPOs to perceive themselves primarily as knowledge workers. A third significant factor is the officer's level of experience and growth in the job. In speaking with officers of differing levels of experience about aspects of the job, both in Edinburgh and elsewhere, it is evident that officers with greater levels of experience view the world in a significantly more complex fashion (shades of grey) than less experienced officers who seek the routine. An experienced frontline supervisor in Edinburgh, in speaking of his officers, emphasized this point: 'Cops are very good with patterns. They like to know "What's my job?" You tell them, "Go do that" and they'll do it. And, they'll do it very well. But if you ask them to see outside the box, that gets a wee bit uncomfortable. They're not too comfortable with that.'

Policing Cowgate/Grassmarket: The Street Perspective

In order to capture more fully the nature of skid row policing in Edinburgh, I compared self-perceptions of police generally, and in relation to the roles they perform on the street, with the views of row denizens and area service providers. Unsurprisingly, given that the bulk of their interactions with police are of the law enforcement variety, residents of the Cowgate and Grassmarket tend to see police largely, if not solely, as law enforcers. The police in this role are often viewed negatively as authoritarian, arbitrary, discriminating – the opposite of members of an inclusionary institution. One addict who had been arrested on different occasions views the police as enforcing exclusion through the mechanism of the law prohibiting a 'breach of the peace' (a fairly ambiguous offence similar to North American laws prohibiting 'disorderly conduct'). As this addict contends, police 'get us for a breach of the peace, even if you never done one ... just to get you off the street ... just to be pure evil.' Others similarly stated that police were arbitrary when asking individuals to 'move along.' However, all residents, including the previously cited addict, agreed that there were good police officers on the street. The following is an excerpted quote from the same interviewee who called the police 'evil':

Q: Have you come across any [police] that are okay?
A: Aye, there are some that are alright. I won't say that here.
[Office door opens and an outreach worker walks in.]
Outreach worker: All coppers are bastards [joking].
A: I won't say that ... There are a few of them that are alright like.

Although residents such as the individual cited above were of the view that there are some exceptional police officers who are 'alright,' others expressed the belief that the majority of officers are 'alright,' and thus those who are not were rather the exception to the rule. This view is expressed in the following quote from an interview with a street drinker in Hunter Square:

Q: How do the police treat you guys?
A: Through the year certainly alright. You get the odd one now and again.

Some residents also accept that the police, even when operating within their law enforcement role, serve a necessary function within their community: 'Some of the police are alright. Some of them are a bit harder. To me, they've still got a job to do. If you never had the police, it would be a worse place.'

One aspect of the law enforcement role that has drawn significant attention within the literature is police use of force (Bittner 1990 [1970]; Black 1980). Its importance can be found in the reductionist vision of police as being defined solely in terms of the legally sanctioned ability to use force to achieve state objectives (Bittner 1990). Early ethnographic work emphasized the importance of force in maintaining order on skid row: 'violence by the police is common ... it appears to be a major tactic used by officers in banishing homeless men from their patrol districts' (Black 1980: 31). However, Bittner's ethnographic work on skid row also reveals that the use of force is at best an irregular occurrence. Similarly, a subsequent body of research shows that police officers tend, for the most part, to prefer non-physical methods to achieve their ends (see Rubinstein 1978; Punch 1979). Fielding (2002: 152) captures this second position in noting that 'in most cases the big stick is locked in a cupboard and the police do not even look toward the cupboard, let alone unlock it.' Given these opposing views within the literature, I made a point of asking about and/or listening for stories that reflected the use of force by police. In particular, I listened for examples of routine force in the context of an arrest (for example, putting someone's hands behind their back in order to handcuff them) and 'extraordinary' force (exceptional or abusive behaviour such as unjustified punching, kicking, or the use of weapons).

Stories involving use of police force had to be elicited from respondents through direct questions, rather than emerging independently as a significant or taken-for-granted characteristic of police activity. Stories told by skid row residents typically reflect the view that the degree of force use by police in effecting arrests is largely commensurate with the amount of resistance officers receive. That is, the amount of force employed was viewed as justifiable with respect to the circumstances either experienced or witnessed. In response to a question on whether police used extra force in making an arrest, one street drinker advised, 'It depends on what you're doing. A few of them, if they've got you for a particular reason, and you're struggling they'll shove your hands in back of you to make you go down.' This particular action is a standard police procedure which is used to minimize struggle and potential for injury when handcuffing recalcitrant individuals.

Even though some street people dislike the police intensely and admitted that they would go out of their way to antagonize officers, none of those interviewed offered any specific allegations of excessive police force. However, two interviewees who did not cite direct experiences involving physical force said that they believed that extra force is sometimes employed when arresting women on the street. One interviewee, a male row inhabitant, stated that women sometimes receive scratches and marks during the arrest process. He was of the view that the women may have been subject to what he viewed as extra force during the arrest process because they were 'stroppy' (abusive) to the officer(s). The view that some police retaliate in response is also articulated by a female addict from Cowgate, who explains that women receive harder treatment from police officers 'because we're being nastier than the guys are.' I note that the 'stroppy' behaviour of female addicts cited is not simply a reflection of women's greater dislike or disdain for police in Edinburgh but can be more properly understood as a part of street-based gender strategy – termed 'going butch' in North America – which is commonly utilized by homeless women to enhance their chances of survival (Passaro 1996).

None of the service providers interviewed offered any allegations of abuse, concrete or otherwise. Rather, the majority felt that stories that they had received from their respective client groups were not credible and that overall the police treated the skid row population better here than in other Scottish cities: 'I think that the drug client group get a very good deal from the police ... I think the police here are very good'; 'they police the homeless community better than perhaps some other forces, and they've got a lighter touch than some other forces.' A senior police officer explains why the police in this neighbourhood generate so few complaints: 'If you assaulted that person, I'm not going to back you up.'

Police in Cowgate and Grassmarket also function as peacekeepers. An excellent example of how this process plays out in the Grassmarket is provided in the following comment from a service provider:

> A lot of the people who beg will have their own spot, and that's their regular seat. So you'll also get fights arising when somebody's gone away for a cup of tea. They come back and somebody else has moved into their slot because it's a good place ... then you'll get someone who'll report them to the police

because they cause problems. [The beggars] can actually use the police to help themselves, to protect their own begging space.

In other instances, police work with other local authorities and/or private agencies to come up with informal measures that result in a keeping of the peace. In the examples that I am aware of, such measures involved closing off public or private areas where street drinkers or addicts congregated. In the following quote, a street drinker describes the loss of an area known as the 'drinking tree':

> Everybody's got their own place where they go, where they do their drinking and all that. Everybody knows that, all we do is drink. The police know that ... We used to sit over here, see over by the bottom there, and there was a bench there and stairs, when it rained you could sit on the stairs and stay covered. The police knew where we was. Never bothered us ... [Some of the street drinkers would] sit arguing against each other. You couldn't control it. [The police] took the seat away and roped off all the area cause there was people complaining. Too much trouble.

What is interesting about this individual's comments is the fact that police knew about the site and accepted its use prior to the receipt of public complaints. For the police, the tree served important purposes. First, prior to the complaints, it created a relatively semi-private space where street people could easily be 'contained' away from public gaze, thus minimizing potential conflicts with shopkeepers. Second, this gathering space and its use by particular individuals meant that the police could easily find an individual and/or use the site as a means of gathering local knowledge. Third, tolerance of activity in this space reveals the use of informal techniques by police to respond to demands from some members within the local community who want to curtail noise and disorder within their neighbourhood. These demands are weighed against the rights of area street drinkers to sit in public spaces, visit their friends, and consume alcohol.

Where row denizens tend to observe police acting out knowledge work is either through requests for information from area residents on local cases or through the warrant checking process. In contrast, service providers are more likely to see police in the knowledge work role through police liaison work and at community meetings – two modes in which row denizens would rarely, if ever, encounter police. Service providers interviewed depicted police knowledge work not only as an important aspect of policing, but as a desirable one with the potential to facilitate their own social work aims. To the extent that police work with service providers, they facilitate inclusionary and/or coercively inclusive goals centred on assisting and/or rehabilitating the skid rower.

At the level of the frontline officer, 'partnership working' typically entails informal, routine meetings with social service agencies to share information regarding service users and to discuss mutual problems and concerns. One service provider, a rarity among those who complained of the lack of CBO presence in the community, described receiving regular visits from the police, which she termed 'a social call,' at which information sharing from both parties occurred: 'They tell me stuff that's been going on on the street and I tell them ... It's a good relationship and it works very well.' The reciprocal nature of information exchange, particularly in connection with police attempts at fostering good relations with service providers, means that shelter workers and others are more willing to give the police information upon request than they might be in other circumstances: 'If there is a very serious crime going on we ... help the police. We keep a record of everyone that comes here, the name, or the name they give us, and we have a very good paper trail of who has been here, and that often is useful to the police ... [but] it's a two way thing with the police.' Another service provider similarly stressed reciprocity as the basis of his working relationship with the police, 'They come and ask questions. If somebody goes missing ... they'll come to us if they can't get any help ... I always say to them, "You help us, I'll help you."'

As is the case with police officers themselves, both residents and service providers placed the least amount of emphasis on the social work aspects of policing. None of my interviews with these two groups yielded stories or discussions that portrayed the police in this role. Even questions to row inhabitants as to whether police officers ever approached them just to ask them how they are doing tended to yield negative responses.

Finally, I also sought to find out from Cowgate/Grassmarket residents and service providers their perceptions on how residents are viewed by the police in order to determine where they perceived policing as falling along the continuum of exclusivity–inclusivity. One street drinker interviewed stated that he believes police view him as 'just another drunken homeless person.' This perception, he advised, resulted in a situation in which he would not seek police assistance from a nearby patrol car when he was being assaulted by a drunken pub-goer when panhandling. This individual's view of the police, and that of other residents who had clearly had negative encounters with the police, stands in stark contrast to the observation of the previously cited service provider who had witnessed panhandlers relying on police for assistance. This suggests that not all area residents view the police favourably and that although some will seek out assistance, this is not a uniform practice. Support for this contention comes in the form of views expressed by other residents who similarly spoke of police seeing them not as citizens but as 'bums' and 'criminals.' This perception is shared by some but not all service providers. As a service provider in the former group stated in reference to her homeless clientele, 'The guys, as far as the police are concerned, they're junkie-bes or alkies.'

As noted previously, though, other street residents and service providers feel that police are reasonably fair and treat them accordingly – that is, in a relatively, if not perfectly, inclusive fashion. We can see this in previously cited remarks, such as those of the addicts and alcoholics who opined that police are 'alright.' These views were also evident in stories told by area residents of positive police encounters.

Effecting Social Change

A key claim of this book is that policing of skid row is a political process and that the police, as political actors, are reflexive about both the roles they play on skid row and the meanings attendant on their actions within these communities. To this end, the majority of interviewees, and all police officers, were asked about how they viewed the politics of policing. Further, police officers were asked about the possibilities of effecting positive social change through the police institution and at what levels of their organization they believed such changes could be effected. In this section I would like to briefly describe the results of these questions in an attempt to lay the groundwork for the further analysis that follows in chapter 8.

With the emphasis placed on knowledge working and community partnering at all levels of the L&B force, it was unsurprising to discover that police managers see their work as political. And, as I have described in sections above, it is clear that police managers within the L&B are pragmatic in relation to understanding the politics of the positions they adopt and the means employed to achieve organizational objectives. Further, all senior officers believed that enormous potential existed for promoting positive social change through the police force and each appeared to be of the view that it was not only possible and a good thing for the police to be engaged in such a process, but that it was imperative in terms of meeting both their mandate and the increasing demands placed on the organization by the general public. This view is based on an acknowledgment that the police often serve as little more than a 'catch all' for a variety of social problems, the causes of which they can have little direct effect upon. However, through shifts in police culture, an investment in partnership working and in varieties of information exchange, they can have some indirect effect on those causes through agencies better placed to meet social needs. Further, in some instances, deliberate changes in police policies and practices can lead to better conditions for those policed. For example, police management were willing to reconsider traditional law enforcement techniques in favour of pro-social policing initiatives. A harm reduction strategy in relation to alcohol and drug use was developed in conjunction with health and social service providers. As of this writing, discussions have taken place which are likely to lead to police working more closely with service providers in offering injection drug users information on both detox services and alternative methods of ingesting heroin (such as smoking rather than injecting). Police officers would ideally be trained in understanding the dynamics of addiction and on how to provide information and service to users.

Police managers interviewed tended to view social change as both a bottom-up and a top-down process within the organization; they believed that the reorganization and its associated culture shift had empowered all ranks to be proactive community problem solvers at their respective levels. As one manager explained, 'we actually encourage our junior officers to take on a problem-solving sort of attitude ... we applaud it and encourage it, and try to stimulate it.' A frontline supervisor advised, 'The beat officers are encouraged to submit initiatives of what they would do [to solve a problem].' The nature of the type of problem a beat officer might solve was described as 'a problem of parking in an area or a problem of noisy neighbours.' As individual officers cannot resolve all local problems, another manager advised that 'if I was a beat officer and I saw something that I thought I could fix, I'd go to my Sergeant and then it'd go up.' Resort to hierarchical authority occurs because larger-scale social problems, particularly those that cross sector boundaries and require inter-agency cooperation, often necessitate the involvement of more senior ranks. For this reason, the majority of police managers tended to place greatest emphasis on the role of the sector inspector, particularly under the new organizational structure, which stresses local police ownership of 'beats' and 'sectors.' However, one manager did acknowledge the influence of 'middle managers' on the lower ranks: 'In the police service ... well ... [the] chief inspector, [the] superintendent, they can have an enormous influence on the local communities and the way things are done.'

In an interview with a senior officer, I asked whether he believed that frontline officers understand the political nature of the work they perform. This question arose out of interviews in Vancouver, where both a frontline officer and a police manager stated that they felt that officers in the street tended to be myopic about the political environment in which the institution operates. In contrast, the senior officer in Edinburgh felt that such a view was patronizing and that the frontline ranks do understand the politics underlying what they do in the street. In conversations with frontline officers it was clear that they do view their role as political, if not as one that is particularly empowered within the organization. In response to the question of whether he saw his role as political, an officer sighed and said, 'Yes ... I'm a pawn in the big game. And you can quote me on that.' His feelings of disempowerment were shared by a co-worker, who expressed deep frustration with a system that constrained her ability to 'do the job' while simultaneously failing to curb public demands for service. As I noted earlier, frontline officers interviewed tended to express dissatisfaction with their inability to realize the promise of community policing, which, as an ideal, empowers both the community and the beat officer.

Some officers interviewed did, however, cite examples in which they felt that they had made a positive change or at least had an opportunity to attempt problem solving rather than simply engaging in reactive policing. Examples include an officer who was working with a local church to reduce problems associated with the use of the church by local addicts, and another who was working with local community groups and giving lectures to school kids. In discussing these situations, it was clear that officers took personal pride in their work within the communities served. However, these examples and others provided by frontline officers point to a central problem with respect to community policing programs generally: the focus is often on providing service to particular types of communities – those that are seen as 'deserving' – rather than to all communities. It may be a function of the interview process that I just happened to draw frontline officers who, because of the nature of their community work or from their individual preference, are discriminating about what they see as community, and so such stories and inferred attitudes should not be treated as representative of the whole. However, as I noted earlier in this chapter, there does appear to be a disjuncture with respect to police manager attitudes towards extremely marginalized communities and attitudes of frontline officers. I would thus hazard to suggest that this disjuncture is manifest not only in stories told of community, but on the street. The perceptions of area residents, whose primary contact with the organization is through frontline officers, certainly offer some support for believing that some frontline officers discriminate in their definitions concerning 'community.'

Conclusion

In this chapter, I explored the policing of Edinburgh's skid row district through an examination of the management style and frontline practices of members of the Lothian & Borders police force. What this examination reveals is an institution that is clearly a product of the larger political environment in which it exists. The system that shapes this institution is one that privileges both the workings of the market and social inclusion. The institutional orientation of the police force mirrors these values through policies and programs that attempt to marry social justice aims with tenets of public managerialism. The result is a community-based policing model that is predicated on a conception of policing as knowledge work.

However, while this model is predominately an inclusionary one, marginalization of the homeless persists, and the police continue to play a role in this process. For example, both skid row residents and service providers cited the discriminatory attitudes and behaviours of frontline officers (both CBOs and patrol), and discriminatory views were noted within the comments of some officers interviewed who were unable to identify skid row residents with conceptions of 'community' (community as consisting of citizens with the right to make demands and be accorded respect). Thus, despite the apparent intentions of the institution, the inclusionary aspects of this model have not yet fully percolated through all ranks.

4 Junkies, Drunks, and the American Dream: Neo-liberal Skid Row

I have previously described San Francisco as representative, in many significant aspects, of the American form of neo-liberal governance. Throughout this chapter, I attempt to justify this characterization through an analysis of local politics and with reference to the ways in which the coercively inclusive/exclusionary nature of these politics is articulated in measures directed against the city's poor. I proceed as follows. First, I describe the political, historical, geographical, and social dimensions of the research site in order to contextualize its key elements and the demands it produces. I then examine more fully the range of inclusionary-exclusionary demands that San Francisco's skid row district produces. This examination leads to a discussion of the larger political context that shapes political processes within and across the row.

San Francisco's Skid Row: The Tenderloin

> The language of poverty and homelessness in this city for the last fourteen, fifteen, sixteen years is that people want to be homeless, they're bad drug addicts, they are mentally ill people ... they just don't want treatment. People are continuously blamed for not being treatable. (mental health outreach worker, San Francisco)

San Francisco's Tenderloin exemplifies a classic American skid row district. It is a patch of decayed and underdeveloped land that sits immediately adjacent to the city's central business district. Geary, Larkin, and Market streets form the perimeter of the Tenderloin, creating the space as a triangle containing some thirty-five blocks, bordered not only by an expensive business district to its east, but also by one of the city's priciest

Illustration 4.1 Streets of the Tenderloin, 2003 (author's photo).

residential areas, Nob Hill, to the west. Its landscape is a conglomeration of porn palaces, cheap diners, single-room occupancy (SRO) hotels, and convenience stores stocked with an abundant supply of alcohol placed on conveniently located shelves. Prostitutes work here, as do panhandlers and drug dealers. Addicts openly puff on crack pipes.

Waters and Hudson (1999) state that the site's name is derived from a historic similarity to a New York neighbourhood where police officers could collect enough bribes in order to afford better cuts of meat for dinner. Today, the Tenderloin is also informally referred to as 'Urinetown.'

The most immediate impression one receives of the Tenderloin is not based on optics – ugly buildings and concrete dull the senses, making the area seem blandly grey and unappealing – but rather on the observer's sense of smell. On any given day, a pungent aroma of urine and sometimes fresh or stale feces wafts up from building corners, laneways, and curbs. This is the smell of an indescribably harsh poverty.

The Tenderloin is not the city's first or only skid row district. According to Blumberg, Shipley, and Barsky (1978), San Francisco's skid row first developed in 1870–80 with the establishment of cheap lodging houses and hotels, medium and light industry, and saloons in the area known as South of Market Street (SoMa), immediately adjacent to the current Tenderloin district. These authors also note that 'by the 1890s there was also a hobo or homeless-man area along Howard Street centered between Third and Fourth' (ibid.: 221). Following the Second World War, still another area of the city – the Haight – developed as a site for homeless drifters: 'a visit to the Haight in early 1974 revealed more evidence of the congregation of heavy drinkers than of street people. There are places which could be identified as hangouts for "winos"' (ibid.: 159).

Redevelopment in San Francisco throughout the 1970s had three noticeable effects upon the Tenderloin. First, the historical Tenderloin district (its population and businesses) drifted north of the SOMA region to the site's present location next to the Union Square retail and business district (Blumberg et al. 1978). Second, redevelopment in residential areas such as the Haight concentrated the city's poor into low-income spaces such as the Tenderloin and areas within SOMA (ibid.; Robinson 1995). This concentration effect was further heightened by the loss of low-income housing stock on the current Tenderloin's borders to a variety of gentrification projects (Robinson 1995). As Robinson explains,

In the last two decades, the Tenderloin has emerged as one of the few remaining areas in which San Francisco's downtown poor can live. As redevelopment and rising rents have eliminated low-income housing units across the city, the deteriorated Tenderloin has absorbed the displaced. Accordingly, Tenderloin population has grown over 20% in the last 20 years, becoming 400% more dense than San Francisco as a whole and absorbing the highest concentration of the impoverished, the service dependent, the drug addicted, and the criminal. (ibid.: 493)

This site is currently home to some 24,000 people, most of whom live below the $8240 U.S. per annum that is recognized as the federal poverty line (Gordon 2002). As is the case in other skid row districts in Canada and the United States, the Tenderloin's population is no longer primarily or solely composed of middle-aged or elderly white males; rather, as a consequence of recent waves of immigration to the city, it now represents an ethnically diverse community that includes whites, blacks, Latinos, and a substantial number of southeast Asian families (Zoellner 2000). The influx of immigrant families has also meant an increase in the

Illustration 4.2 Boeddeker Park. Streets of the Tenderloin, 2003 (author's photo).

number of children living here: it is estimated that some 3500 children live in the neighbourhood (ibid.). Aside from impoverished families and halfway homes for parolees, the Tenderloin also houses a sizable population of the city's homeless and addicted. Service providers have estimated that some 10,000 homeless individuals either reside in or pass through the Tenderloin each day (San Francisco Rescue Mission 2003).

Observation of the site brings other ways to describe the 'T.L.' For example, on a sunny afternoon, the co-existence of a wide variety of humanity becomes the neighbourhood's most striking feature. On a corner of Eddy and Jones sits Boeddeker Park. Older black gentlemen perch on park benches, reading newspapers or chatting among themselves. On another bench a flashily dressed black woman sprays herself with vanilla perfume while another woman walks by loudly muttering to herself. On the other side of the fence, clusters of younger black males 'hang' near the corner, a boombox rapping out a noisy beat. One fact seems painfully apparent in Boeddeker Park: although blacks are only one of the many ethnic groups that make up the Tenderloin, they appear over-represented among the faces of the poor and homeless. This fact appears hardly surprising, though, given historic and contemporary racial attitudes towards African-Americans that are manifest at so many levels of American society.

On another day and in another street, children giggle and laugh as they draw chalk figures on the sidewalk in front of the place that houses

Illustration 4.3 Children's playground. Streets of the Tenderloin, 2003 (author's photo).

their after-school program. Some of the children are black, but many are Asian – from Cambodia, Vietnam, Laos, China, the Philippines, and elsewhere. So too are many of the seniors: an elderly Asian woman with a pull cart full of empty cans is but one of the many faces of old-age poverty.

Other glimpses yield the sight of a transvestite – wearing male clothes, flowered hair bun, and leopard handbag – walking through the 'T.L.' with his/her partner. This is hardly an unusual sight; transvestites, the transgendered, and gays and lesbians come to San Francisco looking for personal freedom but find themselves subject to another form of tyranny: a poverty born of a general lack of decent employment opportunities and affordable housing and the stigma associated with their new place of residence.

Housing is a big issue in the Tenderloin; one that affects almost every person in the community. The most fortunate residents, often seniors and families, live in some form of subsidized housing. Others either live alone or share a room in one of the area's SRO hotels that offer nine foot by six foot rooms that range in price from $600 to $800 per month.

Illustration 4.4 'Nell the homeless cat.' Streets of San Francisco, 2002 (author's photo).

The next step down on the housing scale is shelter beds, which are open on a nightly basis and are run by public and private agencies. The final option is sleeping in public spaces. Whereas many of Edinburgh's 'rough sleepers' have the relative 'luxury' of being able to sleep outside in more or less 'sheltered' locations such as covered closes and quiet graveyards, those without legitimate shelter in San Francisco sleep openly on the city's sidewalks. Walking in or near the Tenderloin, one is routinely greeted by the sight of people sleeping in doorways, covered only in cardboard or a rough grey blanket, their possessions tucked by their heads or hands.

In the 1970s and 1980s, California was at the forefront of a movement to 'de-institutionalize' its psychiatric patients. The result of this 'progressive' measure to 'return people to their communities' was that, as in other cities, San Francisco's skid row became a dumping ground for the mentally ill (Scull 1977). As a psychiatric outreach worker explained,

'People with drug or alcohol problems, or psychiatric illnesses, generally are kept here [in the Tenderloin] ... the Tenderloin and 6th Street have been the discharge place for folks from the hospital for years and years and years.' These individuals, she further noted, are indiscriminately discharged to SRO hotels without adequate support and resources. Thus it is no surprise to discover, as I did, that there seems to be an extraordinarily large number of individuals walking about the Tenderloin and nearby 6th Street areas in what appear to be varying states of psychosis.

Addiction is part of the daily existence for many who live here. Alcoholics can find ready sustenance not only in the neighbourhood's bars, some of which have extended opening hours – Red's is open from 10 A.M. to 2 A.M. daily – but also in local grocery stores which conveniently stock cans and bottles on their shelves. Drug addicts are also easily serviced; dealers, many of whom come into the neighbourhood from nearby Oakland, work through 'runners' who transact business primarily in public spaces such as around Boeddeker Park. Transactions between dealers and potential customers are handled primarily on the basis of eye contact and greetings that, to the initiated, indicate an understanding of their respective roles but look like little more than casual greetings to the uninitiated. I had an opportunity to experience a part of the transaction ritual firsthand one evening while walking in the area of O'Farrell and Jones, which is part of the central drug retail market in the neighbourhood. A man walking towards me made direct and prolonged eye contact as he approached. He then said 'Hello,' as he continued to walk past. My reaction to this greeting was to look at him, then shift my eyes away and not respond. If I had been interested in buying his product(s), I would have maintained eye contact and then responded to his opening by following after him and saying something like, 'Hey, baby.' Had I done so, I likely would have been offered crack cocaine, heroin, or prescription pills – all drugs of choice here.

The streets in and around the upper portion of the 'T.L.' constitute a low-track prostitution stroll – that is, a prostitution area where, because of addiction, disease, and/or the effects of chronic homelessness, the women are often in a worse state of physical shape than others and therefore charge less money for services. In the Tenderloin, the stroll does not stand out as it might in other neighbourhoods because it appears against a chaotic background of traffic, drug activity, public drinking (by both neighbourhood residents and visitors), street corner 'hanging out,' and a lot of street noise.

Although much of the rhetoric around communities like the Tenderloin centres on issues related to disorder, crime is an integral part of the community. And, as is also the case in skid row districts elsewhere, residents of the Tenderloin are as apt to be victims of crime as perpetrators. Much of the violence that occurs in the T.L. – shootings, stabbings, and beatings – is related to the open-air drug market. Police also described the commission of strong-arm robberies,[1] in which perpetrators use intimidation and fear in an attempt to gain money for a fix. However, while much of the drug-related violence is intra-class, this is not always the case; during the course of my fieldwork an undercover police officer whose identity became known to some of the area's dealers was stabbed.

The Politics of San Francisco's Skid Row

In discussing the politics of Edinburgh's skid row I previously stated that skid rows are social and geographical spaces formed through moral codes, where exclusion is typically enforced through zoning regulations, civic ordinances, and criminal laws that define the skid rower as a 'deviant outsider.' Although I then went on to state that Edinburgh's skid row provides an exception in that the space is 'socially' rather than 'legally' defined, San Francisco's Tenderloin stands as an exemplar of the usual skid row: it is the traditional community of outlaws, outcasts, and misfits, restricted and regulated primarily through the legal register of discipline (Foucault 1979). In this section I explore the nature not only of exclusionary demands made of those who live here but also of those demands that are coercively inclusive (as I argue throughout, both are prevalent in this community). Further, I discuss the substance and style of inclusionary demands made on behalf of those who live in this community and the limited impact that these demands have had on reversing the various forms of exclusion and discrimination experienced by residents.

Within urban environments, the production of exclusionary demands made with respect to marginalized communities is often the result of desires centred on gentrification. Skid row districts are viewed by developers, retail, hotel, and other business interests and often by civic leaders as 'underdeveloped' sites that, because of their location next to a city's core, represent enormous potential profits through the conversion of vacant buildings and/or low-rent housing stock into tourist accommodations, high-density condos, and/or retail.

The process of gentrification can be seen in the Tenderloin, most notably in the form of the Hilton Hotel, sited on the easternmost boundary of the neighbourhood, bordering nearby Union Square. The Hilton towers over Boeddeker Park, standing as a constant reminder of past, present, and future encroachment upon the neighbourhood. Future plans for the Tenderloin include the Glide Pavilion hotel/apartment complex and a proposed light rail system through the area that one community group member described as something that's 'definitely going to change what's happening out there [in the T.L.].' According to this individual, developers who had been eyeing the Tenderloin 'got the baby locked down, I think.'

Gentrification produces exclusion in at least two ways. First, the conversion of existing low-income housing stock forces poor people from the neighbourhood as stock shrinks. Second, it generates pressure to 'clean up' an area through the expulsion of 'disorderly' elements. In short, tourists and middle-class residents typically do not visit restaurants in crack-infested neighbourhoods, nor do they like to pay $150 a night in hotel fees to watch the homeless defecate in the streets in front of them. Thus, demands arise that 'something be done' to push the 'disorderly' from neighbourhoods undergoing gentrification. With respect to the Tenderloin, we see exclusionary demands in the form of vocal campaigns urging law and order 'crackdowns' that will remove individuals from the neighbourhood into jails, as well as, more subtly, in the form of pressure applied to local service providers who are seen as attracting the disorderly. Two service providers interviewed advised that a neighbourhood institution that had been helping the poor for several decades had been confronted with demands from area businesses to limit its services because of the crowds of homeless people that it generates.

It is not only local business that produces exclusionary demands directed at the Tenderloin's 'disorderly elements' but also other residents from within the community. As I noted previously, racialized tensions exist within the neighbourhood that are based largely on stereotypes associated with drugs and criminality. As Waters and Hudson (1998: 315) report, when the Bay Area Women's and Children's Center attempted to establish a Tenderloin grade school that would benefit southeast Asian families in the neighbourhood, they were successful, but efforts to create a drop-in centre for crack-addicted mothers and their children, largely African-Americans, were met with what these authors describe as 'fierce opposition' from Tenderloin resident and community groups on the grounds that the centre would bring more addicts to the neighbourhood. Waters and Hudson suggest that stereotypes about the deserving and undeserving poor combine in this neighbourhood with racialized images to create exclusionary demands that are seen to have an impact not merely on addicts but on African-Americans who are frequently portrayed as among the undeserving.

Residents of the Tenderloin are also subject to coercively inclusive demands. Many of these demands are made of the poor generally and not in relation to this neighbourhood specifically, including demanded cuts in public assistance and enforced prohibitions of status offences, such as panhandling, public loitering, and 'camping.' These demands find popular support in the form of a series of punitive bylaws that are disproportionately enforced against those on skid row and other nearby marginalized communities. Throughout the city, and indeed within skid row itself, these demands are finding expression on billboards and other advertising paid for by the San Francisco Hotel Council. The content of their message is intended to regulate two sets of interrelated behaviours: the panhandling of the row's residents and other homeless and the giving of money by tourists and other residents. These advertisements suggest that naive do-gooders foster sexually transmitted diseases and addictions through their donations. For example, one advertisement features a man in a park saying, 'Today I did Tai Chi, donated some change and helped spread STDs' (Mattier and Ross 2002). Another billboard portrays tourists saying, 'Today we rode a cable car, visited Alcatraz and supported a drug habit' (ibid.). To supplement their message, the Hotel Council printed cards to be handed to guests in member hotels, urging them to make donations to local charities instead of to panhandlers. A local advocate for the homeless suggests that 'the message is real clear. Hate the homeless – they spread drugs, disease and close down businesses' (ibid.). These advertisements are read as attempts at forcing individuals – for example, panhandlers – away from what are viewed as morally deficient lifestyles marked by idleness, waste, indiscriminate sexuality, and so on, through targeting facilitating behaviour. Not only do such individuals not contribute to society (i.e., the economy), we are told, but their behaviours have other adverse effects that need to be checked.

Oppression breeds resistance, whether it is in the form of whispered resentments, posters decrying a particular form of exclusion, or mass political action in support of change. Thus, where we find demands for exclusion or coercive inclusion, we may expect to see those who counter with their own sets of inclusionary demands. We find inclusionary discourse in skid row districts, although socially, politically, and economically, such sites are largely isolated from local and other power structures and are often ignored. The Tenderloin is no exception; in many ways it is representative of the battles for inclusion fought and lost by other marginalized communities.

As with other skid row communities, demands for inclusion within the Tenderloin are largely centred on the desire for residents to be treated as full citizens, equally worthy of respect and treated with dignity by both the state and other citizens. Such demands include calls for institutional reform, particularly with respect to the police and this institution's treatment of the poor generally and poor people of colour particularly. There are also demands for the decriminalization of sex work and/or repeals of laws that target behaviours associated with the homeless. Other demands include improved housing, mental health and addiction treatment, and income aid. Interestingly, I note that I found no groups that championed harm reduction or wanted the criminal treatment of addiction replaced with a medical model. One representative of a major community coalition that works with addicts was instead incensed by the perceived unwillingness of police to crack down on the local drug market.

While many local civic organizations are constituted solely of area residents, others represent a mixture of area residents and professionals (such as social workers, lawyers, ministers, health experts). There are also groups that represent a range of constituencies; others are single-issue groups such as those that advocate on behalf of sex trade workers or the mentally ill. Many of these groups in the Tenderloin work together in loose coalitions, although, as I discuss later in relation to Vancouver, tensions exist between several of the major and smaller organizations. These tensions are likely the product not only of differences in ideology, and preferred methods of championing inclusionary change, but also of splits over government funding and access to City Hall. At a time of sharply decreased public funding of social and community services, several organizations find it increasingly hard to make ends meet, while others are continuing to receive funding. This causes splits within the community. For example, it was noted by one community service provider that the organization he represents has experienced difficulties in establishing cross-community partnerships with other groups because his organization receives civic funding, and the perception is that this organization is too closely tied to City Hall and the police. Other groups are similarly viewed as co-opted by City Hall because of their presence on mayoral homelessness commissions, which are sometimes seen as little more than exercises in churning out reports.

Among many inclusion-oriented activists, there is a sense that their work is Sisyphean. Few gains are made and, with a divisive political climate in skid row and a larger community that clearly favours coercively inclusive and/or exclusionary measures, each new gain appears to be met with tenfold challenges. As one organization noted of the treatment of the poor on its website, 'Since the mid eighties the city of San Francisco has been split on how to respond to the impact of homeless people living on our streets and in our parks. Some merchant and neighborhood groups have pushed for more and more use of law enforcement ... so far, the pro-cop sentiment consistently wins' (Coalition on Homelessness 2003). Unsurprisingly, I found that among the majority of those demanding inclusionary change, many were experiencing feelings of demoralization and burnout.

The Larger Political Context: San Francisco as
Neo-liberal City (U.S. Style)

Although homelessness and other social problems have been concentrated in the Tenderloin, they are not contained there. It is estimated that there are between 8000 and 15,000 homeless people, many of whom are mentally ill and/or addicted, who are visible in a variety of spaces throughout the city (Office of the Controller 2002). The visibility of the urban poor in San Francisco, particularly in light of what are perceived by many residents as generous city welfare programs (Lelchuk 2002), has created significant political pressures translating into coercively inclusive and/or exclusionary demands that 'something be done' about the homeless problem.

In response to those voters who feel that income aid payments were too generous and/or were being used to support drug and alcohol intake, in 1994 the city attempted to alter the conditions of its county welfare program (the General Assistance or GA program) (Lelchuk 2002).[2] Voters approved former mayor Frank Jordan's plan to guarantee city welfare recipients a room in a residential hotel in exchange for a $280 reduction in their $345 monthly cheques (ibid.). This plan, had it not fallen through when the city's Board of Supervisors refused to implement it, might have had the desired effect – a reduction of the city's welfare rolls – as individuals moved either into low-paying employment or to another jurisdiction (ibid.).

Jordan also introduced the Matrix program, which promised a multi-pronged approach to reducing homelessness but became synonymous with abuse of the homeless. The most noticeable effect of the city's Matrix program was a repressive policing style aimed at discouraging the presence of the homeless in public spaces through activities such as the confiscation of shopping carts, illegal searches and seizures, and a series of 'quality-of-life' bylaws that made sleeping in public parks or urinating in public offences punishable by fines and imprisonment upon failure to pay (Gardner and Lindstrom 1997; Fagan 2002; Lelchuk 2002). As it may be recalled, quality-of-life regulations are prohibitions against acts of minor disorder that are perceived as threatening the quality of life in a given community. These are typically offences, such as those outlined above, which are noticeably associated with the urban poor. For this reason, they are termed 'status' offences, meaning that the offence arises from the individual's low socio-economic status.

Willie Brown subsequently defeated Jordan in the next mayoral election; Brown ran, in part, on a platform that challenged the Matrix program. Once elected, Brown publicly ended Matrix, while continuing to privately support aggressive police enforcement of 'quality-of-life' bylaws (Edmondson 2000; Nordberg 2002).[3] We see the effects of Brown's tenure in the number of citations issued for quality-of-life offences: approximately 11,000 citations were issued in 1994 under then-mayor Jordan's Matrix program, doubling to nearly 23,000 in 1999 under the Brown regime (Nordberg 2002).

However, none of these measures has been enough to stem growing public frustrations: a poll released in 2002 revealed that 'San Francisco voters overwhelmingly believe homelessness is the city's No. 1 problem' (Lelchuk 2002). Aside from quality-of-life issues, which are frequently touted as problems created by the homeless, the 'problem' of homelessness is actually one of public economics. It is not simply that San Franciscans support county welfare recipients through the provisions of the GA program – only about 2500 people receive GA payments in San Francisco annually (Lelchuk 2003) – but that there are significant costs associated with running a network of civic and non-profit services to support the homeless and other urban poor each year, costs that, given the visible presence of poverty and addiction throughout the city, seem to provide few returns. Nordberg (2002) reports that in 1999 the city spent $57 million of locally generated funds on homeless services, a figure that rose to $82 million in 2002. And, as I document in chapter 8, the services provided do not come close to fulfilling the level of demand.

Article II of the California Constitution allows California citizens to place an initiative of public interest on a ballot for voter approval, thus bypassing the state legislature. In November 2002, San Franciscans were asked to vote on one of two propositions intended to address the homeless issue. Board Supervisor Gavin Newsom's Proposition N, or the 'Care Not Cash' plan, called for a significant reduction of GA payments: from $395 per month to $59 plus food and shelter, with the cash difference – approximately $14 million in annual savings – being used to create low-income housing and to fund social service programs (Lelchuk 2002; Lelchuk 2003). The proposal was supported by major business associations whose members funded Newsom's ballot campaign and/or took out paid advertising with statements that read: 'I don't want to sweep people off my doorstep' or 'I want to know why homelessness is a problem after we spent $200 million last year' (Mattier and Ross 2002).

In May 2003, Supervisor Newsom stated that one hundred residential hotel rooms had been set aside under the Care Not Cash program (Hampton 2003a). Further, the city had requested that hotel owners supply 900 more rooms, budgeted $3 million for drug treatment programs and $1 million to provide assistance to mentally ill individuals to gain Social Security (ibid.). However, funding for these programs is contingent on the cash flow to be received through reducing welfare benefits (ibid.). In the event that the city is unable to provide the services guaranteed under Proposition N, a GA recipient would receive the original full amount of welfare (between $320 to $395) (Lelchuk 2002). In short, under this proposition, funding for housing and services would come from the pool of money allocated to welfare assistance – that is, from the pockets of welfare recipients – rather than from additional taxes or levies.

In contrast, Proposition O, or 'Exits from Homelessness,' sponsored by Board of Supervisors' President Tom Ammiano, would require the city to develop one thousand low-income housing units and seven hundred addiction treatment beds within two years (ibid.). Proposition N received the majority vote, although a later judicial ruling held that welfare limits could only be set by the Board of Supervisors and not by popular vote (Lelchuk 2002; Hampton 2003a). Unsurprisingly, Proposition N was subsequently reintroduced on the agenda of the Board of Supervisors. On 8 July, when Supervisor Newsom was on holidays, the Board passed Ammiano's Proposition O instead (Hampton 2003b). Newsom was subsequently elected mayor in 2004.

San Franciscans, like Californians generally, espouse a typically American style of neo-liberalism. Through public referenda, California voters express their preferences in the form of repeated denials to requests for

Illustration 4.5 Driving the message home. Billboard sign reads: 'Supervisors: the voters have spoken. "Care not Cash" by July. Golden Gate Restaurant Association.' Streets of the Tenderloin, 2003 (author's photo).

funding of social programs that might better the conditions of those on the bottom socio-economic rungs. This includes not only poverty-related programs, which have been continually cut back over the past two decades, but also in areas traditionally seen as existing at the core of the welfare state such as education and healthcare services. Over the past few decades it has become increasingly apparent that California voters do not want to support the majority of basic redistributive schemes.

It could be argued that lack of support for public spending in California through the 1990s was linked to the recession during the early part of the decade; however, by the mid-1990s, the United States, and particularly California, were experiencing economic growth (Baldassare 2002). Job creation in California, coupled with spending restraints, was reflected in county and state budgets posting increasing surpluses from 1995 to 2000 (ibid.).[4] Despite this boom, there was no commensurate willingness to sponsor increases in social service spending. Schrag (1998: 61) contends that the racialization of welfare programs – including

public healthcare services, education, and welfare benefits – is a significant factor: 'the rise of the new minorities and the decline in services
occurred in proportion over precisely the same period (which, of course,
is when the services are most needed) and at roughly the same rate.' In
support of this contention, he notes demographic changes in California's
population that have rendered the state increasingly less 'white.' However, while California's population as a whole is becoming ethnically
diverse, this change is not reflected in voting patterns, which continue to
represent the desires of the overwhelming majority of white voters
(ibid.). In many counties the result has been significantly eroded services, from dilapidated and over-crowded schools to continual cuts in
social service spending leading to lack of treatment facilities and shelters
(ibid.; Gitlin 1995). Underlying these policy choices is a set of beliefs
concerning the inability of the public sector to 'efficiently' supply those
public goods necessary for the proper functioning of society. This is now
seen as the role of the markets, and responsibility for any inequities that
arise are seen as solely belonging to the disadvantaged individual.

Care Not Cash is an excellent example of a public program that
embodies American neo-liberal ideology: the central tenet of faith underlying this program is that the current welfare system, which is perceived as being 'too generous,' reproduces the social problems – poverty,
addiction, and crime – that it is supposed to ameliorate. If 'generous'
payments from an inefficient bureaucracy engender or increase social
problems, so the logic goes, the solution must therefore be to reduce
these payments, forcing recipients to seek employment in order to
better their condition (participation in the market as *the* preferred
solution). These sentiments are echoed in a letter of support for the
program offered by a San Francisco 'citizens' group,'[5] which embraces
such neo-liberal ideals:

> We believe that the Board of Supervisors needs to implement Care Not Cash
> in a timely fashion, to keep San Francisco from remaining an ATM for the
> nation's homeless to buy drugs and alcohol. Instead of a hand-out, they
> need a hand up ... Let's put the homeless on the road to self-respect and
> productivity. (San Francisco SOS website 2003)

Conclusion

In this chapter, I explored San Francisco's skid row district through an
examination of its geography, history, and social dimensions. This was

followed by a discussion of the politics of the site and the demands made of and by its inhabitants. This analysis revealed that the discourse surrounding the Tenderloin is predominately exclusionary and coercively inclusive.

For example, as developers and other business interests seek to utilize space within the Tenderloin to serve middle- and upper-class clienteles, or to present a tidy atmosphere for tourists in nearby shopping districts, we see the production of exclusionary demands centred on limiting services to the homeless in order to push them out of the neighbourhood. Further, exclusionary demands are also produced among residents and often reflect racialized divisions within the neighbourhood that are expressed as moral boundaries.

The site also engenders coercively inclusive demands directed at regulating the 'conduct' of the homeless, the mentally ill, the addicted, and other 'deviants.' These demands find expression in billboards and other forms of advertising that warn tourists against giving money to panhandlers: the ultimate purpose of this advertising is to dissuade the homeless, both within the Tenderloin and elsewhere, away from the practice of begging and into conformity with the existing normative code.

The Tenderloin also produces inclusionary discourse. As elsewhere, this discourse centres on demands that community residents be provided with social assistance – such as shelter and improved access to services – and that they be treated with dignity and respect by the larger society. In contrast to exclusionary demands, countering demands for inclusion receive significantly less support from the larger community. This fact, coupled with limited funding, infighting among activist groups, and the daily realities of trying to keep organizations functioning, has resulted in feelings of demoralization on the part of a number of service providers.

The discussion of the site's politics was followed by an examination of the larger political and social culture in San Francisco that gives rise to the nature of demands produced within and in response to skid row. This analysis provided a context for understanding the influence of the American variant of neo-liberalism on shaping an environment that is at once coercively inclusive while simultaneously subjecting a significant portion of its population to exclusionary treatment.

5 Enforcing the Law with Broken Windows

In this chapter the role of the police as 'demand negotiators' is explored through an examination of the ways in which the San Francisco Police Department (SFPD) responds to inclusionary and exclusionary demands directed at the Tenderloin's skid row residents. The style of policing in this community is, again, consonant with the larger institutional environment in that it embodies key elements of the values and philosophies underlying the American variant of neo-liberalism. In particular, the policing of status offences (quality-of-life bylaws) is work that is at once both coercively inclusive and exclusionary.

The following section offers an introduction to the structure of the San Francisco Police Department and its Tenderloin station. Following this, I explore the orientation of the police institution through the views of police managers, who discuss the delivery of 'community policing' within the Tenderloin. The SFPD's community policing model is based on the broken windows hypothesis and is thus revealed to privilege the law enforcement role over other conceptions of policing. Through analysing the ways in which frontline officers understand their job and the roles they perform in this neighbourhood, we learn that police view themselves as 'general service providers' who embrace the law enforcement role but feel that they must perform social work tasks in order to fill the larger social work service gap. The self-perceptions of frontline officers are then contrasted to those of the individuals policed in order to explore alternative views of the policing of San Francisco's skids. Next, through a discussion of police willingness to effect positive social change in the Tenderloin, we see how police officers at all levels of the institution recognize the politicized nature of policing on the skids.

The San Francisco Police Department

The San Francisco Police Department (SFPD) was founded in 1849 to keep order during the California Gold Rush. Today, the SFPD is a municipal force composed of approximately 400 civilians and 2300 police members.[1] In the fiscal year 2002–3, the force's annual budget was $307,441,724 (Office of the Controller 2003).

The SFPD consists of personnel employed in Administration, Major Investigations, and Operations. The Operations department is responsible for patrol and community policing functions and consists of ten policing districts[2] within two divisions: Metro and Golden Gate. The Tenderloin community and neighbouring Union Square form the Tenderloin police district within the Metro divisions. This district is the result of an SFPD pilot project begun in 1991 called the Tenderloin Taskforce. The project led to the subsequent creation of the city's tenth policing district in October 2000. The station is located in the heart of the Tenderloin, at the intersection of Eddy and Jones. It is operated under the authority of a district captain, with seventy-six officers assigned. Officers are deployed to beat functions in one of three sectors; patrol primarily consists of car and bike beats and foot patrols (when there are deemed to be sufficient bodies available). The department operates staggered ten-hour shifts supervised by a sergeant who is responsible for five patrol officers. The night watch also consists of two inspectors who are tasked with assisting patrol in responding to serious offences.

The SFPD claims a 'community-based' policing approach, with community policing functions said to be vested at the local level within each individual patrol officer. However, the organization also operates some community-based programs at the institutional level. These include the Police Activities League, a program in which police officers serve as mentors and role models for impoverished children, and a Citizens' Patrol Academy, which offers a series of seminars on policing topics to interested civilians. Department policy also requires each district captain to hold monthly police–community relations (PCR) meetings.

Policing the Tenderloin: The Organizational Perspective

The city of San Francisco and its police department view the Tenderloin as a criminogenic site necessitating a dedicated police presence. Despite this presence, the Tenderloin is not the focus of specialized policing programs mandated by command staff; rather, the SFPD's programs and policies, like those of the city itself, tend not to be neighbourhood-specific because the target of public fears is less a geographically defined criminogenic community than a perceived criminogenic status found throughout the city: homelessness. In the section that follows I explore the policing of this status within the context of a discussion of the SFPD's 'community policing' practices. These practices reveal the institutional prioritizing of a law enforcement role that is at once both exclusionary and coercively inclusive.

Among the SFPD's various policies is one entitled 'Community Oriented Policing and Problem Solving' (COPPS). This policy mandates 'community policing' as 'an integral part of district station policing' (SFPD website). COPPS is further described as 'a policing strategy that assists station personnel in helping to prevent crime and to maintain order and fulfills the Department's commitment to help solve neighborhood problems while providing a highly visible presence in San Francisco neighborhoods' (ibid.).

Previously it was noted that the broken windows–style policing which has gained enormous popularity in the United States has often been erroneously described as a variant of community policing. As will be recalled, Wilson and Kelling's (1982) 'broken windows' model hypothesizes the existence of a positive correlation between serious offences and low-level disorder, stating that the former can only be addressed through community surveillance and aggressive policing of disorder. The differences between the community policing and broken windows models are significant. For one, community policing depicts police as service providers, whereas broken windows focuses on 'quality-of-life' issues, thus permitting police to retain a largely mythical conception of themselves as aggressive crime fighters. Second, public consultation and oversight of policing practices, hallmarks of the community policing model, are lacking from the broken windows approach, which is more concerned with preserving the power of the police institution than rendering it accountable to the public. For example, where community policing defines the role of the public as co-producer, with the police, of local crime prevention and safety strategies, broken windows casts the public as mere surveillance agents of the police – as 'eyes and ears.' This privileging of the police role at the expense of the community is made explicit by Wilson and Kelling in their original articulation of the broken windows model (1982: 37): 'The police are plainly the key to order maintenance.' Third, whereas community policing attempts to bring neighbourhoods together to find common ground on local issues, broken windows creates and/or reinforces community divisions by categorizing people as orderly or disorderly according to moralistic premises (see, for example, Huey, Ericson, and Haggerty 2005; Herbert 2001a; Harcourt 2001, 1998).

I raise these distinctions in order to support my contention that the community policing approach that the SFPD lays claim to is really a version of broken windows and that these two models are conflated by the organization. This conflation was made explicit during an interview with a police manager who opined that 'community policing is fixing the broken window.' Further, this conflation serves as a rhetorical strategy that obscures the lack of public oversight of the police department, both at institutional and local levels. As in other communities, 'community policing' is less a practice here than a term misappropriated in order to hide the unwillingness of an organization to launch meaningful and needed reforms: 'The police do not want to officially commit to doing anything other than command and control' (community activist).

Quality-of-life enforcement is central to the style of policing in San Francisco. Status-related bylaws – against public loitering, camping in public, and so on – provide the tools necessary for enforcing treatment for some 'disorderly' elements and/or effecting the dispersal of others. For police managers interviewed, these bylaws serve as tools that enhance their ability to respond to demands concerning the public presence of the homeless. Not only does the organization support quality-of-life enforcement strategies, but police members, through the San Francisco Police Officers Association (SFPOA), actively lobby for new measures that are seen as enhancing their ability to 'maintain order' on the streets. Police managers can also lobby Council directly: one senior officer spoke about his involvement in having a bylaw passed that would prohibit public urination and defecation. Prior to the enactment of the new law, frontline officers attempted to deter such behaviours through 'innovative' means, for example, citing individuals for the offences of 'public exposure' and 'dumping toxic waste' (Lelchuk and Guthrie 2002). The new bylaw is seen as an improved method for preserving order because it limits the exercise of judicial discretion: previously, judges would throw out tickets for 'public exposure' or 'toxic waste' offences as being offences too broadly defined by police in their bid for public order (ibid.).

In interviews, some officers referenced quality-of-life policing during discussions of their work: 'a lot of times people will steal shopping carts from stores ... and use them as their own vehicle. It's stolen property because they're not purchasing them ... we used to be able to confiscate those carts.' Similarly, an officer spoke of confiscating the bedrolls of homeless people on the grounds that 'I deem things as being hazardous waste if I see flies buzzing around it and it smells like human waste.' During fieldwork I also had multiple opportunities to observe instances of 'quality-of-life' policing activity conducted by Tenderloin patrol officers. On several occasions, I witnessed officers waking up individuals who had been sleeping on sidewalks, using their voice or taps of their feet to prod someone into moving along. I also noted days, which seemed to correspond with major events in the city, when individuals who had been sleeping on nearby streets could no longer be found. Most incidents observed involving requests to 'move along' were conducted with minimal resistance. However, one afternoon in front of the exclusive St Francis Hotel in the Union Square tourist district I noticed a homeless man sitting on the sidewalk. Standing over him was a female officer, who alternately talked into her radio and ordered the man to get up and move along. When the man appeared to be refusing to move, the officer responded by yelling, 'I'm the authority here. You'd better fucking get out of here.' During this exchange, the officer's hand was firmly placed on her sidearm, a gesture interpretable as an implicit threat. Given that multiple interviewees had reported incidents where witnesses to such exchanges had been harassed or intimidated by police, I moved along when I noted that I was attracting the attention of a hotel staff member with security functions and was therefore unable to see how this incident was resolved. However, the portion of this incident that I did witness, combined with evidence of periodic sweeps of the homeless from the nearby tourist and retail district, illustrates the geographical dimensions of exclusion here and the role that police play in enforcing that exclusion. Individuals caught outside of the Tenderloin or the nearby Mission district are forcibly shunted back into these sites or are removed to jail through the expedient of bylaws that prohibit the status offences with which the disorderly are most commonly associated: public sleeping, panhandling, loitering, and so on.

Although the bulk of the targeted law enforcement activity that takes place in San Francisco occurs at the local level and is often manifestly exclusionary, there is at least one institutionally mandated 'quality-of-life'–based program aimed at fostering coercive inclusion: the San Francisco Campaign Against Drug Abuse (SFCADA) program. This program utilizes routine crackdowns on addicts for what is termed 'rehabilitative' purposes. Once or twice a month, plainclothes officers identify individuals under the influence of crack or heroin in the Tenderloin and Mission districts. The offence of being 'Under the Influence of a Controlled Substance' is contained within section 11550 of the California Health and Safety Code. As one officer described this work, 'They'll have days here where they'll bring people in ... and that's all they do; they arrest people who are under the influence of drugs or whatever, mostly drugs.' Addicts arrested on a 11550 violation are then given the choice of accompanying an officer to a treatment centre or being charged and potentially prosecuted. In a documentary produced by members of the SFPD, an officer depicts SFCADA as progressive. The overall message in this segment of the video is that police are engaged in 'community policing' through providing order on the streets while actively assisting addicts in the provision of treatment. We are told that 'this is where police work is going' (SFPOA 2001). However, the ultimate message of this program is revealed through the fact that in the first two years of its operation, it has been estimated that only 150 of the 1200 individuals arrested for being under the influence have agreed to enter treatment; no statistics are available as to the overall success rate for those 150 individuals (Forbes and Gumper 2002).

Bureaucratic decentralization is a standard feature of the broken windows style of policing, which urges practitioners to devolve responsibility for policing reforms onto the local level. As a senior officer explained, the organization's commanders have 'basically said' to the captains who occupy the middle-management ranks, 'Here's your area, go fix it. Take care of it. I don't want to hear about it. No news is good news; keep crime down, and get a handle on it.' Proponents of the broken windows model Kelling and Coles (1996) and Jerome Skolnick (1999) posit that devolved responsibility within police organizations is democratic. However, despite the appearance of community input into policing practices – for example, the department's mandatory monthly PCR meetings – the SFPD model is anything but democratic.

Bureaucratic decentralization in San Francisco allows district captains the discretion to implement local policies and programs as they choose. There are no standardized evaluation criteria in relation to 'community policing,' and performance evaluation for captains is not linked to meeting established 'community policing' standards or goals but, rather, as a police manager noted, on whether captains are seen to have 'gotten a handle' on local crime problems. Further, some captains do not support community policing at all. This was made clear during interviews with service providers and community groups, who complained about the withdrawal of 'community policing' services under a previous district captain.[3] Indeed, the only mechanism I am aware of for providing internal accountability with respect to 'community policing' issues is the problem-solving worksheets used by district stations (illustration 6.2). These sheets, utilized for a variety of local complaints, require follow-up by individual officers and periodic reviews by higher-ranking officers (to the level of captain). Again, I am not aware of any such review process with respect to the implementation and performance of 'community policing' initiatives at higher levels within the organization, and comments by police managers suggest that there is no such internal oversight process. Support for this contention can also be found in an annual report on the SFPD, prepared with the department's assistance by the Office of the Controller (2003). This report lists four key responsibilities of the police department: preventing crimes, responding to crimes, investigating and solving crimes, and managing the department (ibid.). In its literature, the SFPD places 'community policing' under crime prevention (SFPD website 2003). The Office of the Controller similarly treats 'community policing' within its section on the SFPD's crime prevention duties (ibid.). It is in this section that the report's authors pose three troubling questions: 'How successful have [crime] prevention programs been?' 'How does the Department measure success?' and 'How do the crime prevention programs relate to SFPD's community policing strategy?' These questions are posed rhetorically; no attempt is made to address a disconcerting lack of evaluative criteria with respect to this institution's performance and its 'community policing' commitments.

External accountability signals an institution's desire for public acceptance and legitimacy. Ideally, the negotiation of demands by police organizations occurs through the development of policies and practices that are informed by public input (from all members of a community and with recognition of individual and group rights) and are supported or modified through subsequent public feedback. In San Francisco, I found that structured means of providing external accountability by the institution, as well as avenues for gathering public input into policing practices, were sadly lacking. For example, I was unable to obtain an annual report of the SFPD either through their website or through several direct requests (which remain unanswered). This is a fairly standard document for most public organizations in an age of increased public accountability.

With respect to the issue of public input into policing practices, the only formal avenues available are Police Commission meetings and the monthly PCR meetings. These meetings are not attended by a large number of residents or service providers from the Tenderloin, most of whom do not see the police either as responsive to their input or as representing their interests. Service providers also spoke extensively about their frustrations in attempting to be heard by senior police staff on issues that they deemed critical to community well-being. One asked in frustration, 'How can we get these people to talk to us?' Another, who had attended meetings with high-ranking officers, advised that, 'We really didn't get anything but, "We'll look into it, we'll have training."' But ultimately, 'they don't do anything in terms of making change.'

One potential source of community input into policing practices is a program funded from within the police budget: Safety Awareness For Everyone (SAFE). SAFE is a crime prevention and public safety program that operates to educate the public about safety issues, creates neighbourhood watches, works with local agencies on local crime and safety problems, and liaises with local police districts. SAFE's twin program, the Neighborhood Safety Project (NSP), coordinates resources to assist local community groups in organizing watch programs. One of these local watch programs is TCOP (Tenderloin Community on Patrol), which a senior officer cited approvingly as an example of local ownership of neighbourhood problems. However, in my conversations with community groups within the Tenderloin, it is apparent that SAFE and its local watches have no more influence on local police policy than other groups and that their demands may receive little extra attention if they do not accord with SFPD operational dictates. This was most readily demonstrated when 'community policing' services were largely withdrawn under the previous captain's administration. I asked a local community worker if he felt that the replacement of what he saw as an 'anti-community policing' district manager with what he believes to be a 'pro-community policing' manager was in response to community demands. The interviewee's answer reveals the perceived shallowness of institutional commitment to local communities: 'It was just a switch and we lucked out.'

The SFPD's COPPS policy further follows the broken windows model by devolving responsibility for the assumption of 'community policing' practices onto all patrol officers. In an earlier incarnation, the SFPD utilized special liaison officers who worked out of each of the police stations; however, this program was abandoned because, as one police officer explained, the specialist positions 'created a lot of tension and resentment' on the part of regular patrol officers. Liaison officers were not perceived as 'being a "juice" person,' that is, 'not doing so much work – realistic work.' What this officer is referencing is the common belief held within many police organizations that community policing does not constitute 'real work' because it is inconsistent with the image of police as macho crime fighters (Van Maanen 1978a; Herbert 2001b). This was not the only time I was made aware of the low esteem in which real community policing is held within the organization. Indeed, one of the reasons why I initially was drawn to San Francisco as a research site was an interaction I had had with a desk officer at a district police station three years prior to the present study. Upon asking about community policing within the city, I was told by this officer, 'We don't do that shit here.' Instead, he likened the SFPD to the New York Police Department, an agency notable for its aggressive crime control tactics. Residents also referenced the organizational culture's traditional masculinist approach when describing an individual that they see as a 'good cop' – a police officer whose attitude towards street people is perceived as decent and fair. These interviewees noted that other Tenderloin officers referred to this officer as a 'pussy' – feminine and therefore weak – because of his friendly treatment of neighbourhood residents.

In response to resistance from the rank and file, the SFPD implemented General Order 3.11, which mandates that 'community policing' is to be done 'on an individual basis, meaning everyone is a community policing officer' (police officer). The inability of community policing programs to significantly alter institutional policies is most frequently attributed to the unwillingness of organizations to embrace changes that are seen as degrading their traditional law enforcement mandate and associated occupational role (Herbert 2001a; Saunders 1999; Greene 1998). There can be little doubt that the SFPD privileges the traditional view of policing as law enforcement that was central to the professional model that community policing was intended to replace. Certainly, we see this in the department's willingness to accede to internal demands for the removal of the 'soft' liaison officer positions and in the enthusiastic adoption of quality-of-life enforcement, which renders social problems crimes to be responded to with aggressive policing tactics. In his examination of the Los Angeles Police Department, Herbert (2001b) captures perfectly the dichotomous treatment of police officers as either 'hard chargers' (aggressive, action-oriented law enforcers) or as 'station queens' (weak, pencil-pushing community police officers). I suggest that this treatment is also found within the occupational culture of the SFPD, which similarly prizes the 'hard charger.'

For community policing advocates within the SFPD, the embedding of 'community policing' functions within the patrol function is seen as inherently problematic. A primary concern cited by an experienced officer is 'training decay': recruits are taught the principles of community policing at the Police Academy, but these lessons are often forgotten or undermined upon leaving the Academy (Chan, Devery, and Doran 2003). New officers are typically partnered with older, more experienced officers, who may reject community policing principles in favour of a crime control orientation. Further, the new officer becomes acculturated to the organizational culture, which privileges a conception of policing as 'crime control,' over the 'soft' community policing approach. According to this frustrated officer, the overall result is that, within the SFPD as a whole, 'we don't have community policing.'

Under the current captain, the Tenderloin district claims a 'community policing' approach. It is of a style that is in keeping with that endorsed by the organization: the SFPD utilizes neighbourhood watches to carry out street-level policing activities – becoming 'eyes and ears' on behalf of the agency. 'Police officers can't be everywhere,' a neighbourhood watch brochure exhorts potential watch recruits, 'they depend on the community to be their eyes and ears and to call them when suspicious activity occurs' (SAFE undated). Members of watch groups are largely supportive of the SFPD's style of 'community policing'; rather than viewing the department's responsibilizing efforts negatively, they saw resident and service provider involvement in low-level policing activities as necessary in order to free up police officers for law enforcement purposes. One individual stated that 'community policing to me means that police officers are really doing their police officer role ... You can't have a police officer on every block, and what community policing means to me is that it's like peer responsibility.' For members of community groups that work towards improving the 'quality of life' in the Tenderloin, the appropriate role for police officers is as law enforcers, an attitude that accords well with the views of the SFPD's organizational culture. As one community group member complained:

> Now [the police] do everything. They do social work ... they'll be like, 'Yeah, we help little old ladies cross the street.' I'm like, 'Damn, you're a police officer and you're doing that?' That's something someone on the street should be doing, and you should be like looking out for the next armed robber. So [I want to see] more emphasis on getting the community involved, and getting the police to do what they're supposed to do, which is work on drug issues.

One of the most interesting things that I noted not only in the interview with the pro–law enforcement resident cited above, but more importantly in interviews with community residents and group members critical of the police, was the level of support from variously situated community members for the 'war on drugs' and the police role in that war. One outspoken critic of the police, who complained to me about the exclusionary tactics that police support, also decried the presence of drug dealers in the neighbourhood and what he perceived to be the unwillingness of the police to effect arrests that would clean out the neighbourhood (which was deemed to be a more important use of police resources than going after the homeless). Whereas in other jurisdictions local groups have sprung up whose members have recognized that the exclusion perpetuated by the war on drugs has had a devastating impact on local communities, and now demand the replacement of the 'war on drugs' with a medical approach to the treatment of addiction that stresses inclusion over exclusion, I could locate no such organizations within the Tenderloin community. It would appear as though, for those groups dedicated to the inclusion of marginalized residents, that the line remains firmly drawn at the feet of the addict.

Returning to the issue of inter-agency police work, the only other form of 'partnership working' noted at the local level is the cultivation by police of ad hoc and/or informal relations with other public agencies and groups in order to address local quality-of-life issues. In response to questions to police managers concerning the development of inter-agency networking within the Tenderloin, examples cited of institutional problem solving were limited in scope and instrumentalist in nature. A notable example was a request by police for the Department of Public Works to increase the number of street cleanings in the Tenderloin to three times a day, in return for police assistance in moving homeless people off the streets in order to have them cleaned. This request was made in response to demands from local and nearby businesses to do something about the fact that 'there's urine and feces right on our sidewalks' (police officer). This problem is, of course, ultimately tied to the lack of affordable housing for the urban poor. Since the homelessness problem is increasingly seen by many within the public sector as unsolvable, and policing districts typically lack wider institutional support for their local efforts and/or the ability to cut across ideological boundaries to effect new cooperative solutions with other agencies, the focus of police 'demand negotiation' work in this instance becomes the much narrower concern with acquiring resources for street cleaning.

The Tenderloin police do provide other services to the community outside the scope of law enforcement–oriented policing. For example, while I was there I attended a planning session for a Halloween festival and party for local children, organized by a number of community organizations including the police. Similarly, I am aware of a number of other police initiatives aimed at developing positive relations with local neighbourhood children and their parents. Police also attend safety talks for seniors' groups. Such activities call to mind a comment that I heard in relation to the Vancouver Police Department but that seems to more accurately summarize the nature of police–community relations in the Tenderloin: 'The police picks their community.' As Herbert (1996) notes, youth and seniors are two groups that police often feel a moral obligation to provide assistance to. In contrast, no local policing initiatives that provide assistance to addicts or prostitutes were cited, with the exception of an informal local policy permitting officers to assist homeless individuals who ask for assistance in securing shelter. Addicts and prostitutes are generally not among those considered 'deserving' of citizen status and the rights that fall from this status.

This treatment is central to broken windows policing with its emphasis on the moral division of community members and groups into one of two distinct categories: legitimate citizen (morally worthy) and criminal or potential criminal (morally unworthy) (Harcourt 1998, 2001). The 'democratic' broken windows model is seen to be responsive only to the concerns of the former, who are permitted to have input into policing services and who also receive the bulk of services (ibid.; Websdale 2001). This division is implicit in the following statement offered by a frontline officer in response to a question asking her to articulate her 'community policing' practices in the Tenderloin:

> Talking to people who live in the neighbourhood who have been citizens in the neighbourhood. Getting to know them, what their concerns are, what particular problems they are having, whether it be with a homeless person who's always coming into the store or they're having problems with ... people sleeping in their doorways. That's what community policing is.

The community that this officer attends to clearly does not include the homeless person, who is instead viewed as a real and/or potential problem rather than as a citizen. Thus it is clear that for this officer, negotiating demands necessarily entails resolving issues that arise from demands made by 'legitimate citizens' against the disorderly rather than responding to conflicting sets of exclusionary-inclusionary claims. As in the previously cited situation involving area street cleaning, the negotiation takes place largely with other institutions who may either assist (through providing facilitating laws) or provide barriers (judicial review, unwilling prosecutors, lack of laws) to what this officer sees as the proper disposition of the legitimate citizen's claims.

One apparent feature of community divisiveness in the Tenderloin is its racialized nature. During interviews with police, community groups, and residents, the racialized dimensions of the neighbourhood were repeatedly referred to, and, in many instances, residents and community groups noted that local determinations as to who are 'law-abiding' citizens (morally correct) and those who are not are often made on the basis of colour and/or ethnicity. Given the history of race relations within the United States, it is hardly surprising to discover that black residents are among those typically associated with the morally undeserving category. As a community group member explained, '[In the Tenderloin] you have this race dynamic where it's like, what do you see on TV? I watch *Cops* and I'm like, "Oh my god, every black person is bad." So if I'm a senior, and I'm looking out my door, I'm like, "Damn all these people are bad, I live in a bad neighbourhood."' As this community group member explained further, 'you have certain people going, "Well, we're law-abiding and they're not."' Racist attitudes evidenced by both white and Asian neighbours translate into exclusionary demands that become centred on the aggressive use of police resources to disperse African-Americans from the neighbourhood.

It is not only 'citizens' who form discriminatory attitudes towards their neighbours based on race, culture, deviant (addict) and/or socio-economic status, but also the police who are tasked with responding to demands that 'something be done.' As Plotkin and Narr (1997) note of police attitudes towards the homeless, an officer's perceptions are likely to be based on the quantity and quality of contacts. Given the prevalent social and institutional view of homelessness as a source of disorder and crime, and the fact that a significant number of the homeless are African-American, as are a number of the local drug dealers, it is hardly a leap in logic to draw a connection between race and aggressive policing. Harcourt (1998) and Roberts (1999) both note in relation to quality-of-life policing that minorities are disproportionately arrested for misdemeanour offences. Websdale's (2001) field work in Nashville's projects documents the experiences of black men who see that city's version of 'community policing' as marking them out as targets of the criminal justice system. In San Francisco, a frustrated service provider stated that 'people of colour do not see the police as protectors. If we have a conflict in our community, we solve it ourselves, because as soon as the police come there's a whole lot of chaos. Children get taken away, people get beaten up, people get [charged].'

Policing the Tenderloin: The Frontline Perspective

When asked to describe the nature of their work, frontline officers tended to give responses that emphasized their patrol functions. For example:

> Basically, we do patrol. We do street patrol. We answer runs. If you call 911, it will get dispatched to our district, and then we'll go respond to those calls, whether it be a 911 hang up, a burglary report.

Similarly, another officer stated: 'We're driving by and we'll see what we see.' A third officer described his work as 'community policing': 'interacting with the people or the citizens.'

Given that the SFPD's COPPS policy vests patrol officers with 'community policing' responsibilities, I was curious to know how police officers whose primary function is patrol and emergency response would describe their 'community policing' work. Their responses indicate a style of policing that has evolved little from Bittner's (1967) description of police work on skid row circa the 1960s. For example, in the following exchange with two frontline officers, they describe 'community policing,' like the officer above, as a discrete set of informal interactions with residents that produces both local knowledge of the street and leads to informal dispute resolution through peacekeeping activities (such as removing the homeless from doorways):

> Q: How is community policing done here?
> A: I guess we do it every day, but we kind of don't see it.
> A1: It's just talking to the people in the neighbourhood basically, knowing who's who ...

My contention that contemporary skid row policing in San Francisco is akin to that described by Bittner in the 1960s is also supported by the views of a frontline supervisor who described 'community policing' as follows:

> Well community policing hasn't really ... that's just a title ... Before the guy on the beat would have more discretion and he would kind of handle the

problems on the beat by himself. He would maybe call different resources
and tell him to take care of this and that, but it's more formalized now ...
The basis of policing has not changed at all.

The institutional privileging of the law enforcement role, through
both policies and department-mandated practices, resonates throughout the organizational culture. When asked about the police function in
light of the theoretical frameworks employed, all officers emphasized
the law enforcement role. As a senior officer advised, 'our main job is
the protection of the citizens in this community. Law enforcement.'
Another manager similarly explained: 'We go with our mission and our
main mission of course is very traditional within police culture: it's the
protection of life and property.' However, both managers and frontline
officers saw the latter's function on the street as significantly more
diverse. Frontline officers, in particular, saw themselves as 'generalists'
who function variously as law enforcers, peacekeepers, social workers,
and knowledge workers. As one officer claimed, 'we're a combination of
all those [roles].'

In relation to law enforcement, a major portion of the police work
performed in the Tenderloin centres on the crime and disorder associated with addiction. As one police manager wryly noted, 'How many
bank robbers are there in the Tenderloin? Not that many.' Instead, the
drug dealers who proliferate on neighbourhood street corners are a
major focus of activity. As one officer stated with respect to the area
dealers, '[We've] targeted them pretty religiously.' As in other police
jurisdictions, arrests are linked to positive performance evaluations, and
the dealing in the Tenderloin provides ample opportunity for effecting
arrests. Some patrol officers, recognizing that performance is linked to
drug arrests, have adapted by becoming 'specialists' with respect to the
drug activity in the street. Another frontline officer explains: 'There's
certain officers that specialize ... you know they like dealing with people
who sell crack, they're more familiar with the crack dealers ... then
there's some who like to [police] methamphetamine.'

One of the central features of law enforcement generally is its 'dirty
work' aspects. Two particular 'dirty' aspects of the job were mentioned in
discussions with Tenderloin officers: dealing with waste and filth and
concerns over infectious disease. A frontline officer explained that she
had concerns about 'people who you know have TB [tuberculosis] and
hep B [hepatitis B], hep C [hepatitis C] and all this stuff, and we have to
have these people in our car.' Another stated: 'Sometimes we deal with
people ... they live on the streets so they're not the cleanest people, you

know? And there are times when you find out later on that they have scabies or lice or bugs, fleas.' Because contact with others is part of the arrest process, frontline officers see 'dirty work' as necessary, if not particularly enjoyable:

> If you're going to have to be dealing with someone that's a little dirty then you just put the gloves on. You know, I'll just put the gloves on, that way I don't have to touch you, skin contact ... and then you wash your hands a lot. You know, we always carry the wipes. After we deal with someone, we'll use the wipes or the sanitizer. To me it's just part of the job ... In the beginning I was just kind of like, ugh, he's dirty, he stinks ... but then you just kind of have to deal with it and do what you do.

As in other jurisdictions, it is standard procedure for officers who are conducting a search to ask if the individual is carrying needles or other sharp objects. As an officer explained, 'it's pretty much known if you tell us you got needles we're not going to charge you with them, we just need to know [for safety reasons].'

Police interviewed also discussed the peacekeeping aspects of working skid row. As the exercise of police discretion is often central to this role, discretion and discretion-related concepts featured prominently in discussions. In multiple interviews with frontline officers and their managers, emphasis was placed on adhering to the 'spirit of the law' (moral principles) in situations where the application of the 'letter of the law' (formal legal rules) would lead to perceived unjust or unreasonable outcomes. The following illustration was provided by a frontline supervisor: 'You could go and stand in front of the police headquarters right now and cite every attorney, judge, and the chief for jaywalking across the street. You could do the same thing over here and over there. Do you do it? No. There's the letter of the law and there's the spirit of the law.' A senior officer advised that this concern for effecting moral outcomes is central to the organizational culture. Banton (1964) and more recently Herbert (1996) have also noted a tendency within the police institution towards seeing its members as imbued with both moral and legal authority.

Such a concern, when applied to the homeless and other marginalized residents of the Tenderloin, can be interpreted as a limited form of inclusionary treatment. For example, an officer noted his use of discretion in relation to quality-of-life violations: 'We have our own discretion, you know, letter of the law to the spirit of the law. So I tell the homeless guys on the street, if nobody calls, I don't care. You have to sit somewhere. You're homeless; I'm not going to solve the problem, the city's not going to be able to solve it, so if no one calls, no big deal.' The decision to invoke discretion by ignoring a violation of a quality-of-life bylaw is seen as 'morally correct.' However, moral concepts invoked by police are also flexible and subject to individual weighing. The decision to turn a blind eye to the sleeping vagrant can and will be revoked, regardless of the 'spirit of the law,' if a complaint is lodged. For the officer, the 'spirit of the law' encompasses the need to balance what are perceived to be competing rights and, perhaps equally importantly, the need to reduce potential problems for the police. In short, discussion of moral precepts is really a guise for talking about negotiating demands on the street, with privilege largely attaching to demands that can be justified under law.

Police officers interviewed in San Francisco often depicted themselves as social workers. When asked about performance of the social work role, a senior officer responded by saying 'that's exactly what we are.' A frontline officer claimed that working in the Tenderloin, 'especially down here ... it's social work.' Another frontline officer who similarly saw himself as a social worker, expressed the view that policing in the Tenderloin had evolved from strictly law enforcement to a more general service type work:

When I first came here it was more law enforcement, fighting crime, catching crooks. We still do that but we've become more of a resource to these homeless people. It may be detox, taking them to a shelter when they become an annoyance with the business owners and even the people that live in this area. So now we take them to the shelters or detox centres ourselves, rather than when I first came in and the paddy wagon would have to drive around; if they were sleeping in a doorway in they went. So it's changed a lot. You've become more of a resource officer than a police officer.

Each of those who identified with the social worker role saw their adoption of this role as a response to two factors. First, as the officer quoted above makes clear, frontline police are tasked with responding to low-level demands that 'something be done' about issues identified as forms of disorder – for example, the alcoholic sleeping in a doorway. In negotiating citizen demands, it is easier for police to assist 'problematic' individuals in finding treatment beds or detox facilities as a means of satisfying these demands, if only temporarily, than spending hours processing a stream of people through the criminal justice system to similar effect. Second, officers' views of their social work role are also shaped by the larger institutional environment. As exasperated officers explained, there are not enough social work resources for police to rely on; thus individuals attempt to fill service gaps as best they can. This often means ferrying inebriated individuals to different shelters and/or treatment centres in hopes of finding a bed, providing encouragement and support to youth 'at risk' in the streets, or offering other forms of support to those in need.

The views of both frontline officers and their supervisors as to what constitutes social work tended to cohere with traditional views of police work articulated by scholars. Such activities as working with youth and developing positive relations with local kids in order to steer them away from the temptations of the street are seen as important social work activities, as are activities such as finding individuals shelter or pointing people to resources. However, as examples of some of these activities reveal, it appears that such actions can also serve peacekeeping ends. This again points to a central problem with attempts to categorize police activities according to a unidimensional model: police clearly utilize strategies that can serve multiple related purposes simultaneously. For example, two Tenderloin officers described regularly attending a disturbance call at a home where 'there's one guy who always gets drunk all the time. We always go when him and his wife are fighting.' They advise that the man has been repeatedly told, '"There's AA right down the street. We'll come and get you."' As they explain to me, 'It's like we'll take him. Just let us know when.' On one level, the officers are functioning as social workers by offering to assist this individual in securing treatment services. However, the act of providing treatment also serves a peacekeeping function: getting the man to stop drinking is seen as a means of reducing the strife that his alcohol consumption produces, thus reducing future calls for service.

Other officers described inebriated individuals being arrested 'for their own good.' A police manager in San Francisco described the arrest of inebriates as 'like a non-arrest.' Individuals who are conscious and non-violent are given the option of being taken to a drop-in centre for detoxification. Again, as with the example of the 11,550 arrests, there is a coercive edge to the choice offered. As one officer stated, 'If they don't go there, their only other option is jail and they usually choose the centre. So, we encourage them to do that.'

Knowledge work was primarily referenced within discussions of local knowledge-gathering efforts. For example, a frontline officer explained knowledge work in the following terms: 'We do like talking. We try to talk and get to know a little bit about [residents'] lives.' Again, this is often the sum of local 'community policing' efforts, as was made clear during an interview with a senior officer who advised that 'community policing' is about developing relations with area residents in order to acquire access to local knowledge: 'We have a lot of officers who are friends with a lot of the street people, and that's our source of information, a major source of information.' In San Francisco, police knowledge gathering at the street level is a function not only of the style of policing employed – the broken windows model – but also of the economic realities of policing in many jurisdictions: as a consequence of budget woes, the SFPD has lacked the funds to purchase and maintain some of the most basic communications technologies that police use.

Manning (2003) and others, notably Ericson and Haggerty (1997), have argued that technology is increasingly shaping the nature of police work, particularly in relation to the production, processing, and relaying of information through routinized communications formats. We see the uses and impacts of technology within the San Francisco Police Department in a variety of ways, ranging from mobile data terminals in police cars to the automated fingerprint technology used to process arrested offenders. However, the SFPD also offers an example of a major police department that lacks what many other organizations would consider to be basic policing technology. As one officer complained, 'We're twenty-five years behind everybody else in technology.' In support of this contention, a frontline supervisor noted, 'I should have an email, voice mail ... we don't have it and this is [a] newer facility ... If someone wants to call in or send me an email, they can't. They have to use the old pink slip; you have to leave a little pink slip on the board – a "while you were out" type thing.' While most organizations routinely use computerized geographical systems to track criminal activity, in this district I was told, 'We still use the pin maps.' The lack of technology and other resources has not been limited to this patrol district alone. In 2002, it was reported that detectives within the Investigations Bureau were sometimes unavailable to leave the office because of a lack of assigned cars (Parrish and Van Derbeken 2002). Further, due to city-wide budget constraints, investigators lost the use of department cell phones and 50 per cent of the Investigation Bureau's hand-held radios were reassigned to the Patrol Division (ibid.).

Whereas officers in Edinburgh and Vancouver gave little attention to non-computerized communication forms, this was a topic raised by one of the frontline officers interviewed in San Francisco in the context of a discussion of how little policing has changed over the years. I was advised that officers continue to use various paper-based forms to communicate both internally (to supervisors and managers) and externally (other agencies, local businesses and residents) (see, for example, illustration 5.1). These forms include traditional call sheets that are used externally to notify a business or resident of a potential or low-level problem. As one frontline supervisor explains, 'We have a situation where there's a problem ... you just pass out call sheets in the car as we go by.'

I was advised that problem-solving worksheets are intended for addressing problems of a more serious nature that require a formalized approach. As one officer suggests,

> For a problem-solving worksheet, that would be more if there's a problem with drugs at a certain corner or someone selling narcotics, or it could be as simple as a park with garbage in it. It's a scripted form where someone says they did something, you can go back to the community ... they want a follow-up and you have to tell them.

It is clear from this explanation of the worksheet, however, that the purpose is less for addressing serious problems – a garbage-strewn park can hardly be termed a pressing police problem – but more for the purpose of supporting an image of the police as responsive to the community. Problem-solving worksheets serve as a means by which the demands of area residents can be shown to have been addressed by the police, although the nature of the problems defined and the boxes for listing contact with allied agencies suggest that much of this activity involves little more than calling other institutions for resources. Regardless, they do represent one of the few formal avenues for providing internal and external accountability that I am aware of.

However, the content of the form itself raises a concern again as to the nature of the community to be served. If we look at the contact information on the problem-solving worksheet (illustration 5.2), we see that the form is designed for use in facilitating responses to individuals who have homes and/or employment as well as access to regular modes of contact. This is not a form to be used for responding to individuals who are homeless or who have only intermittent shelter. The inference to be drawn is that such individuals are more often identified as the problem to be addressed than as a legitimate citizen-complainant.

It could reasonably be suggested that the identification by police officers of homeless individuals as problems necessitating a 'solution' is

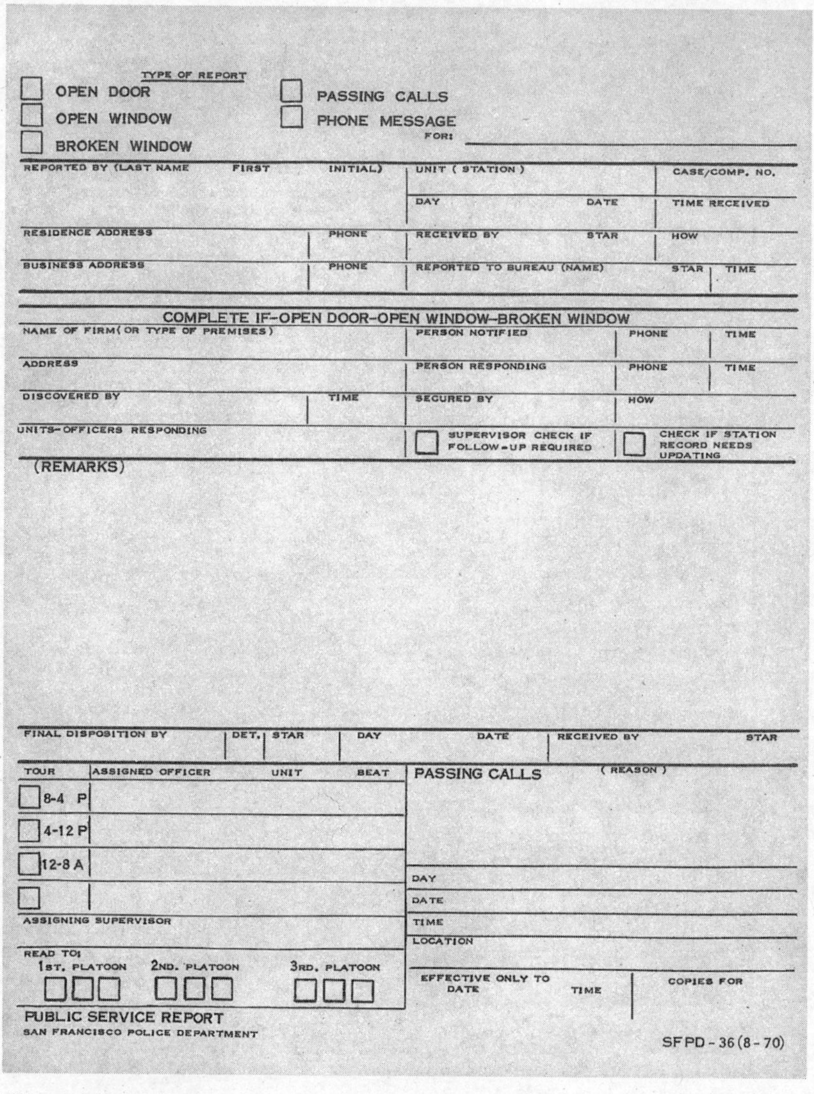

TYPE OF REPORT
OPEN DOOR
OPEN WINDOW
BROKEN WINDOW
PASSING CALLS
PHONE MESSAGE
FOR:

REPORTED BY (LAST NAME FIRST INITIAL) | UNIT (STATION) | CASE/COMP. NO.
DAY | DATE | TIME RECEIVED
RESIDENCE ADDRESS | PHONE | RECEIVED BY | STAR | HOW
BUSINESS ADDRESS | PHONE | REPORTED TO BUREAU (NAME) | STAR | TIME

COMPLETE IF–OPEN DOOR–OPEN WINDOW–BROKEN WINDOW

NAME OF FIRM (OR TYPE OF PREMISES) | PERSON NOTIFIED | PHONE | TIME
ADDRESS | PERSON RESPONDING | PHONE | TIME
DISCOVERED BY | TIME | SECURED BY | HOW
UNITS–OFFICERS RESPONDING | SUPERVISOR CHECK IF FOLLOW-UP REQUIRED | CHECK IF STATION RECORD NEEDS UPDATING

(REMARKS)

FINAL DISPOSITION BY | DET. | STAR | DAY | DATE | RECEIVED BY | STAR

TOUR | ASSIGNED OFFICER | UNIT | BEAT
8-4 P
4-12 P
12-8 A
ASSIGNING SUPERVISOR
READ TO:
1ST. PLATOON 2ND. PLATOON 3RD. PLATOON

PASSING CALLS (REASON)
DAY
DATE
TIME
LOCATION
EFFECTIVE ONLY TO DATE | TIME | COPIES FOR

PUBLIC SERVICE REPORT
SAN FRANCISCO POLICE DEPARTMENT
SFPD - 36 (8 - 70)

Illustration 5.1 SFPD police service report, 1970 (courtesy of the SFPD).

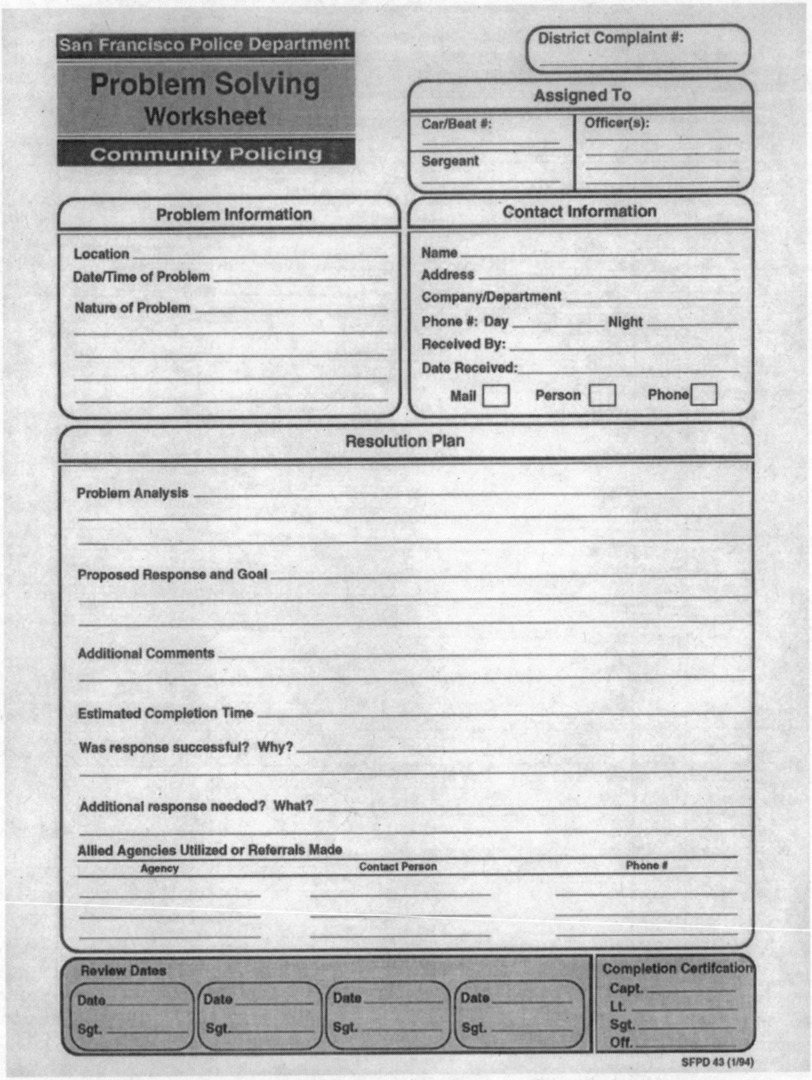

San Francisco Police Department

Problem Solving Worksheet

Community Policing

District Complaint #: ____

Assigned To

Car/Beat #: ____

Sergeant ____

Officer(s): ____

Problem Information

Location ____

Date/Time of Problem ____

Nature of Problem ____

Contact Information

Name ____

Address ____

Company/Department ____

Phone #: Day ____ Night ____

Received By: ____

Date Received: ____

Mail ☐ Person ☐ Phone ☐

Resolution Plan

Problem Analysis ____

Proposed Response and Goal ____

Additional Comments ____

Estimated Completion Time ____

Was response successful? Why? ____

Additional response needed? What? ____

Allied Agencies Utilized or Referrals Made

Agency	Contact Person	Phone #

Review Dates

Date ____ Sgt. ____

Date ____ Sgt. ____

Date ____ Sgt. ____

Date ____ Sgt. ____

Completion Certifcation

Capt. ____

Lt. ____

Sgt. ____

Off. ____

SFPD 43 (1/94)

Illustration 5.2 SFPD community policing report, 1994 (courtesy of the SFPD).

itself a form of community or pro-social policing. After all, the identification of homelessness as a problem and subsequent referral to a social
service agency, which the form's referral section seems to require, would
appear to represent an attempt at dealing with the issue, if only on an
individual basis. However, during my interviews with various police officers it was readily apparent that the bulk of inter-agency networking on
homeless issues was not between the police dealing with street people in
need and social service providers but, rather, between the police and
other city agencies responding to the 'problems' that the homeless
cause while sidestepping the issue of homelessness itself. As one officer
explained of the department's problem-solving approach, 'You have
closer ties with the Department of Public Works, the Water Department,
the Health Department, and it's more formalized on paper, paper wise,
problem-solving worksheets and all that.'

I was also curious to discover how officers view those they police.
During interviews, I received only one comment that suggested a recognition of all row residents as community members, as opposed to 'disorderly elements' plaguing the community. This comment was offered by a
particularly enlightened police manager, who noted that in order to
effect real social change in the neighbourhood, the police need to sit
down with all community groups in order to find common ground,
including those that represent the homeless, addicts, prostitutes, and
other marginalized residents.

Unsurprisingly, given the bifurcated treatment of individuals under
the broken windows model and the divisions within the Tenderloin
community generally, police officers interviewed reflected views of area
residents that divided the latter into distinct moral categories. One
frontline supervisor described the community as 'a good area ... there's a
lot of saints and sinners here.' Other officers distinguished between
addicts and dealers, noting that 'addicts, they need help, they need to
get the programs and get off the dope.' In contrast, 'the dealers, they
need to go to jail.' Since officers did not directly reference the fact that a
sinner can also behave like a saint or that addicts also deal in order to
support their habits, I asked two frontline officers about this fact. The
response received indicates some awareness of the complexity of life
here: 'Today [someone's] a victim, tomorrow he's a suspect.' However,
the implications of trying to categorize a sinner–saint dual status along
dichotomous lines were not abstracted from this acknowledgment. Instead, this officer spoke about how the dual status impedes his work:
'There's been times when you check them both [victim and suspect] and

they both get arrested because they both have felony warrants. Some of the inspectors are like, "Oh, that's cool, I know where they both are." I don't get to talk to my victim.'

Policing the Tenderloin: The Street Perspective

In a city where the urban poor are frequently targeted by the police for their presence in public spaces under a plethora of quality-of-life bylaws, it is hardly surprising to discover that area residents and service providers most frequently referred to police as law enforcers, and often using negative terms. Indeed, stories of the police told by residents and some service providers generally depicted officers as bullies and harassers of the poor. For example, two residents described an officer who singles one of the men out for abusive treatment. As the targeted man explained, 'he goes out of his way to make my life miserable. He arrests my friends. Because I didn't have a warrant, he said, "Well, I'm taking him" [indicating his friend].' The friend also described abusive behaviour by this officer:

It's the oddest thing. It's like a bully having a favourite kid in the classroom. It's amazing. He busts anyone that's hanging out with him [points to the other man] ... And every time he's like, 'I'm going to arrest you next time. I'll never catch you around here again.'

In *Powers of Freedom* (1999: 240), Nikolas Rose contends that in the present age 'subjects are locked into circuits of control through the multiplication of sites where the exercise of freedom requires proof of legitimate identity,' adding that 'it is impossible to participate in almost any contemporary practice without being prepared to demonstrate identity in ways that inescapably link individuation and control.' He then goes on to list a variety of what many of us would consider routine or non-exceptional activities, such as purchasing products with credit cards, withdrawing funds using bank debit cards, travelling with computer-readable passports, and so on. These are activities of the mainstream society, those who are counted among the 'included.' For those who are excluded from such activities, the freedom imperilled by the loss of identification is not the freedom of consumptive choice that Rose describes but rather the loss of liberty itself. On San Francisco's skids, individuals without state-issued identity cards are subject to arrest if they fail to produce identification upon police request – that is, they become doubly excluded.

I point this out because some of the residents interviewed complained about what they perceived to be the deliberate loss or destruction of their identity cards by arresting officers. The imputed rationale behind the loss is that individuals subsequently coming into contact with police could be re-arrested if they failed to produce an identity card upon demand. On another level, such activities, if true, represent a doubly exclusionary measure aimed at controlling and punishing the city's rowers.

Exclusion is also marked out along racial lines, according to those policed. Both residents and service providers pointed to what they see as disparate treatment of blacks by the police. One white resident noted, 'Come to think of it, I can never think of a time where I've seen an Asian person arrested in the Tenderloin, and I can only think of maybe like one or two white guys. They were like really gross bum white guys.' Some community groups and service providers placed individual incidents of racism within a larger institutional context. An outspoken critic of the SFPD's policies noted that with respect to poor black neighbourhoods, 'what we see in both San Francisco and Oakland is that the officers are not being held accountable for their actions. They're basically just given licence to go into these communities and behave however they want to.' Another frustrated service provider, speaking of recent police actions against communities of colour in both San Francisco and nearby Oakland, likely echoed the sentiments of other black residents similarly disempowered within the larger political system: 'I hate to say this, but I'm going to say it because I don't care and I'm not afraid: the way [the police] kill us we need to kill some of them. I feel like they need to deal with some of the things that we deal with.' In short, this is a community whose demands for a greater inclusionary treatment by police have fallen on deaf ears.

The primary peacekeeping activity reported by residents and service providers is the act of 'moving people along.' For some residents being moved along is seen as the police benevolently exercising their discretion: 'Some of [the police] are pretty nice though, I have to admit. Some of them, all they say is, "Let me see your hands." Then they say, "You can't sit here" ... And I say, "OK, I'll go."' For others, this activity is viewed as an abusive one that serves to reproduce class privilege by pushing the poor away from their home communities in order to respond to the demands of moneyed interests (businesses, tourists) that wish to be protected from contact with the lower orders. For example, a resident stated of the Tenderloin police: 'If you've just come out the store with a container [of alcohol], right? And you are walking home. They'll tell you to open the container, tell you to go to the south side of Market ... Everybody who lives on the north side is high class. Everybody on the south side is low class.' By ordering the resident to open the can of alcohol, the officer ensures that the direction to move to another neighbourhood will be followed. Both the officer and the resident know that if the latter wants to keep his alcohol and avoid being cited for violating the bylaw that prohibits open alcohol in public, he will have to go to the south side, which is a designated containment site away from the central tourist area. The resident obeys the command to open the container because he wants to avoid a confrontation with the police. It is common knowledge within the street community that, as another resident explains, failure to obey a police command means that the police 'will kick their ass.'

Both residents and service providers noted that the peacekeeping role also serves as a means of avoiding the paperwork associated with an arrest. A resident said of the Tenderloin police, 'They don't really want to go through all the paperwork and stuff sometimes, [so] they will pull your beer out, they will smash that crack pipe.' Similarly, a service provider offered the following story:

> They let things slide in this neighbourhood. Maybe that's a good thing ... I don't know if they told you this, but police officers often say, 'I don't want to arrest people because that's a waste of my time' ... I went to Boeddeker Park, and I'm like, you're right. You spend two hours on paper work just to find out that the guy is probably going to walk out of there before they even finish this whole transaction.

When I asked some residents for their response to the belief held by officers interviewed that the police should generally be seen as service providers who periodically engage in social work functions, the response was sometimes laughter or scorn. For example:

> Q: So part of the social work [police] say they do is helping people find shelters.
> A: The drunk tank. Here's a shelter, here's a blanket, on the concrete. I've seen them give it half-ass tries. There's a need for it. I'll be in the backseat of a car and they'll be like, 'So, what's your problem? Why do you do drugs? Why don't you stop it?' [laughing] I'm like, 'Oh man, you don't know who you're talking to.' He's like, 'You can just cut that shit out.' I'm like, 'Thanks.' [laughing] They're not educated in social work. Social work isn't slapping people around.

Service providers felt that police were unable to effectively deal with situations that demanded a non–law enforcement response, particularly when an individual appeared to be heavily intoxicated or to be having a psychotic episode. A service provider who works with the mentally ill noted the unwillingness of police to arrest obviously ill individuals under a voluntary detainment order:[4] according to this person, the process and associated paperwork are seen as 'a real pain in the ass,' so individuals in need of immediate help are often released by police. I asked this service provider if she would be surprised to learn that police officers interviewed tended to see themselves as routinely performing social work functions. Her response: 'It doesn't surprise me at all because they see anything outside of enforcement as social work.' This individual felt that, in critical episodes involving the mentally ill, 'police [don't] take the time' to assess the situation. It was also felt that police were often unwilling to seek advice or direction from social workers with respect to their clients.

A service provider in an unrelated field similarly told a story of an individual under the influence of drugs who had been picked up by police for threatening people with a chair, only to be subsequently released and then arrested an hour later for a violent incident in another facility. This service provider felt that 'if [the initial officers] had been more sensitive, they would have just kept [the man] for observation ... I don't feel like he was a criminal justice person, but he just needed time to detox.' Other service providers simply noted that they are often unwilling to call the police in emergency situations involving their clients because they do not perceive the police as effective in responding to situations where a social work response is needed.

I note that both residents and service providers did single out individual officers for praise because of the respect and decency with which they treat the area's residents. One officer in particular, an experienced frontline supervisor, is seen as a model for the type of policing that various residents and community groups would like to see in the Tenderloin. As one shelter worker explained, 'he's the coolest officer that you can meet because he understands what it's about, and he treats people in appropriate ways.' What I find interesting about the respect that this officer commands within the community is that he is someone who sees himself as performing 'social work' and utilizes a 'service-style' orientation in his work (Brown 1981). Although he works within a system that privileges the treatment of the marginalized in exclusionary and/or coercively inclusive ways, this officer responds positively to the inclusionary demands made by local residents and service groups by treating skid row residents with courtesy and respect.

In discussions of policing practices with both area residents and service providers, the least emphasis was placed on police performing knowledge work. Few of the service providers interviewed referenced knowledge brokering. Harcourt (1998) has suggested that order-maintenance policing draws on the use of local surveillants and the transfer of information. My research suggests that while this is the case, information exchange in San Francisco is largely unidirectional (flowing from informants to the police) rather than reciprocal. This finding lends some credence to the claim that broken windows maintains police power and privilege while reducing opportunities for meaningful community participation (Herbert 2001a). The exceptions to the general trend noted were public agencies or private groups that access police security knowledge for community safety projects.

I do note that one service provider did reference the institutional knowledge uses of crime reporting:

> Have you ever reported a crime at a police station? It's ridiculous. They just go, 'Okay, what's your name, etc.' Like, you could have written this information down and given it to them. You didn't even need to talk to the guy. They don't like really look into it ... They're like, 'Well we can write a report ...' And it's just like great, now there's another crime stat. Yah, that's helpful.

Residents and service providers also shared their perceptions on how they believe frontline police officers view them. In the context of discussing how he viewed the harassment received from Tenderloin cops as 'impersonal,' a resident revealed his belief that underlying this harassment was the fact that 'they hate you.' Another resident shared his perception of what a given police officer thinks: '"Look, I busted four bums today. I didn't do any real work, but I filled my quota."'

Effecting Social Change

Police managers interviewed acknowledged the political nature of their work, largely within the context of discussions on the difficulties of implementing local-level changes. One police manager opined, 'there's such fractured special interest that they're just a reflection of the governance as a whole in the city right now, which is very fractured.' Another manager, in discussing attempts at having a quality-of-life bylaw passed, similarly referenced 'special interests': 'it becomes very, very special interest oriented, and to get consensus for the full board to get laws changed ... it's unbelievable.' In contrast to 'special interests,' police managers who lobby for change see themselves as representing the mainstream of a given community; however, the 'community' that is often represented by the police is constituted of those individuals and groups who are not completely disaffected by the system and its political workings. These are the people and organizations that lobby the police because they see this agency as representing their interests. This 'community' does not often include the poor and addicted. As one senior officer acknowledged, there is a need to 'make a paradigm shift and say ... it's all about being one city, and [including] all the marginalized elements of that city.'

Whereas police managers in both Edinburgh and Vancouver spoke extensively of the role of the police institution as a whole in effecting social change, in keeping with the decentralized nature of policing in San Francisco, the bulk of discussion in relation to social change was on the role of local managers in trying to provide assistance to specific communities. One manager offered the following assessment of the current policing model: 'The captains are the ones who can drive the police resources ... so whatever calls they can make, whatever power they can broker.' Further, no examples were provided of how the organization itself attempts to address the social problems that affect local communities. For one police manager, the lack of direction and support for social change initiatives from command staff is seen as an impediment to effective policing: 'With bottom-up [policing] what happened was it was almost like the tail wagging the dog in a way, and the [captains] would set their own priorities not seeing the bigger picture, and we'd commit resources that we couldn't necessarily deliver on. That was a problem and there was conflict there.' Further, the decentralization of other city services similarly presents difficulties in effecting change: 'It's so decentralized you have each individual [political] district fighting amongst themselves, and then within these special-interest districts, you have the special interests fighting amongst themselves.' To combat the problems created through decentralization, one manager believed that the organization needs to move more closely to a governance-based policing model that is structured on city-wide accountability. As this individual explains,

It's saying the problems can come up from either way, externally or bottom, but we better listen to them and identify the trend, and then hold accountability at the bottom levels from the top to make sure that they deal with those problems out there, and being in touch with what they're doing. So I think you still have to have that accountability from the top down, but you have to make that accountability result-oriented. Those results have to be for the greater good of the community, with some clear directions from the top that are flexible.

I also asked a senior officer about whether he believed that frontline officers saw themselves as political actors empowered to effect changes within the community. The response received could have been taken straight out of a community policing manual: 'The officers at their level can really make a difference out there. They can really help people out and they really understand that.' In contrast, frontline officers did not see themselves as empowered political actors. Rather, as one frontline officer acknowledged, 'There's tons of [situations] where we can be political pawns.' Another officer explains:

> I think when it gets political they're going to say, 'OK you have to do this for a while.' Like for a while with the homeless people, the mayor was going to have us go out and confiscate all the shopping carts. They're stolen property and ... then someone got wind of it and it was like, 'Oh no, we're not going to do that.'

In this fashion, external political pressures translate into internal demands that dictate frontline policing practice. The shifting political winds leave many frontline officers feeling like 'pawns,' a process that 'community policing' has done little to alleviate. In response to some of the community policing rhetoric heard from a senior officer within the SFPD, I asked a frontline officer about the supposed shift within the organization towards empowering the frontlines. His response: 'It hasn't taken place yet.'

Frontline officers also acknowledged the politics of dealing with demands made by activist organizations concerning policing practices. One officer spoke of how 'we have organizations here who actually do nothing, but their goal is to actually sue the police department for every citation and arrest issued by an SFPD officer. In fact I have a copy in my locker at work; they put out a pamphlet on how to sue the police, DPW [Department of Public Works] for taking your matted bedroll.' In response, this officer is careful to engage in standard police behaviour: CYA (Cover Your Ass). As she says in relation to requesting that items be removed from public space by the Public Works Department, 'you just have to be careful how you word things and know exactly why you do what you do ... what I'll usually do is if I have a camera, I'll take a picture of it. If not, I'll just make a note of what it was, say it right on the tape or on the radio why I'm asking that it be removed.' Similarly, another officer acknowledged the impact of police complaints on her practice: 'It's like, "Do I want to do this and get a complaint?"'

Conclusion

In this chapter, I explored the policing of San Francisco's Tenderloin district through an examination of the management style and frontline practices of members of the San Francisco Police Department. What was revealed is an institution that reflects many aspects of the larger American neo-liberal political environment. For example, policing practices are shaped by, and in turn shape, the production of demands that are both coercively inclusive (reform-oriented) and exclusionary (punitive). In order to effect a response to these demands, the police institution utilizes an aggressive law enforcement–centred approach (the broken windows model) which operates under the guise of community policing.

Racial and class divisions within the Tenderloin have resulted in a divided community. The police contribute to this divisiveness through their construction of 'community.' Through interviews with officers, it is clear that 'community' consists only of those individuals who are viewed as 'decent' and 'law-abiding,' a definition that excludes a sizable population within the neighbourhood: addicts, alcoholics, prostitutes, the mentally ill, and others who sleep outside, disturb the peace, or urinate publicly. Not only is 'law-abiding' a class-based moral construct but it is also racialized. Many of those who view themselves as 'law-abiding' are whites or Asians, some of whom equate blackness with criminality. For the law-abiding, police represent their interests, although imperfectly. Residents and neighbourhood groups ally themselves with the police but complain that the organization fails to fully enforce the law, particularly with respect to preventing and solving violent offences, but also in situations involving quality-of-life infractions.

For those who are not part of the group that the police define as 'the community,' and for the service providers who assist them, the aggressive law enforcement approach that other residents demand and that the police supply is perceived as harassment and bullying.

To the extent that the SFPD policing model lacks both internal and external accountability at all levels of the organization, both sides in this neighbourhood can claim that the police are unresponsive to their demands. However, more often than not, it is the inclusionary demands of skid row residents and their supporters that remain unheard.

6 Crazies, Crack Addicts, and the 'Middle Way'

The current political situation in Vancouver could best be described as an incomplete mixture of Canadian welfarism and U.S. neo-liberalism – that is, as a 'middle way' between these two forms of governance. Throughout this chapter, I expand on this characterization through a discussion of some of the ways in which this unique political configuration has affected this city's skid row district.

As in previous chapters, I discuss the political, historical, geographical, and social dimensions of the research site in order to contextualize the demands it produces. I then examine the most salient demands made of, by, for, and against inhabitants of the site. This examination leads to a discussion of the larger political environment within Vancouver as a form of 'middle way' compromise.

Vancouver's Skid Row: The Downtown Eastside

The Downtown Eastside of Vancouver (DTES) has garnered a reputation across Canada as one of the most physically and socially decayed areas in the country. Local mythology suggests that it serves as little more than a holding tank for alcoholics, drug addicts, the mentally ill, criminals, and the most indigent of the poor. I find some support for this contention each time I walk through this site. Dealers stand openly on the corners of the area's major intersection – Main and Hastings – keeping a very close eye on their workers, who peddle drugs to a plethora of addicted prostitutes, thieves, panhandlers, business people, and, all too frequently, teenage suburbanites looking for a thrill. Those who score their drug of choice shoot up or 'puff' in nearby alleyways, or retreat to a room in one of the many cheap hotels. The area's alcoholics are also well served; the DTES has one of the highest concentrations of licensed premises in the city (City of Vancouver 2001).

The Downtown Eastside of Vancouver is 205 hectares of land divided into seven sub-areas: Oppenheimer, Gastown, Victory Square, Chinatown, Thornton Park, Strathcona, and Port/Industrial (City of Vancouver 2000). It is abutted by the Burrard inlet to the north, the city's business and retail district to the west, historic Chinatown to the south, and the working-class neighbourhood of Grandview to the east. The central hub of the area is the intersection of Main and Hastings, with Main Street running north/south and East Hastings running from neighbouring suburb Burnaby to Vancouver's business district.

The city of Vancouver was originally founded in the DTES; it was both the original commercial site of Vancouver, and the first city centre, housing a population that was substantially composed of single male labourers who worked in the railyards and on the railways and as loggers, miners, construction workers, and seasonal workers (Tasker 1992). To cater to this population, inexpensive lodgings, diners, beer parlours, and brothels sprung up. Missions and other charitable organizations shortly followed. Throughout the 1920s and 1930s, the site was home to both transient male labourers and a number of working-class families who laboured in the area's commercial factories and businesses (Tasker 1992).

By the end of the 1950s, the DTES became firmly associated with moral delinquency. The first news article that I could locate that discusses Vancouver's skid row as a site of social decay was a pictorial series featuring photographs and texts on life here:

> The typical Skidroader seldom eats, although meals are cheap in the neighborhood restaurants. He spends his time drinking the alcohol from canned heat, consuming cheap wine and picking over the dumps ... All skidroad habitués are not bums. The sordid three blocks harbor pensioners, ex-loggers and other respectable but poverty-stricken people who live in the slum area because rents are cheap. (Young 1951: 8)

By 1960, it was estimated that Vancouver's skid row housed a core population of some six hundred chronic alcoholics (Obe 1960). Heroin became increasingly popular throughout the late 1960s and 1970s (Vancouver Police Department *Annual Report* 1977); crack cocaine was introduced in the 1980s (MacPherson 2001). Today, both heroin and crack cocaine are prevalent in the DTES, and a well-established open-air drug market exists on the corner of Main and Hastings.

Illustration 6.1 Listerine, a street cocktail. Streets of the DTES, 2002 (author's photo).

Some 16,000 people live here (City of Vancouver 2001). As is the case with skid row districts generally, the residents are not all convulsing crack addicts and staggering drunks as seen on the evening news. While it is often difficult to overlook the obvious presence of these groups on the street – and, even when not present, the empty household product containers and other street detritus alert one to their occupation of various spaces – it has to be remembered that this is a neighbourhood with a varied population. There is a mix of young and old: almost 1800 residents are under the age of twenty, and 3600 are sixty-five and over (ibid.). Men make up 63 per cent of the population; women 37 per cent (ibid.). The DTES is also becoming increasingly ethnically diverse: whites, Aboriginals, Asians, and Latinos all live and work here. What these individuals and groups have in common is poverty – the median household income is approximately $11,000 per annum, with 68 per cent of residents defined as 'low income' (ibid.) – and the stigma associated with living in the skids.

The images of swaying junkies that have come to signify the DTES draw attention to the fact that the site does contain a sizable population of addicts. Service providers and police sources estimate that some four thousand residents – one-quarter of the area's population – are addicted. This figure includes not only alcoholics but also crack, heroin, and, increasingly, crystal meth users, many of whom suffer from infectious diseases such as HIV/AIDS, hepatitis C, syphilis, and tuberculosis (Adilman and Kliewer 2000). Included among the addicted population are a large number of individuals who are 'dual-diagnosis' (mentally ill and addicted).

The presence of the mentally ill here is generally attributed to government policies of the 1980s and 1990s that 'deinstitutionalized' the mentally ill, removing them from treatment facilities without providing adequate community-based treatment alternatives (MacPherson 2001). The city estimates that the DTES mental health caseload represents 20 per cent (984 cases) of the overall monthly mental health consumption (City of Vancouver 2001). However, this figure does not include those residents who refuse mental health services or many of those who are dual-diagnosis and are left untreated because of the refusal of mental health agencies to work with individuals with active addictions (Allen 2000). Thus, it is likely that the number of mentally ill residents in the DTES is significantly higher than figures suggest.

Like other skid row districts, the DTES houses both long-term residents and transients. The most fortunate residents live in fairly decent rooms; throughout the years, the city has invested some money in providing livable accommodations. However, the bulk of low-income housing in the neighbourhood is found in single-room occupancy (SRO) hotels. I had an opportunity to visit one of these hotels while doing research for a previous project (Huey, Ericson, and Haggerty 2005). The hotel's outward appearance was that of a vacant, boarded up building; thus I was surprised when a police escort pulled a handle and we entered. The hotel itself seemed to consist of a long, dark corridor, marked with dirt and god knows what, reeking of an overwhelming stench of chicken fat, from which a series of tiny rooms hung off. In one of these rooms, a knock on the door revealed a small group of residents, sitting together watching a small black and white television. The rooms themselves were generally no more than six feet by six feet, lit by a bare light bulb and furnished with a mattress on the floor and a rickety dresser. The 'unsheltered' are even less fortunate. Some bunk with street friends in one of the hotels, barter sexual favours in exchange for a place to stay, seek an overnight bed in one of the shelters, or sleep out on the street.

As in other skid row districts, in the DTES crime is largely intra-class and many perpetrators are also victims in a long cycle of abuse. Petty theft is very common and people will steal from friends, even when there is every expectation that they will be caught. I observed an instance of this involving a female addict who was 'camping out' with others in a group and was caught by camp members with pilfered items (she was subsequently thrown out of the camp). This theft is not merely for personal use; it also fuels the underground economy. Had I been inclined, I could have bought men's runners, jewellery, watches, and other personal items from 'street vendors.' Strong-arm robberies and 'rolling' people for their welfare money are also not infrequent occurrences.

The Politics of Vancouver's Skid Row

The message in illustration 6.2 was found written in chalk next to a squatter's camp in the middle of the Downtown Eastside. It reads: 'The lies: It's not more dangerous down here than it is in your own home – the problem isn't crack and heroin, it is loud abusive alcoholics, high-priced, highly addictive and highly toxic tobacco.' In chalk, we thus find again evidence of the divisions that occur both within and across marginalized communities. As elsewhere, Vancouver's skid row generates exclusionary, inclusionary, and coercively inclusive demands aimed

Illustration 6.2 Addict's message, written in chalk. Streets of the DTES, 2003 (author's photo).

at, or on behalf of, its various residents. Whereas the alcoholics interviewed in Edinburgh decried the presence of heroin addicts in their midst, an addict in Vancouver represented in chalk the desire of similar others to exclude from their midst the alcoholics and tobacco smokers deemed noxious. Interestingly, the message itself is addressed to another group: those from outside the community who seek to quarantine themselves from the poor of the Downtown Eastside on the grounds that the latter group, as a whole, are not simply noxious but represent a criminal menace.

In this section I intend to focus on recent sets of exclusionary and inclusionary demands in order to illustrate the increasing politicization of this neighbourhood and some of the effects that this politicization has had on its inhabitants and those who profess to speak for them. In similar sections of previous chapters I also looked at coercively inclusive demands directed at row residents; however, I have opted to reserve discussion of coercively inclusive demands found in Vancouver for later chapters. This is as a consequence of the fact that the most significant recent set of coercively inclusive demands made of row residents are articulated through a style of policing discussed in the next chapter – the saturation policing program known as the City-wide Enforcement Teams (CETs). While I introduce the CET program in the chapter that follows, the coercively inclusive demands that are embedded within it are discussed in fuller detail in chapter 8.

Over the past few years, residents of the Downtown Eastside have been the subjects of repeated, sustained exclusionary calls from business and resident groups who desire to have the area's 'social problems' dispersed to other places within the city. The argument advanced by these groups is that the concentration of poverty-related industries within this site harms area residents and businesses by attracting more alcoholics, addicts, and other street people into the neighbourhood, increasing crime and creating a concentration effect that has crippled the community's economy. To further their demands, these groups formed an umbrella organization called the Community Alliance. In 2000, Alliance members tested their strength through staging a demonstration in support of their demand that City Hall reverse decades of containment-oriented policy by reducing the number of future poverty-related projects in the DTES. Their demonstration met with moderate success: the previous City Hall administration declared a ninety-day moratorium on any new social services within the DTES. However, following the moratorium's lapse, poverty-related projects not only continued but have since escalated under the current civic regime.

Although Alliance members were meeting with little overall success in dealing with the city and had drawn significant hostile responses from local service providers and harassment from some poverty activists, they were not deterred. When an application was filed by the regional health authority to open a Health Contact Centre near Main and Hastings to assist addicts in accessing addiction services and health treatment, merchant and residence groups sprang into action, signing petitions and appearing at zoning meetings to demand that the proposed facility be opened elsewhere (Bula 2001). Again, the central concern voiced was that such a site would attract more addicts to the area (ibid.). In the face of possible success by the health authority, the vice-president of the local Chinatown Merchants Association vowed that 'if the health board wins here, we're not going to lie down and play dead.' Subsequently, when the centre opened, DTES business owners filed suit against the city, arguing that it had violated its zoning bylaws to permit a health facility in a site zoned for retail (Morton 2002).

Although the DTES has historically served as a site of containment within the larger city, exclusionary demands directed at shifting its population elsewhere are hardly new; such demands first began to receive significant political support with the province's successful bid to host the 1986 World Exposition (Expo '86). The fair's siting – immediately adjacent to the DTES – provided developers and local businesses with the financial incentive to convert existing rooming stocks into tourist accommodations The result was that approximately one thousand low-income residents were displaced (Blomley 1998). In turn, this mass eviction sparked the birth of local community activism in the form of a loosely defined anti-gentrification movement centred on the belief in a 'collective entitlement of poor community members to the use and occupation of the neighborhood as a whole' (ibid.: 471). Although this belief underlies much of the inclusionary work that takes place today, this original movement subsequently developed into a constellation of individuals and organizations advocating for a broader range of inclusionary goals.

The range of inclusionary demands produced here is diverse and includes: increased income for aid recipients, more social housing, community development (in benefit of the poor), improved access to healthcare and addiction treatment, harm reduction measures, the decriminalization of sex trade work, improved resources for youth, and better treatment of residents by the police, among others.

In contrast to other marginalized communities where residents and their advocates are often simply too demoralized by a lack of institutional or popular support to attempt efforts at social change, individuals and groups within the DTES have launched several recent notable campaigns. During the research period, for example, local residents and community activists erected a tent city in the Downtown Eastside's Victory Square park to protest a lack of available quality social housing and continuing provincial welfare cuts (illustration 6.3).

Literally hundreds of social service providers work within this community, representing varied interests and advancing different sets of inclusionary demands that compete not only with the exclusionary demands heard from merchants' associations and neighbouring resident groups but also with each other. As one long-time community activist wryly noted, 'if you put two people in a room in the Downtown Eastside you get a non-profit society. If you put three people in a room in the Downtown Eastside, you get two non-profit societies.' Some of these groups are organized from within the community; others are primarily

Illustration 6.3 Tent City (Victory Square protest). Streets of the DTES, 2003 (author's photo).

composed of interest groups from without who see themselves as filling gaps in local services. For local activists outside of the community, the DTES represents an opportunity to advance their political agendas, which run the gamut from organizations demanding better housing or enhanced police accountability to those seeking a Marxist-style regime change. Indeed, poverty activism has become 'cool' for many youths from better neighbourhoods – a fact that creates tensions with older residents and established community groups, who prefer to work within the existing power structure in order to effect change rather than to engage in what are viewed by many as counterproductive confrontational activities. Indeed, many groups within the DTES find the confrontational methods employed by some poverty/community activists – such as camp-ins, protest parades, critical media campaigns, disruptions of City Hall meetings, and/or shouting down civic officials at public gatherings – as divisive and ultimately harmful to the overall goal of social inclusion. The tensions produced within the community by such disparate political aims and tactics were referenced in the course of an interview with a local resident who noted the divisive effects that so many different competing interests have on the space:

> It's like the DTES, it's becoming a political symbol. It's like everyone's hobbyhorse for whatever political issue they're interested in. Sometimes that's benign, but sometimes it's really, really damaging. And it comes at the cost of people not being involved in their own community. But there's a lot of cachet ... 'Oh, I'm working in the DTES' ... It's this real cultural phenomenon on its own.

Aside from facilitating inter-community divisions, the 'hobbyhorse' phenomenon also engenders another significant problem for local resident-activists. It is used to support the claim, often heard with respect to pro-inclusion and/or anti-exclusion actions in the Downtown Eastside, that most of the organizers and participants are 'professional activists' or 'agitators' from other areas of the city rather than local residents. Such claims are common, both in Vancouver and in other cities. For example, Passaro (1996) notes the pressing of such claims with respect to the installation of a homeless encampment in New York's Tompkins Square; she found that while squatters there did ascribe to radical politics and participate in a variety of demonstrations and pro-inclusion actions, these activities did not render them any less homeless. In my own field research, which included observing a homeless encampment in the Downtown Eastside over the course of several days, I encountered both varieties of protester: the 'professional agitators' as well as area residents concerned with pressing legitimate inclusionary claims for the benefit of their neighbourhood.

In short, it is evident that years of containment-oriented policies and social decay have spawned what some in the DTES refer to as a 'cottage industry' of poverty. Older established and/or more mainstream groups are given wider access to city officials and are often invited to participate in local policymaking, whereas other groups are excluded, most notably those who are seen as holding extreme views or utilizing confrontational tactics. These inclusions and exclusions from formal policy channels increase divisions within the community. Thus, despite some recent advances with respect to funding for local housing and the provision of medical services – most notably the purchase of the historic Woodward's building as a site for social housing and community development, increased healthcare services, and the opening of the city's safe injection site – there continues to be an overall lack of social cohesion within this community with respect to advancing inclusionary goals.

The Larger Political Context: Vancouver as a 'Middle Way'

> I think there's some renewed hope, and I think that's warranted given what
> we can do. But I do sometimes wonder if it's a little ... if there are more
> expectations than the city can possibly take care of. (city official speaking of
> the DTES, Vancouver)

Since the 1960s, when the city formed various 'skid row task forces,' one
common area of agreement among community stakeholders from both
within and outside the DTES is a shared view that 'something needs to
be done' about the site. For the past few years, the city of Vancouver and
provincial and federal governments have recognized the need to address
the significant social problems that maintain the DTES as a skid row
district. To this end, in March 2000 the three levels of government
brokered a five-year collaboration aimed at developing and implementing a comprehensive tripartite drug strategy that incorporates social
housing, employment, community safety initiatives, and the development of social and economic infrastructure within the DTES and in the
larger community (MacPherson 2001). This collaboration is called the
Vancouver Agreement.

In 2002, the city of Vancouver, in support of the Vancouver Agreement, adopted its own plan for engendering positive social change in
the DTES. This plan is called the Four Pillars plan because it is founded
on four principles: prevention, treatment, enforcement, and harm reduction (MacPherson 2001). Prevention-oriented programs to be developed by the city include city-wide education that focuses on the dynamics
of addiction and its prevention. Treatment is to consist of intervention
and support programs, including detoxification and health services.
Enforcement strategies are intended to restore public order in the site
and to shut down the open drug market that flourishes there. Finally, the
city is to institute harm reduction programs, such as safe injection sites,
aimed at reducing the negative health and social impacts associated with
addiction. As of June 2003, the only programs in effect under the Four
Pillars plan are those associated with law enforcement (a massive police
crackdown on the area's drug dealers was begun in spring 2003). Newly
elected officials had promised a January 2003 opening for the city's first
safe injection site, but the city was unable to obtain approval from
federal health authorities until June (Luba 2003). The facility, the first of
its kind in North America, finally opened in September 2003 (ibid.)[1] and

is now serving some five hundred addicts, averaging six hundred visits per day (Bermingham 2004).

In Edinburgh and San Francisco, the political philosophies underlying social and economic policies of city and state are largely in line with each other. That is, the city of Edinburgh and the country of Scotland both embrace a social market model, which incorporates inclusionary goals, whereas policies and programs in San Francisco, and within the larger state of California, are distinctly neo-liberal in the American mould. With respect to Vancouver and the province of British Columbia, there is a curious dissonance between the political philosophies of the parties currently leading the two levels of government (municipal and provincial), which has resulted in a political environment that is a strange and uneasy amalgam of both Keynesianism and American neo-liberalism.

British Columbia, like Scotland and its regional councils, differs significantly from California in that voter input into policy decisions is provided largely through the general election process rather than through public referenda. Voters elect officials to the provincial legislature for a period of up to five years and are provided few other avenues through which to offer input into the shaping of public policy. For example, there are no legislative mechanisms in place that require public officials to hold public forums on particular economic and social policies, and there has been only one public referendum in the province within the past twenty years, which turned out to be disastrous.[2] Because of the lack of avenues for public input, voters must choose officials based on their political platforms and/or those of the various political parties. It could reasonably be argued that this process resulted, for some years, in British Columbia's electorate being largely insulated from many of the vagaries of U.S. neo-liberal governance that overwhelmed its referendum-loving neighbours to the south. However, voter fatigue, combined with public debt, eroding public services, little growth in the private sector, and a widespread lack of confidence in the government of the day, led to the ushering in of a new style of politics in British Columbia, one that it is explicitly and unabashedly neo-liberal in many key aspects.

In 2000, the provincial Liberal party of Gordon Campbell promised to reverse the province's debt position by bringing in a balanced budget within four years of election. Campbell's balanced-budget platform rested on four familiar U.S.-style neo-liberal strategies: massive budget cuts, privatization of public corporations and their subsidiaries,[3] increased public–private partnerships (facilitated through moving the provision of goods and services to private markets), and lowered provincial income taxes (to stimulate consumer spending). In an effort to reduce public spending and produce a 'lean, mean' government, the provincial civil service, which already contained one of the lowest rates of public sector employees in Canada, was further reduced by over ten thousand jobs (McNulty 2002). Courthouses and jails were closed, legal aid services slashed, funding for drug and alcohol programs eliminated, forestry and agricultural programs were abandoned, spending freezes on healthcare and education were instituted, and public services were 'contracted out' to the private sector. Further, the welfare rolls in British Columbia became a principal target of 'waste' elimination.

The extent to which the provincial Liberal government has adopted neo-liberal economic and social policies modelled on the Chicago School approach is most readily apparent with respect to their treatment of the provincial welfare system, a system that is becoming increasingly similar to those found at county and state levels in California. This change is most clearly reflected in the new rhetoric surrounding receipt of welfare assistance: 'We'll be pushing hard for people to get training and get a job ... People have to make the most of their potential so they can participate in the economy and society' (Murray Coell, Minister of Human Resources, cited in Smyth 2001: A3). The phrasing of the second sentence is revealing: people's potential rests first on market participation, and second on participation in society. As occurred in California and other U.S. states, strict time limits on the collection of assistance were also put into place: individuals were barred from collecting benefits for more than two years during a five-year period. The dependent welfare recipient of yesterday is to be replaced with an active, reflexive market participant who assumes risks and responsibilities for choices made.

In 2002, the residents of the city of Vancouver elected a left-of-centre political party into power, seating a new mayor and seven city councilors[4] from the Coalition of Progressive Electors (COPE) party. COPE members ran on a platform that included promises that would effectively increase rather than decrease the social safety net. These promises included the implementation of the city's Four Pillars plan and commitments to increase funding of local school boards,[5] increase low-income housing stocks, and improve public transit. Further, the party promised to increase direct democracy by holding a plebiscite on the city's Winter Olympics bid, which it did shortly after taking office. A COPE-led City Hall also immediately purchased a historic landmark in the DTES from the provincial government to be used for low-income housing and neighbourhood development. And the city's new mayor held meetings with federal health officials to push for federal authorization of the city's first safe injection site, which was approved some seven months after he took office.

Vancouverites currently find themselves in a paradoxical situation. On the one hand, many voters, both within Vancouver and throughout the province, elected a provincial political party that ran on a distinctly American neo-liberal political agenda. On the other hand, a majority of the city's electorate overwhelmingly selected representatives from a party that ran not only on a welfarist platform, but moreover gave the concerns of a marginalized community prominence among their election promises. Three questions arise from this situation.

First, to what extent can it be suggested that the victory of the provincial Liberal party represents a shift towards an American style of neo-liberalism? There is, unfortunately, no clear-cut answer to this question, as the available evidence conflicts. It has been suggested that what voters were seeking in the Liberal party was an improved economy and an opportunity to remove a scandal-ridden New Democratic Party (NDP) from office (Smyth 2003). Whether voters at the time of the election explicitly understood the consequences of their acceptance of the (neo)Liberal platform is unclear. Since the election, the province has faced massive labour unrest, a series of demonstrations against spending cuts, and several recall campaigns. Recent polls suggest that support for the Liberal government has waned considerably.

Second, can we understand Vancouverites' civic election preferences as indicative of a response to provincial politics? It is worth noting that voters in Vancouver and in the province have historically tended to elect oppositional parties to power simultaneously (Tielman cited in Ward 2002; Johnson 2002).[6] This is a practice that could be described as an informal checks and balances system. A quote from a voter interviewed after leaving a civic polling station captures this voting tendency perfectly: 'It's time for a change. We've got an extreme right-wing government in Victoria – which I voted for. This election is about balancing that, about humanitarian concerns' (cited by Lee 2002: B1). However, Kennedy Stewart (2003: 5), a political scientist from Simon Fraser University, suggests that the COPE victory should be understood as a consequence of a party running 'an almost perfect campaign under ideal circumstances,' which include not only voter frustration over provincial spending cuts, but also an incumbent civic party (the NPA) lacking clear policy options. Again, no clear-cut answer emerges.

Third, is Vancouver's current political climate unique within Canada? The answer to this question is a clear 'no.' Vancouver's somewhat ambiguous political climate is also mirrored, albeit to a lesser extent, at the national political level. This can be explained as a consequence of Canadian culture and history. In analysing Canadian politics over the twentieth century, Bradford (1999) contends that there have been two dominant political paradigms: technocratic Keynesianism (liberal welfarism) and American-style neo-liberalism. In support of this contention, he reviews the nation's history, which ranges from policies and programs during the post-war period that reflect, first, the 'investment control, and actuarially sound, contributory social insurance programs' that are hallmarks of Keynesianism and its focus on fiscal policymaking, then, later, an overwhelming political preoccupation with monetary policies, deregulation, fiscal conservatism, globalization, and an emphasis on enshrining individual choice that are each tenets of neo-liberalism (ibid.: 31). The result of the latter has been, Bradford argues, 'high unemployment and the proliferation of junk jobs, rising inequality, growing debt, and the dismantling of public services and social standards' (ibid.: 53). Bradford is quite right to point to these symptoms of neo-liberal rule as indicative of a larger political trend, a shift not merely to the political right but moreover towards market fundamentalism; however, he underestimates the extent to which Canadian voters remain invested in the production and reproduction of public goods and services provided by the welfare state under the former Keynesian system.

While American-style neo-liberal programs and policies offer potential means of modifying aspects of the welfare state that are seen by voters to be 'inefficient' (Stein 2001), the basic message of neo-liberalism is a hard sell in Canada. Certainly, the emphasis on individual over collective action is anathema to a Canadian frontier culture that developed through norms stressing community cooperation and mutual assistance over rugged individualism. As Jeffrey (1999: 35) explains, 'risk-taking and entrepreneurship [have] never figured prominently in the Canadian identity. Thus, in crisis situations, where Americans would typically turn to individuals or charitable organizations for assistance, Canadians would expect government to look after them.' The neo-liberal drive to privatize is another sticky point for Canadians, particularly in relation to attempts to privatize such basic redistributive schemes as healthcare (Heath 2001). For these and other reasons, the neo-liberal agenda remains incompletely realized. We see the incompleteness of this project most noticeably in the fact that Canada continues to retain several of the key elements of the welfare state, albeit in noticeably eroded forms. These elements include, but are not limited to, fiscal policies that cushion unemployment and programs that provide universal healthcare coverage, unemployment and old age pension schemes, social assistance benefits, and public enterprises such as a national passenger rail service (Stein 2001; Heath 2001).[7] As Heath suggests of Canadians, 'people like these programs and they tend to vote against politicians who tamper with them' (ibid.: 179; see also Jeffrey 1999, who claims that Canadians view many of these programs as 'rights of citizenship').

How ought we to understand the current political situation then in both Canada generally and in Vancouver specifically? I suggest that voters at the municipal, provincial, and federal levels are currently experiencing a form of governance that can be characterized as an amalgam of oppositional political styles, a creep to the right that, because Canadians cannot completely distance themselves from their welfarist past, has resulted in the creation of an indigenous form of 'middle way' politics that incorporates elements of both traditional Keynesian and market economies.

To be clear: I am specifically employing 'middle way' rather than 'third way.' Both terms are commonly understood as describing a political position beyond the traditional left and right (Giddens 1994). However, Giddens (1998) also uses 'third way' to describe a political project centred on the renewal of social democracy – a meaning not generally found in U.S. politics (O'Connor 2002). In order to avoid confusion, I use 'middle way' to describe a political form that does not adhere too closely to either the left or the right but rather represents a blurring of elements of both political conservatism and liberalism and/or economic neo-liberalism and Keynesianism. This 'middle way' does not comprise a set of policy principles reflecting a distinct brand of political beliefs – for example, social democracy – but rather a compromise position undertaken out of political expediency (see O'Connor's [ibid.] discussion of the Clintonian version of 'third way' politics).

With respect to Vancouver, because of its relationship to/dependence on the province, the blending of ideologies is incomplete and, if it does happen successfully, will emerge as a set of compromises between two levels of government representing oppositional politics rather than as a set of shifts as one political party after another (left through right) attempts to grapple with the domestic effects of market liberalization on a global scale. However, at this point it is unclear whether a blending will occur or whether, as a response to some of the ambiguities found in the present state of affairs, there will be a decided tilt towards neo-liberalism or a return to the politics of the welfare state.

Conclusion

In this chapter, I examined Vancouver's skid row district through a discussion of its geography, as well as its historical and social dimensions. This was followed by an examination of the politics of the site and the demands made of and by its inhabitants. What this examination revealed is that the discourse surrounding the Downtown Eastside is both exclusionary and inclusionary (as well as coercively inclusive, as I shall discuss in further detail shortly). Exclusionary discourse found here centres on demands by merchants' groups and residents' associations that zoning regulations and other measures be put into effect that limit social housing and facilities used by the poor and addicted – that is, that steps be taken to exclude poor people from the site – and that force others within the site who need services to look elsewhere. These demands are made on the grounds that the city has over-concentrated facilities for the poor here, damaging the local community and its economy. The preferred solution for those advocating for this position is that the poor be dispersed to other parts of the city.

Inclusionary discourse here consists generally of demands that skid row be treated as a legitimate community and that the needs of its residents be understood and accepted by the larger society. Such demands involve, among others, increased income aid, improved access to healthcare, housing, and employment services, as well as the treatment of area residents as full citizens instead of as outcasts existing outside the social sphere. However, even among those advocating for a greater inclusion of skid row by the larger society, there exist ideological, political, and other divisions.

The discussion of the increased politicization of the DTES was followed by an examination of the larger political and social culture that gives rise to demands produced within and in response to skid row. This analysis provided a context for understanding the influence of the middle way politics that emerged in Vancouver on shaping demands for both social exclusion and inclusion.

7 Peacekeeping through Saturation

In this chapter I explore the police as 'demand negotiators' through an analysis of the responses of the Vancouver Police Department (VPD) to inclusionary and exclusionary demands directed at and produced by Vancouver's skid row residents. I advance the argument that the VPD's style of policing mirrors the institution's larger political and economic environment: it reflects aspects of both welfarism and the U.S. variant of neo-liberalism, melding both inclusionary and exclusionary goals in its policies and practices. Thus, we see a force that has recently adopted a saturation policing model on skid row – a mode of policing that is typically aggressively punitive (exclusionary) – that is utilized in advancing a social work (inclusionary) purpose. This melding has created a unique hybrid that is at once exclusionary (policing directed at pushing drug dealers and other forms of illegitimate business out of the DTES), inclusionary (not targeted at drug addicts), and coercively inclusive (policing areas in order to push addicts into using the new safe injection site).

This chapter begins with a brief overview of the structure of the Vancouver Police Department. I then offer an institutional analysis of policing in Vancouver's Downtown Eastside through an examination of two recent structural changes to major policing programs and their effects on this neighbourhood. This analysis reveals the ways in which each of the four frameworks is utilized as a set of responses to the often conflicting demands placed upon police, demands that range from total inclusion of residents to their total exclusion. From this, the analysis turns to street-level policing, and I explore these four frameworks in relation to understanding how frontline officers in Vancouver's skid row view and perform their roles and functions. In this section, we again see how frontline officers utilize these frameworks as a means of negotiating demands that are placed upon them by different interest groups. Officers' perceptions are then compared with those of the residents policed and local service providers in order to flesh out important similarities and differences. I then turn to the subject of police willingness to effect positive social change in the DTES, and through a discussion of the politics of policing, we see how police officers at all levels of the institution recognize their work as political and themselves as political actors.

The Vancouver Police Department

The Vancouver Police Department was created as a municipal force in 1886 through the city's Charter. In 2002, there were approximately 1100 uniform members and 300 civilians serving in the Operations, Administration, and Major Investigation branches (VPD 2003). Vancouver City Council funds the force's annual budget; for the fiscal year of 2003–4 the force budget was $133,214,000 (Klein 2003).[1]

According to its mission statement, the organization operates under the community policing ethos. It contains a community policing section, administered by a sergeant within the Operations branch. This sergeant is responsible for overseeing the nine community policing centres (CPCs) that operate throughout the city and the neighbourhood patrol officers (NPOs) assigned to each centre. There is also a Community Services branch which operates liaison programs with retail and other businesses, organizes a Citizen's Police Academy, and posts a constable to City Hall to review public building proposals for crime and safety issues (Crime Prevention through Environmental Design or CPTED).

The Patrol division falls under the Operations branch and is geographically subdivided into four policing districts. The Downtown Eastside, Strathcona, and Grandview Woodlands neighbourhoods comprise the VPD's District 2 (D2). There are approximately two hundred police officers in D2 assigned to patrol, specialized details, and/or administrative tasks. Patrol officers are primarily deployed in cars (throughout the district) or on foot (within the DTES). Officers are assigned to one of ten squads in the district, typically consisting of twelve officers reporting to a patrol sergeant. The DTES is also the current home of a specialized policing program called the City-wide Enforcement Teams (CET). This program is administered by a sergeant, who oversees forty foot patrol officers tasked with maintaining order and providing assistance to a new supervised safe injection site in the neighbourhood. There are also three neighbourhood policing officers (NPOs) who liaise with one of three community policing centres (CPCs) within the district: Chinatown, Grandview Woodlands, and Hastings North. Officers work with these centres, providing assistance to CPC personnel and volunteers and liaising with other local organizations on community safety projects.

Policing the DTES: The Organizational Perspective

Two recent interrelated developments within the Vancouver Police Department reveal an organization in the process of change. The first of these discussed is the introduction of the force's City-wide Enforcement Teams (CET) program. As the program's name suggests, its mandate is city-wide, but its purposes and practices are centred primarily on the DTES: the program is a form of saturation policing introduced with the intent of breaking up and scattering the illicit markets of the DTES. An examination of this program shows two important things about the organization. First, the prioritizing of policing services within the DTES reveals a site that is viewed by police and by the larger community as not only distinct from other neighbourhoods but as desperately disordered. Second, although CET's order-maintenance mission privileges peace-keeping over a strict law-enforcement (crackdown) approach, law enforcement and knowledge work remain primary policing strategies in pursuit of CET's social work goals. To the extent that this combination of strategies is mandated through public policy, as outlined within the city's Four Pillars model, they mirror the current predominant political mood in the city – that is, they reflect an uneasy compromise position between welfarist and enterprise goals.

The most significant demand placed upon police with respect to the policing of the DTES is found within the city's Four Pillars plan, under which the police are tasked with restoring public order in the DTES, ostensibly in order to lay the groundwork for an inclusionary project aimed at recreating the neighbourhood as a stable, economically viable site for local residents (MacPherson 2001). The policing mandate is to be accomplished through 'a redeployment of officers in the Downtown Eastside, increased efforts to target organized crime, drug houses and drug dealers and improved coordination with health services and other agencies to link drug and alcohol users to available programs throughout Vancouver and the region' (ibid.: 4). In April 2003, citing the September opening of the first supervised safe injection site within Canada in the DTES as a critical factor, police implemented the City-wide Enforcement Teams program as their response to public demands for order in the neighbourhood, as articulated within the city's policy documents.

CET utilizes frontline officers primarily as peacekeepers tasked with restoring order to the community through an expanded and very visible presence. To support the program, police management initially redeployed forty officers – reassigned from community policing offices, administration, and operational sections – to the DTES, creating a pool of sixty officers to patrol the site (Rich and LePard 2003). Although CET was launched immediately following 'Operation Torpedo' – a drug enforcement project that resulted in the arrests of ninety individuals suspected of dealing – police have been careful to characterize CET as an 'order maintenance' program that emphasizes peacekeeping over law enforcement. One district manager stated that 'the focus [of CET] was never to totally rid the streets of dealers, but to restore public order to the community' (Howell 2003a: 7). Public order is to be achieved in the DTES, as one senior officer advised, by 'break[ing] up the large pockets of critical mass into smaller pockets which are more manageable.' To this end, CET targets those who fuel the illicit markets of the DTES – for example, drug dealers and vendors of stolen property – to drive their businesses into other neighbourhoods. Officers are then to be redeployed to these new sites, continuing the dispersal cycle until the major markets are smashed.

In interviews, police managers repeatedly stressed that the focus of law enforcement activity under CET is the drug dealers and sellers of stolen goods and not addicts. This was seen as an important distinction for the organization, whose members were clear to distinguish their order-maintenance–based program from 'order-maintenance' models that utilize quality-of-life bylaws and other forms of legalized harassment to target the urban poor. The reason for emphasizing this distinction is clear: the police wish to be seen to be acceding to a particular set of inclusionary demands, expressed by the public through media and through their local representatives, that centre on the treatment of addiction as a healthcare issue rather than as a criminal justice problem. Public legitimacy of the police mandate – crucial in a time of fluctuating police budgets – is frequently, although not always, predicated on the public's belief that they have some say in shaping the institution's policies, that the police are working in the public interest. The organization thus must appear not only to be accountable to the public but moreover to value their input. Unsurprisingly, news stories in which police representatives discuss the new CET program tend to minimize arrests of drug addicts, emphasizing instead arrests of dealers, although many addicts are also small-time dealers.

In support of this reading of the politics of the VPD, I note that CET was initially implemented as a VPD-funded three-month trial project, to be extended pending a request for additional funding to City Hall. It was the hope of police managers that CET-generated successes would lead City Council to provide a more permanent funding arrangement for extra police resources in this community. However, the mayor and the majority of councillors denied a request for additional funding until a study could be completed showing that the program worked without producing deleterious effects on the community – that is, they wanted to ensure that the policing they were paying for was not leading to the further exclusion of area residents. Some seven months after its initial implementation, CET continued to be funded solely by the police, with a reduced contingent of officers (forty-eight instead of the original sixty),[2] while Council awaited the production of the police study.

During the course of my fieldwork in the DTES in July and August 2003, I walked through the space in order to observe the effects of CET on the ground. Two things were immediately evident: the presence of police officers along the street and the lack of noisy, chaotic crowds. Officers were observed walking in pairs, on mounted horses, in patrol cars, on motorcycles, and standing in pairs or groups in various public spaces. Whereas the Hastings strip had a slightly chaotic and dangerous feel to it prior to the implementation of CET, the street now seemed relatively calm and quiet. People still congregate in the street, but the large crowds of drunks and addicts have largely dissipated. Dealers no longer approach strangers on the street with the greeting 'Up, down?' Several of the alleyways that formerly served as shooting galleries are now largely empty. Indeed, during a walk in the laneways behind the Carnegie Centre at Main and Hastings – an activity that I would never have attempted alone prior to CET – the only presence I observed was two officers on patrol. Some critics have suggested that this new police presence in such numbers represents a 'mini-occupation force.' This description is intended to invoke the feeling of a neighbourhood held under close guard by an oppressive military presence. My own experience of this neighbourhood under CET is rather the reverse. For the first time in many years, I felt that I could walk freely through the space, a feeling that several neighbourhood residents interviewed cited as not only a positive experience but indeed as an inclusionary development.

Those who had formerly hidden away in their tiny rooms out of fear of the open circus – including senior citizens and other vulnerable individuals and groups – are now visible in public spaces.

Although the 'optics' – a police term referring to a neighbourhood's appearance – have improved in parts of the DTES through displacing drug dealers and their clients into local hotels or to other downtown areas, dealing still takes place on the streets. At the time of writing, Oppenheimer Park, a few blocks away from Main and Hastings, has become a central site for dealing in the DTES. Whereas previously I could walk to Oppenheimer and see older residents sitting out and enjoying sunshine, more recently the park has become overrun with dealers and addicts. For some residents, the park has become a serious concern. One interviewee described drug-related shootings that had recently taken place there: 'You've [got] 120 kids surrounding the park, and they can't even go into the park to play because of the drug deals that go on and the shooting.'

There is little consensus among residents and community groups concerning CET. The split within the community is perfectly captured by the following comment offered by a local addict: 'A lot of the residents do [like CET]. Those of us that are involved in the other side of life don't like it.' It is tempting to explain the nature of the split in resident opinion, as the addict cited above does, with reference to the question of whether one is an addict or a provider of addiction-related services. Certainly, those interviewed who are addicts or addiction-related service providers tend to see CET as generating rather than alleviating social problems in the DTES. For example, an addict explained to me what she saw as the negative effects of the increased police presence: 'a lot of the people who live here ... are getting frustrated and angry. They're starting to rip each other off ... a lot of fighting. It seems like a lot of people are ripping each other off that wouldn't normally do that.'

A number of objections to CET have been raised within the Downtown Eastside community. Some of the concerns cited centred on the program's perceived potential to have an adverse impact on the provision of healthcare services in the neighbourhood through the creation of a climate of fear. Addicts were said to be too afraid to access services because they believed that they might be stopped by police and arrested for outstanding warrants. For individuals with HIV or hepatitis C, gaps in treatment can have serious consequences, and some service providers interviewed suggested that treatment compliance had declined following the implementation of CET. One healthcare worker identified the following as negative health impacts attributable to CET:

Huge displacement. Dealers are no longer in their same locations, so there's just been a displacement of all activities ... People can no longer use their same source, so the purity of their drug is unknown. There's a lot more riskier injections because people are constantly rushing to inject outside ... there's a lot more bunk artists out there. That in turn increases the violence. There's a lot more riskier needle usage because people are less likely to go return their needles, go get new ones.

These are significant concerns that cannot be properly addressed within the context of the present study. Future research is necessary in order to examine the impacts of an increased police presence on health services provision in marginalized communities and whether negative effects are of a shorter or longer duration. I do note though that the presence of police within the neighbourhood appears to have had little adverse impact on the success of the new safe injection site. It has been reported that the site receives some five hundred visits a day from area users (approximately 2100 of an estimated 4700 addicts within the DTES have registered as site clients) (Saskatoon Star-Phoenix 2003).

There is also a significant level of support for CET within the community. Again, it is important to remember that a majority of the 16,000 residents of the DTES are not addicts and that, as far as the notion of 'a climate of fear' is concerned, the violence associated with the drug market has long had severe negative impacts on residents' feelings of safety and security that have led many to feel excluded within their own neighbourhood. As one resident advised following the implementation of CET, 'Well I feel real safe down here ... there's areas where there's crackdowns on the users, which makes this whole area a little more safer to walk around.' When asked if the increased police presence was a positive thing, this individual replied, 'Oh, yeah. It's been real positive.' Another resident, who is also a service provider, noted that 'this community has the largest per capita in terms of disabled people, never mind just addicted. These are people who are physically disabled and mentally disabled and they are really vulnerable. And they were excited to see an officer. They feel safe.' A longtime activist in the DTES likely summed up the views of others in this neighbourhood when he said of CET, 'For right now it simply seems that the city-wide enforcement team has achieved a level of public order on the streets, and that's fine with me.' In response to charges that public order has been achieved at the expense of the very marginalized, this interviewee responded that, to the extent that it is the very marginalized who are most affected by crime, protecting people from crime and their safety-related fears 'is not a class issue.' Thus, although some residents view CET as displacing community policing, or as an exclusionary form of policing aimed at cracking down on the neighbourhood's marginalized, for others it is an enhanced form of community policing that has restored a sense of security to the neighbourhood. For these residents, CET affords those who had formerly felt excluded as a result of the open crime and disorder an opportunity to use public space freely – that is, to participate openly and without fear in the life of their community.

The second major development to be explored is the recent structural changes made to the force's delivery of community policing services. The emphasis on citizen-led local policing programs appears to be giving way to a new police-oriented model of community policing, one that retains a knowledge-work orientation but favours the development of inter-institutional relationships over local-level intelligence gathering ('eyes and ears'). This shift, which was accomplished in part by reducing the number of community policing centres throughout the city and the reassigning of NPOs to CET, lends further support for the contention that the problems of the DTES, long ignored through policies of containment, are now a focal point of civic public policy.

In its literature the VPD claims to embrace community policing; however, the redeployment of officers to CET was accomplished through the reassignment of neighbourhood policing officers from community policing centres (CPCs) that were closed down. Prior to April 2003, much of the community policing that took place in Vancouver occurred at the local level through the work of volunteers and NPOs at Vancouver's seventeen CPCs.[3] CPCs organized and operated a variety of knowledge work–based programs, such as Citizens' Foot Patrols, Block Watches, and Bar Watches. As of this writing, eight CPCs have either closed or are operating as neighbourhood safety offices independently of the VPD.

The rationale offered by the VPD for reducing the number of CPCs and NPOs in their discussion paper to City Council is threefold: insufficient funding, lack of police resources, and concerns with a inadequate public accountability under the previously existing operational agreements (Lee and Goodard 2003). A fourth factor, not articulated in the Council discussion paper, is that the restructuring of the community policing model was necessary to the success of CET. The department lacked the resources to carry out both programs simultaneously, without modifications to one or the other. In the restructuring of the CPC-based model, and the use of newly freed resources for CET, we see the VPD's privileging of CET over community policing. This privileging is directly acknowledged by a senior manager in response to the claim by a community policing advocate that police do not value community policing: 'It's not that we don't think that that work is important; it's just that we think [CET] is more important at this time' (Howell 2003b: 7).

It may seem surprising that the force would move away from citizen-led community policing programs, particularly as such initiatives are often seen as an effective means of offloading safety and security responsibilities to local citizenry. However, as VPD management has learned, citizen-led programs are not always the most effective or cost-efficient method of offloading policing responsibilities. To the extent that such programs are largely dependent on enthusiastic and committed volunteers, they may provide little return for the institutional investment. One frontline supervisor who has worked with citizen-based programs in the past noted a central problem with such programs is that the initial enthusiasm of volunteers often fades over time:

> [Volunteers] could come out with some enthusiasm, want to fix up the neighbourhood, want to be accountable. It reminds me of ... when somebody comes out for a police ridealong or is maybe interested in policing, and maybe comes out for a couple of nights and they think they have an insight into the job. But the one thing they'll never understand is the effect that it has on you night after night, after thousands and thousands of nights. Maybe the same thing is happening to these volunteers. They volunteer for a whole bunch of nights, and they realize it's eternal.

Without citizens actively patrolling the streets to deter crime and supply police with low-level intelligence, police managers experience such programs as little more than expensive public relations exercises with little value. Recognizing this, the force pulled funding from those CPCs that were not deemed to be providing 'best value' – to use new public managerialism terminology – in favour of those that were seen as effective at maintaining and/or attracting resources (both volunteers and independent funding). At a time when the force is experiencing heightened personnel demands, as one police manager explained, public demands for all of the CPCs to continue operating is seen to represent 'an example of a desire for a Mercedes-type service on a VW-type budget.'

Despite the fact that the VPD has initiated a partial retreat from community policing as articulated within the CPC-based model, this does not mean that community policing does not take place, but rather that it is increasingly becoming police- rather than citizen-driven. Whereas citizen-led community policing frequently involves frontline officers functioning as street-based knowledge workers acquiring low-level intelligence from citizens in exchange for their security expertise, the VPD is increasingly turning to more formal modes of knowledge work involving citizens less and other institutions more (this work also increasingly takes place at higher levels of the organization, utilizing sergeants and inspectors instead of constables). This overall shift pre-dates the restructuring of the CPC model, and it is likely that earlier successes in inter-agency partnerships influenced the decision to prioritize inter-agency work over citizen-based programs. Some support for this contention can be found in the claim made by a senior officer in discussing these earlier efforts: 'The police department is only effective if we work with other agencies as well to effect change.'

For the VPD, inter-institutional relationships are seen as being more cost-effective and less resource-intensive, and as having the ability to produce effects on a larger scale than local citizen-led policing initiatives. Simply put, they require little or no administrative overhead, require fewer dedicated officers, and allow for responsibility to be shifted onto partner agencies with the means and powers to effect changes. Further, for agencies concerned with issues of accountability, as many police organizations increasingly are with the new emphasis on public managerialism, inter-agency partnerships are built upon the need for mutual accountability. In contrast, without police oversight of civilian programs, ensuring accountability among partner civilian societies has proven more difficult. This fact was referenced in the VPD community policing discussion paper: 'There has been a general recognition that there are wide inconsistencies in how the different CPCs are operated and managed, and there is a need for improved accountability' (Lee and Goddard 2003: 3).

In the remainder of this section, I examine two community policing initiatives as examples of inter-institutional knowledge work. Each initiative represents a mix of the theoretical frameworks explored, in the pursuit of effecting improvements in the conditions of row life.

A key site for drug dealing has been the area outside of the Carnegie Community Centre on the corner of Main and Hastings. Police and private security patrols had little impact on the presence of dealers and addicts. The site was formerly so forbidding as a consequence of the open dealing and drug use that on at least two occasions when I walked past the Carnegie with police escorts, I still felt a little unnerved. This reaction is especially remarkable given some of my experiences here and in other marginalized communities. It is common knowledge within the community that many seniors were afraid to use the community centre or other public spaces because of the street-carnival atmosphere. In order to establish a more orderly atmosphere that would encourage people to use the centre, a number of agencies – including police, city officials, and Carnegie staff – worked together to convert a portion of the space on one flank of the building into an enclosed open-air patio for centre patrons. Police brokered their knowledge of the site and their expertise of Crime Prevention through Environmental Design (CPTED) to assist the Carnegie and other agencies in creating an open-air patio that would supplant some of the drug activity outside the centre. CPTED principles are most noticeable with respect to the use of barred gates and entranceways that serve to limit street access (in order to gain access to the patio, one must enter the centre, passing security staff). As a senior officer explained, 'I think one of the things that we [have] learned is if you want to control imperfect conditions, you have to control the environment.' The effects of this lesson were stunning. During several visits to the patio, I observed seniors and other residents enjoying the warm sunshine, smoking, chatting, reading, or sitting quietly. Again, those residents formerly fearful of using public space because of the violence associated with the drug trade, either real or perceived, view the patio not only as a welcome respite but as an inclusionary space. Undoubtedly, the dealers and some addicts see this space as representing an exclusionary attempt at pushing their business to other areas.

Other inter-institutional partnerships serve knowledge work, order maintenance, and social work functions, but through the utilization of enforcement strategies. For example, police officers are assigned as liaison officers to the city's Neighbourhood Integrated Services Team (NIST) program. NIST is aimed at ameliorating conditions of life on Vancouver's skid row and in other local communities through active partnerships. Police, fire department, liquor enforcement, social workers, and members of other government agencies work jointly to target businesses that exploit area residents. NIST inspection teams perform surprise inspections of local businesses, levying fines and issuing warnings. Businesses identified as 'problems' by NIST personnel are repeatedly targeted until compliance with all laws is gained or the business is closed down. NIST teams also work with allied agencies at improving policies and practices that are exploited by problem businesses in the DTES. Although one experienced police officer expressed skepticism over the efficacy of NIST, a police manager illustrated the benefits of this program by pointing out that prior to NIST, business compliance enforcement was done haphazardly and often only at the discretion of overworked police sergeants.

Before concluding this section I want to note that in response to the accurate perception that the force is effecting a shift away from frontline community policing services, the organization has promised to 'strive to immerse the entire Police force into the philosophy of community-based policing' (Lee and Goddard 2003: 6). This promise, if implemented, could result in a model not entirely dissimilar to that of San Francisco. Such a move represents a substantial concern because, as we have seen with respect to the latter force, community policing without institutional investment in the model as both policy and practice at all levels of an organization – which includes organizationally mandated goals, effective oversight and evaluation of those goals and clearly defined lines of internal and external accountability – renders such programs as little more than 'rhetorical strategies' (Saunders 1999: 479) for the legitimation of existing police practices.

Policing the DTES: The Frontline Perspective

As occurred elsewhere, frontline officers interviewed discussed the nature of the work they perform. One officer stated:

> When people ask me what I do it's pretty hard to describe. It's a lot of preventative stuff. It's community policing ... handling things before they get to the sort of crisis stage.

Another officer on a specialized detail describes the work performed by him and his partner as follows:

> Our job, if you look at it, we more or less drive down the streets of the Downtown Eastside. Hastings, Main, down that way, and look to see if there's kids that don't fit in there.

Officers were also asked to what extent they saw their role on the street as law enforcement, peacekeeping, social work, and/or knowledge work. Their responses were then contrasted with those of police managers, who were also asked to discuss frontline officers in light of these frameworks. No particular role was prioritized; rather, both sets of officers tended to see frontline work as a contingent mix of each of these roles. As one frontline officer said, 'Our job has changed so drastically over the years that I think now you have to be a bit of everything.' The nature of contingent role-shifting is neatly illustrated within a story told by a police manager of an experience he had had while working on the frontline:

> In the context of one incident you will work many different roles ... I worked in the Downtown Eastside in the mid-nineties when it was really a bad place ... paramedics [called for an assist] for a woman ... she's on coke, she's very paranoid. So, she's in a hotel, and it's one of those hotels that scare the hell out of you because the stairwell is entirely open ... you look down, and you can look down like seven stories, and it's just railing there. And as EHS [Emergency Health Services] are trying to approach her, we were staying way back. You could see it in her face, and she's backing up the stairs. My trainee actually said, 'Well, why don't we go to your room and discuss this?' thinking that would be a place where she'd feel more comfortable in her environment, and maybe she'd be more cooperative. Unfortunately from my stance ... I was weighing the stairwell versus in [her] room, [where] you also have potential weapons. And so she scooted back to her room, we scooted up the stairs after her, [and] the paramedics went in the room with her. Very small typical SRO room. So she sits down on the bed and they're talking to her and I look down and there's a needle half-filled with blood. But it wasn't like a small diabetes type needle, it was like a really thick needle. She followed my eyes ... she grabbed the needle and said, 'This is mine.' I yelled at the paramedics, 'Get out of the room.' I closed the door part way and she's standing there. So we'd gone from helping to not being in a very tactful situation. So I took out my baton, reached in and smacked her with the baton. She dropped the needle. We rushed in and grabbed her, handcuffed her, sat her down on the bed, and then let the paramedics back in. And then we were very caring, trying to get her a place to go, get her to the hospital because she was sick. So in the context of one incident we had to wear all different hats and we had to flip. Part of the trick to becoming a police officer, a good one, is to know which hat to wear at the appropriate time.

One reading of this story is that officers enact contingent role-shifting as a negotiating strategy between the twin pulls of exclusion and inclusion. For example, in the story the officer states that he used force to gain the woman's compliance so that she no longer posed a threat to himself, herself, or the others in the room. This is a necessary precondition, he implies, to treating her as an individual who needs help (inclusion) rather than as a dangerous criminal (exclusion).

In the example cited above, the officers play out two seemingly incompatible roles, those of law enforcer and social worker. This would seem to be a highly unusual occurrence, and yet I heard several other stories concerning frontline workers who combine roles, including the following:

This is a lesson I learned from [name deleted]. [He's] on the street one day and he heard that a prostitute had been sexually assaulted and beaten. He also knew that she was heavily into using drugs at this point. [He] knew ... from other working girls that this girl had been seen around, and she'd been badly beaten up, but she didn't want to come forward because she had a warrant out for her for drugs. We're duty bound when someone has a warrant out ... our responsibility is to arrest them, to make sure the warrant's served. And what [he] did is he got the word out on the street that he wanted to talk to her, that he wasn't going to execute the warrant. He wanted to talk to her, to find out what happened. Within a day or two she met with [him] and [he] got the information, and the bad guy was identified and arrested. When she was in a better medical condition ... where she wouldn't be in a lot of pain from heroin withdrawal ... [he] met with her and executed the warrant ... it couldn't have been done any other way ... without showing proper respect to the person – to the victim – and taking the asshole[4] off the street.

In this story, we see a police officer who is again attempting to successfully negotiate two sets of demands. On one level, we can interpret his dilemma as the product of conflicting demands produced within the criminal justice system: the system mandates that he execute the victim's warrant, and yet his duty as an officer also compels him to investigate and arrest the perpetrator of a serious crime (an action that requires the victim's cooperation). Alternatively, we can understand this dilemma as again the product of the twin pulls of inclusion and exclusion. The system demands that the officer execute the warrant without regard for the victim's situation, an action that would have had an exclusionary effect because the victim would not have had the opportunity to be accorded the full rights of a citizen who has been victimized.

This second story was told to me by the individual's senior officer, who, rather than viewing the frontline officer's actions as a failure to carry out his duty with respect to the exercise of the warrant, offered the story as an example of 'good police work.' These actions constitute good police work because, although the officer involved did not adhere strictly to the legal rules, he successfully negotiated two conflicting system demands while obeying two of the internal rules of the organizational culture: he 'showed respect' to the victim and arrested a 'bad guy.' I note that when I told this story to frontline officers in Edinburgh they stated that they would be unwilling to use their discretion with respect to the exercise of warrants, even under the circumstances described. In contrast, VPD frontline officers were much more willing to admit using their discretion in cases where they felt that the 'spirit of the law' and 'the letter of the law' conflict. Cultural norms within the VPD organization – such as getting 'bad guys' off the street – support this flexibility because they adhere to the institution's moral code.

Thus far I have been emphasizing the importance placed on role-shifting by members of the VPD. However, discussions also centred on police officers within specific roles. In discussing frontline work, members of both groups – police managers and frontline officers – tended to prioritize both their law enforcement and social work roles. Frontline officers with specialized (i.e., non-patrol) roles also referenced their knowledge work. Surprisingly, given both the peacekeeping orientation of the new CET program and the traditional reliance on peacekeeping measures on skid row, the least emphasis was placed on this role by both groups.

The police as law enforcers on skid row spend an inordinate amount of time dealing with alcoholics, drug dealers, and addicts. This is undoubtedly the source of greatest frustration for many officers. As law enforcers, their duty requires them to act as the gatekeepers of a system that does little to address the problem of addiction. For some officers, the blame is placed squarely on a judicial system that is seen to be weak and ineffective at meting punishment:

> If you look at any addict on skid row that I would stop and check, and run his record, yeah, he's been dealt with. He'll have a record this frigging long. He'll have been arrested, and busted over and over and over again. You want to talk about hands-on policing? The courts just don't want to do anything about it.

In interviews it was clear that, for some officers, the ineffective response of the exclusionary-punitive system to the problem of addiction had resulted in an attitude shift whereby harm reduction and/or increased emphasis on treatment were seen as worthwhile goals. For others, such as the officer above, punitive-exclusionary measures – arrest and incarceration – were viewed as necessary parts of a coercively inclusive process that has as its end the inclusionary goal of rehabilitation.

Echoing Bittner's contention that at the core of the police role is the willingness to employ coercion, one police manager stated of his occupation, 'What it really boils down to in many ways is the gun. I mean do you want to carry the gun? Do you want to have all that responsibility?' For many skid rowers, the employment of force by the police is perceived not as a responsibility but as the ultimate manifestation of the institution's exclusionary powers. This is particularly seen as the case in light of recent allegations of abuse raised against police involving not simply physical violence but also 'starlight tours.'[5]

Rather than attempting to downplay this aspect of the job, a few officers raised the subject themselves as a result of frustrations over what they perceived to be misunderstandings about their use of force.[6] Force is viewed in light of two considerations: the need to carry out one's duty (arrest) and the need for self-protection and/or to reduce harm to others (see Rubenstein 1978). As one officer explained:

> We don't walk up to people and say, 'Hi, how's your day going? And you're under arrest. Would you mind coming with us?' People run, they fight, they do all sorts of things ... Our training hopefully enables us, plus the equipment they give us, enables us to resolve something in the quickest way possible, so we don't duke it out with the guy. I'll use my pepper spray. I'll hit a guy really hard sometimes to make him go down real quick, so I can get it over with. I'm not going to punch it out with a guy.

Police officers' views on their use of force offer limited support for Bittner's contention that force is employed by police 'in accordance with the dictates of an intuitive grasp of situational exigencies' – that is, the level of force employed is often dictated by their 'reading' of a situation (1970: 46). This use is not however entirely contingent; police also employ 'recipe rules' that dictate how they will respond to given situations (Rubenstein 1978). An example of such a rule is that governing police conduct when a dealer is arrested in the DTES: the dealer is taken down from behind, with some force employed – possibly his or her face pushed into a sidewalk or even a kick to the groin – to ensure minimal resistance. As one officer explains: 'If you ... are out there dealing drugs and you get taken down by a police officer, you get hurt on the way to the ground. Guess what? That's part of the game.' Police believe that these rules and the underlying justifications are known and accepted by older residents as part of the norms of row culture but that younger residents, relative newcomers to skid row, do not adhere to the rules. These newcomers, many of whom are crack addicts, 'lack respect' for the police and for the skid row community. As the police see it, 'respect' is necessary for their effective functioning on the row, including their ability to negotiate the demands they face when policing here.

In relation to the issue of police employing excessive force against residents, one officer acknowledged that 'there are guys that shouldn't be on the job ... I don't cover up that fact. There are some guys who are heavy-handed.' Since no officer admitted to being 'heavy-handed,' I cannot offer an account of motives for employing excessive force. Officers interviewed on the subject revealed a distinct distaste for having to use force, which is essentially viewed as a form of 'dirty work' (Harris 1978). This distaste is revealed in repeated references to wanting to get physical confrontations 'over with quick.'

Order maintenance is an important function of the peacekeeping mission of police on skid row generally (Bittner 1967). This point was emphasized by a police manager while discussing the work of patrol officers: 'Their primary responsibility on the street, when they're not assigned to calls, is dealing with disorder issues. The number one thing is to maintain the peace.' Yet frontline officers spent the least amount of time discussing peacekeeping aspects of the job. One possible explanation for this discrepancy – between what officers speak of and what they perform on the street – is that peacekeeping is so integral to skid row policing that it fails to elicit mention.

Where officers did reference their peacekeeping role was in relation to the perceived ineffectiveness of arresting people who they knew would be back out on the streets shortly: 'In the old days you'd whack somebody, arrest them and haul them off. That's not effective. The first couple of years on the job, I was arresting the same people over and over again and I thought "How effective is this?"' Similarly, 'You don't just go and arrest somebody ... there's a whole other side to it. So certainly part of our role is peacekeeping.' Bittner (1967) has described peacekeeping as a resort to authority by police in order to gain conformity of behaviour from 'troublesome' individuals. Another means of describing this strategy is as a form of coercive inclusion: police rely on the possibility of arrest (exclusion) in order to gain compliance with directions aimed at restoring order. To the extent that individuals are not simply hauled away, but rather directed to correct their 'troublesome' behaviour, they are being treated, albeit coercively, as members of society capable of functioning in society.

The exercise of discretion is central to the peacekeeping function.

Some row residents have exceedingly long arrest records for narcotics possession, theft, and minor trafficking offences. Re-arresting addicts for possession of a few rocks of cocaine becomes an exercise in futility that achieves little, other than generating paperwork. For this reason, police routinely exercise their discretion by 'warning' individuals and confiscating and destroying open containers of alcohol, drugs, and/or drug paraphernalia. However, even the simple exercise of smashing crack pipes can become a burden, given their number. So it is not unusual to see police officers walk by individuals they know are 'holding.' This too can have something of a deterrent effect. A couple of years prior to the recent study, when walking through the DTES with a colleague and a police escort, we had the opportunity of seeing addicts dropping rocks of cocaine on the ground at our approach. Ultimately, consumption is merely impeded, not prevented. Row denizens were observed, both here and in San Francisco, poking at sidewalk cracks with straightened paper clips to retrieve dropped rocks.

Social work is also seen by many frontline officers as an important role that they perform on skid row. As one individual explained, 'You've got to be a bit of a social worker, a bit of a counsellor. A lot of my job is counselling.' The necessity of utilizing a social work approach is seen to arise from the special conditions of row life: order maintenance in a socially chaotic space can often be most effectively achieved through providing assistance to an individual, such as finding shelter for a vulnerable person (for example, a senior or youth). For some officers, they may simply be touched by the circumstances of vulnerable individuals: 'We've got some guys will send a girl on the bus, send her home.' Such instances exemplify, on the individual level, the desire to advance modest forms of social inclusion: police know that a young girl on skid row will likely never leave, becoming instead a permanent victim of poverty, despair, abuse, addiction, and marginalization. Through sending her away – ironically, a form of exclusion – they attempt to prevent the more significant social exclusion that follows from living on the row.

Working on skid row can take an immense personal toll on individuals over time. Frontline officers carry with them an awareness of the fact that ultimately there is often very little that they can do as individuals to address the social problems of the community they patrol. The social worker response permits some police members a positive outlet through which they can deal with the realities of what they witness – the 'dirty work' aspects of their job – as this skid row officer makes clear:

I talk to junkies in laneways for a living. Crawl through the muck. And I always say to them, 'Have you ever thought maybe God wants more for you than this? Maybe He could help you out. Maybe you could get clean?' And some of them say, 'Yeah, you're right.' A couple of times I've gone and pulled strings with friends in the recovery community and son of a gun if they didn't really make it.

While frontline officers interviewed appeared willing to acknowledge that they perform social work as a routine part of their job, on the whole it remains a devalued role within the organization. This is because the organizational culture of the VPD follows the predominant policing ethic, prizing a traditional masculinist approach (Harris 1978). As one officer interviewed stated, 'If you told a sort of normal police officer or a correctional officer that the best part of our job that we do is put kids in touch with social workers and stuff, they'd laugh.' In discussing community policing, another officer complained that 'some of our guys have that sort of male, police attitude, where "You're not going to tell us how to do things. We're going to tell you."' The privileging of masculinist conceptions of policing within the organization is also made clear in the following story told by a police manager:

I can't remember who it was ... but they talked to one of the neighbourhood community policing centres and the first thing [the residents] said is, 'So and so and so and so are the best community based police officers we have.' And the sergeant, who I think heard this, said, 'Well I don't want to tell them that.' In other words there's a perception of a community-based policing officer as being this soft little thing, versus what it really meant was being a good deep cop. So there's still an element of that. The same thing with social work: it's 'Oh, I don't do social work,' but yet they'll do all those little things.

To the extent that social work consists of coercively inclusive and/or even inclusionary practices aimed at assisting even the most marginal of marginalized individuals, this continued privileging of the masculinist conception of policing, with its roots in 'law and order' ideology and its emphasis on the police as 'crime fighters,' is problematic for the positive treatment of the skid rower who, as we see in San Francisco, is often the target of the crime fighter's activities.

In contrast to discussions of the social work aspects of policing, frontline officers made few direct comments about performing knowledge work and did not portray themselves as knowledge workers unless it was in relation to networking within an inter-institutional context. For example I asked a frontline officer:

Q: How much of your time is just spent with information gathering?
A: Not a lot of mine. We have areas within the department, like our crime analysis guys. My knowledge is the knowledge of being in the area so long, and working with the organizations.

This response reveals the split that frontline officers in each of the jurisdictions studied perceive between information and knowledge. As this officer's answer indicates, information is viewed as 'data' to be input into organizational formats and used for institutional or extra-institutional purposes, whereas knowledge is seen as accumulated wisdom to be used in guiding action on the street. Although most readily accepted that they performed the latter task, they seldom saw themselves as performing the former. And yet police officers, whether patrol or community based, process a substantial amount of paperwork, providing knowledge that is consumed by the police organization and other institutions. Further, frontline officers and their immediate supervisors are often tasked by the organization with gathering knowledge that will inform internal and external security-related programs and policies. For example, aside from generating routine apprehension statistics, youth squad officers were also at one time expected to fill out 'data capture sheets' in order to gather statistics on youth picked up over a two-month period. These statistics were produced in order to support police demands for City Hall funding of a 'Youth at Risk Database'[7] that would permit the police and partner agencies to pool information on apprehended youth.

Manning (2003: 179) observes that 'traditionally, the patrol officer is expected to act as a buffer, translator, information channel and receptacle of information and fact, all the while scanning the environment for information that should be either processed at that time or processed and passed on subsequently to investigators, internal affairs, juvenile officers or vice officers.' This is exemplified in the DTES by the fact that patrol officers routinely call youth squad members upon locating young people in the area who might be 'at risk.' Youth squad members advised that this process of inter-department knowledge sharing permits them the opportunity to 'identify new faces' in order to build up knowledge of 'who's in our area and where they're coming from.' This knowledge is then brokered to other agencies through statistics, reports, and case conferences.

Of the various officers interviewed, those performing non-patrol functions such as community-based policing or specialized details were the most likely to speak of their job in terms of knowledge work because of their involvement with inter-agency partnerships and knowledge sharing. Through their work, we see the response of inter-institutional demands for the production of knowledge. For example, youth squad officers advised that should a juvenile be picked up by squad members, he or she will become not only a record in a police database, but moreover a social service casework file, and possibly have corresponding entries in other agencies' files (school files, health service provider files, probation files). Every subsequent interaction between police and a given youth results in information being 'memoed' to a social work case file. Each strand of information gathered thus accumulates into a body of knowledge used by the police and other agencies to assist in the disciplinary function of the social worker, whose task is to assist a delinquent youth into becoming a productive member of society. The participation of the police in this process facilitates the social work role by lending a potentially coercive element to a coercively inclusive process.

From interviews with frontline officers, their views of the skid row residents whom they police emerged both directly and indirectly. These views largely ranged from the inclusionary to the coercively inclusive, such as discussing area residents in compassionate terms and expressing the view that they required help from both the police and other agencies. Each of the frontline officers interviewed expressed a desire to help skid row residents, who they felt were often the objects of inadequate or unfair government policies. Even addicts, who are usually seen as the lowest of skid row denizens, were discussed in sympathetic terms. We can see such attitudes present in the following comments offered by a frontline officer within the context of a discussion of service provisions for addicts in the DTES: 'I don't think I've ever heard the word cure once from anybody ... [Health and service providers are] not concerned with curing. They want to show them how to live with the disease. I think that's really irresponsible. I think these people [addicts] deserve better and they're not getting it.' Police managers interviewed similarly expressed sympathetic views towards row residents. These views were typically offered within discussions of how police could help the neighbourhood as a whole.

Policing the DTES: The Street Perspective

Here, as in the other two sites studied, residents and service providers who spoke about policing in the DTES tended to speak of the police primarily in terms of their role as law enforcers. When referencing this role, residents frequently used highly negative terms with which to portray police officers or offered stories of abusive, discriminatory, and/or arbitrary police conduct. Stories were told of 'shake downs' – illegal searches – of skid row residents. One resident stated, 'I see cops roughing people up. Searching them for no reason.' When interviewing this individual, I noted that he was watching a police car turn down an alleyway. He suddenly halted mid-interview, becoming hyper-alert. As the police cruiser stopped mid-alley, he explained that it was likely that the police were talking to crack addicts; thus he was watching in case the police 'move on them.' I asked him what he would do if he thought that was the case and he replied that he would go into the alley to be a witness. This response reflects the growing politicization of skid row policing in Vancouver, where row residents are increasingly encouraged by some community groups to watch the police and to report any real or suspected police misconduct to a local group that documents police behaviour – a form of community-based counter-surveillance and knowledge-gathering for the purpose of reversing what is perceived by some within the community to be exclusionary policing practices. In this instance, the police car my interviewee was watching simply drove on, and the interview was resumed without further incident.

When asked, some residents who were critical of police were willing to acknowledge that they had also had positive encounters with some officers, even when the latter were operating as law enforcers. The following story was told by a young homeless person:

There is one good cop. When I was inside Woodwards[8] and the SWAT team came in; there was 180 cops to 67 of us. This one cop I knew because I was drinking so much ... I used to drink so much bottles of sherry that I'd get chucked in the drunk tank ... he'd be the one, if he was working, he'd be the one who'd pick me up and he'd be the only officer that could ever calm me down ... This cop came down to me at Woodwards ... I looked up over my left-side shoulder and what do I see but it's an officer and I'm like, 'Okay, here we go.' I ignore him. And he still keeps calling my name, and then he comes down and he taps my left-hand shoulder and ... he looked at me and he said, 'You know something? If you go with me now, I'll make sure that you don't get beaten up by the SWAT team. I'll make sure.' And I go, 'How do I know that? How do I know?' He says, 'Cause I'll walk you there.' I said, 'All the way right through? All the way to the paddywagon? Lock me up with the cuffs?' And he said, 'Yup.' I said, 'Okay, take me. Let's go. I'm ready to go.' And I went. And he made sure. Not one cop touched me. Another cop tried to take me, and he said, 'No, no, no, this one's mine.' There's one good cop out there, and I still thank him.

Service providers and other community groups held mixed views on the police, particularly as law enforcers. Some community groups are very critical of the police, believing that not only does the organization not represent their constituencies, but that it is a significant part of the exclusionary process that keeps their members marginalized. This view was largely expressed through comments that the VPD is brutal, corrupt, and/or inefficient. One community activist, who feels that the state and its agents marginalize his constituency, granted that the police have a legitimate function to serve but that they 'have been abusing their authority in the DTES.' In support of this contention, this individual pointed to the findings of a local affidavit campaign alleging police misconduct, undertaken by a local activist organization. However, other groups held opposing views, feeling that law enforcement was weak within the community and that the police should have enhanced powers for dealing with the neighbourhood's drug markets, which they saw as the primary exclusionary factor preventing their members from enjoying neighbourhood life.

Some residents offered stories or comments that portrayed the police functioning as peacekeepers. One area resident stated that 'sometimes the cops have to come here and straighten out our own people because they drank too much.' For this interviewee, the peacekeeper role is clearly necessary to public order maintenance. Only one service provider referred to police as peacekeepers; she felt that, prior to CET, police had been gradually moving away from arresting addicts for possession in favour of confiscating and destroying drugs and drug paraphernalia, which was seen as a positive development toward a greater inclusion of marginalized addicts.

Some community groups view the police as social workers who utilize law enforcement and/or peacekeeping strategies to achieve social work outcomes. For example, in a letter to a local newspaper on the subject of children at risk, a service provider references the case of a teenage prostitute with serious addiction and health problems:

Agencies, police and community members all worried she would be dead soon. She would not bond with anyone, and wouldn't accept help. Police tried to arrest her for any offence just to get her off the street and off the 'pipe' long enough for someone to help her. (Turvey 2000: A13)

This letter's author is describing a classic form of police social work: arresting people 'for their own good' (Blumberg, Shipley, Jr, and Shandler 1973; McSheehy 1979). Other service providers noted that police members assist them in their own social work by 'hassling' kids in the street. That is, they serve as a coercive element in aid of rehabilitative efforts. For example, one interviewee stated that 'the kiddy cops will just see one of the kids on the street and say, "Hey, aren't you supposed to be home?" Or, they'll tell them, "You better get home, because if I see you again ..."' As with some of the other examples cited, the process of 'hassling' kids to get home serves dual purposes. Pushing the kids out of the street and into their foster homes is a peacekeeping measure in that it reduces opportunities for kids to be both victims and perpetrators of crime in the streets, while simultaneously serving the social work goals of other agencies.

None of the residents interviewed spoke of the police as social workers. This is interesting given that I witnessed multiple examples of police operating within this role on the street. Further, I observed several instances of residents actively seeking out the attention of officers they know, approaching them, chatting with them, asking for cigarettes or the time, or simply reciting a litany of complaints or woes. It is clear that, for some residents, police officers they know serve as street-based resources, providing cigarettes, advice, and so on. It could be suggested that actions of police who stop and chat and/or provide assistance to residents is largely as a result of the observer's presence. However, such an explanation does not satisfactorily account for residents' behaviour in seeking out the police in the first place.

As is the case in other cities, resident experience with police as knowledge workers in the DTES is often limited to warrant checking. However, research previously conducted in this neighbourhood on inter-institutional knowledge networks between police and private security shows that some residents do encounter police as knowledge workers within the context of being targeted or apprehended by private security agents (Huey, Ericson, and Haggerty 2005). One local resident reported that police officers stood by while security guards photographed him for their own security purposes (they advised that his picture and personal information were to be put up in local stores; it was subsequently learned that security agents also maintain a database of 'suspect' individuals) (ibid.). This knowledge is used entirely for exclusionary purposes: security guards maintain a database of knowledge on 'suspect individuals,' who are subsequently targeted through overt surveillance practices intended to drive them from the neighbourhood (ibid.). To the extent that this information is used to resolve potential police problems through pushing 'problem' individuals out of the neighbourhood, or is used to assist in identifying potential suspects, police have a vested interest in its acquisition and use.

Service providers who work with the police on social issues affecting the DTES were more likely than residents to see the police as knowledge workers. One service provider discussed at length police participation in an inter-institutional network aimed at assisting youth at risk and described the benefits of pooling government and community resources. In other instances, the knowledge worker role was expressed in discussions of informal knowledge-sharing with service providers: '[The youth squad] is really good I find at passing information or even phoning me and saying, "Hey, we just found one of your kids downtown on the East Side."' Service providers who provide security, either as their core function or to support their main work, referred to expertise, knowledge, and/or training that they had received from police. Such assistance ranges from criminal records checks on new volunteers, to advice on securing property, to offering training services to local crime prevention groups that operate independently of the CPC structure.

Some residents and service providers also discussed their perceptions as to how they believe police see area residents. Their views were again mixed. Both residents and service providers singled out individual officers as being 'good cops.' A 'good cop' on the street is one who treats people with respect, regardless of their condition and who understands the norms of the row community. One service provider, for example, singled out an officer as a 'good cop' on the grounds that 'he knows the norms and values of the people' and is therefore seen as representing an inclusionary form of policing. This individual was contrasted with other cops – 'outsiders' – who see a resident as a 'junkie, not as someone with a health problem' – that is, as representing exclusionary policing. In short, for many community groups, the 'good cop' is one who exhibits support for inclusionary demands and responds through treating residents respectfully despite their marginalized status or the fact that they behave according to skid row norms, which sometimes conflict with the values of the larger mainstream society.

However, several residents and service providers expressed the view that the police discriminate against alcoholics and addicts. One service provider who is critical of the police commented on the mental fatigue and frustration produced by months and years of working in such a chaotic, dirty, and often hostile environment. She believed that the cumulative effect on the frontline officer's psyche was likely to produce individuals who begin to hate their work environment and the people who populate it. For her, the officer's perception of the 'job' on skid row could be described in the following terms: "'Fuck, I'm so tired of walking these dirty lanes. It's making me hate the people.'" The result, this individual suggested, was the production of officers more willing to accede to exclusionary demands.

Effecting Social Change

Police managers interviewed were keenly aware of the political nature of their work. I recall that while attempting to set up an interview with one senior officer, I had to explain to another the nature of my research. In response to being told that one of my interests was the politics of policing in the DTES, this individual snorted and abruptly told me, 'You get that everywhere.' He then proceeded to explain that politics is an integral part of the police manager's job, regardless of the community. However, as I discuss in the next chapter, the demands made upon police management with respect to the policing of the DTES are unique. Further, these demands are generated within a politically charged, highly fractious environment.

All senior officers interviewed expressed the belief that their organization could play a role in effecting positive social change within the DTES. Moreover, it was felt that such participation was critical not only to maintaining order within the community but also to improving social conditions on the row. Several examples of police programs and strategies were offered in support of this contention.

Police participation with the new supervised safe injection site provides an excellent example of the melding of different policing frameworks in the pursuit of improved social conditions on the row. Rank and file are expected to utilize a combination of these roles in order to assist in creating environmental conditions that will enhance the ability of the site to operate successfully. However, as with CET, the primary emphasis is on frontline officers operating as 'peacekeepers.'

The model police are intending to use represents a form of coercively inclusive policing that is similarly found in Amsterdam, where police are required to act as law enforcers to create a 'bubble zone' around sanctioned injection sites. The bubble zone is intended to insulate the site from open drug use and trafficking. Within this space, addicts who want to use are thus 'encouraged,' under the threat of arrest, to use the safe injection site to fix. However, as a police manager in Vancouver acknowledged, it's unlikely that VPD members will employ as strict a law enforcement approach as occurs elsewhere: 'We'll never have a bubble zone in Vancouver. We'll probably just [be] directing [addicts] to the centre.'

Although strict law enforcement might be a preferred method according to the model currently in place in Amsterdam, such an approach would be both impracticable – because the VPD does not have the resources necessary to carry out a total enforcement policy – and lacking in wider political support. In response to the harsher neo-liberal agenda being pursued by their provincial government, Vancouverites have expressed a desire for a more welfare-oriented approach to the treatment of social issues. Despite their vaunted institutional independence, VPD management recognizes that a City Hall pursuing welfarist aims is not likely to support zero-tolerance policing, and certainly not on a sustained basis. Thus, we have a resort to peacekeeping, with limited law enforcement targeting, in aid of social work goals. Police will also provide limited social work services, through such activities as offering addicts assistance in accessing the site. Knowledge work also arises through recasting frontline officers as street-based 'mini-experts' on addiction and addiction services. At the management level, knowledge work occurs through routine knowledge sharing with safe injection site workers, health agencies, and other service groups.

Inter-institutional networking increasingly frames police-driven community policing initiatives centred on effecting positive social change in the DTES. Previously I cited the examples of the NIST program and the Carnegie Centre remodelling project, a new initiative undertaken by the VPD that underscores the organization's view of the neighbourhood as a site for positive change and of its addicted population as part of the larger community that the police serve. After extensive consultations with community groups that serve addicts, local health service providers and emergency services personnel, and a public forum to discuss the new policy, the VPD proposed to its Police Board that the department implement a trial policy that would remove the requirement of police attendance at drug overdose calls. The policy was approved. In an interview conducted before the matter went to the Police Board, a senior manager advised that the impetus behind advocating for this change was research conducted in Australia, where it was found that overdose deaths could be prevented if addicts who witnessed an overdose were not fearful about attending police issuing charges. As this officer explained, 'We don't go into an overdose call and charge the survivor ... We don't charge because you've got a dirty needle. We don't charge because you've got heroin in your body ... But the perception here is that if you call for an ambulance, that the cops will show up, and they'll charge you.' In order to prevent unnecessary deaths, the organization took the position that police would only attend in situations involving a fatality or in circumstances where ambulance crews felt they needed police support. For the senior officer who spoke of this harm reduction initiative, it represents a form of inclusionary policing – treating addicts as individuals who need medical help rather than punishment – that also creates resource efficiencies: 'What value do we add when we go [to an overdose]? ... I don't see value being added by police attending an overdose.'

The organizational culture of the VPD stresses the importance of adaptability. At the management level, adaptability is necessary in the face of constant demands for change and a political climate that alters every few years, variously demanding containment of the marginalized, then their dispersal. Contingent role-shifting, particularly within a community that is undergoing change and within an organization that is itself in a state of flux, can lead to role strain for members. We see this potential with respect to drug use in the DTES and the demands that police enact conflicting roles, often simultaneously. This strain is evident in the words of a police manager who drew attention to the apparent contradictions that exist for officers: 'We are for harm reduction. However, we are also against drugs. So we have issues both ways.'

When asked at what level within the organization social change occurs, VPD managers did not succumb to conventional community policing rhetoric by offering a bottom-up vision of policing. Instead, it was acknowledged that many of the police initiatives aimed at effecting social change that have been undertaken were driven by frontline supervisors rather than by beat officers (constables). As one police manager explained, 'sergeants have a tremendous opportunity working with other agencies. They speak for their people, they're working for opportunities, for competitive advantages, they're looking to trade off things. Sergeants have the latitude, they've got the time and they've got the responsibility.

It's delegated to them.' This officer felt that, in terms of driving effective change within and through the organization, it was necessary to encourage frontline supervisors to be outspoken leaders because 'they're right there in the organization to tell us if something's working or not.'

In contrast, frontline officers are not similarly empowered to effect change. As one manager stated, 'a lot of [frontline officers] don't feel that they have the ability to drive tremendous change in terms of programs, process or whatever. So, an awful lot of legwork's done one at a time, person by person.' Further, workload was cited as a factor prohibiting officers from becoming proactive problem solvers. This was felt to be particularly the case for patrol officers: 'We are incident-driven at this point – this is our frontline people – they're going from call to call to call ... people's computer screens are full from the time they get in to the time they leave.'

In light of Bittner's claim that skid row police are not reflexive, I asked a frontline officer whether officers in the street understood the political nature of their work on skid row. His initial response was:

> Not so much the guys on the job, I don't think ... The street-level police, I don't think they see themselves like that. I would say higher up, the management certainly do, the inspectors. But not so much the guys on the job. Most of them just go out and they do their thing and don't worry.

It was also explained that 'the majority of guys that go out on the road, they got their thing in mind that they're going to do. They're going to go after drug arrests ... I don't think they see themselves that way [as political actors].' However, this claim was later contradicted by another set of observations from this same officer: 'The DTES is a hard area to work in. Not a lot of the guys choose to be down here for that long. The politics are fierce ... there's really very little thanks.' In his view, '[beat officers] get shit upon by everybody.' He further stated that, 'To some extent guys are even pulling back from their doing their jobs, thinking why are they going to get into a scuffle arresting a guy when there's somebody across the street videotaping with a camera.' These statements suggest that street-level officers are very aware of the fact that their practices are political.

Awareness of the politics of policing by frontline officers was also manifest in frontline officers' responses to requests for interviews. Previously, when I undertook research for a project on private security (Huey et al. 2005), I contacted police officers for interviews. Interviews were granted at what appeared to be the discretion of the individual officer; to my knowledge, none of the officers sought department approval. For this project, I again contacted officers directly. Most contacted declined the request or simply failed to respond. One of those who did not respond was a frontline officer who had previously granted an interview but who had at that time expressed concerns over how his words might be misused by community activists. Frontline officers who declined a direct request referred me to the department, stating that they would only accommodate requests approved by their managers. One officer indicated that his desire for management approval stemmed from concerns over negative reactions from community activists to the implementation of CET.

Frontline officers' views concerning the organizational levels at which social change could be effected tended to accord with those of managers. Officers interviewed wanted to see row conditions improve for area residents, believed that they had a part to play in effecting such change, but their comments and stories indicated that they felt, for the most part, an inability to generate change. This was particularly the case for patrol officers, who can usually, at best, only provide individual assistance to area residents. Community officers and those on special details felt slightly more empowered as a consequence of their participation in inter-agency knowledge work, which provides enhanced opportunities for networking, developing new ideas, and strategizing about effecting change.

Overall, what I took away from interviews with frontline officers was a keen sense of their frustration with the current situation on the row. Each of the officers interviewed pointed to the lack of adequate addiction treatment options as both a frustration and a concern. As one officer stated: 'You know what's the real embarrassing shame and tragedy down here? It's that there's no treatment available.' The number of existing treatment beds was seen as inadequate; treatment upon demand was deemed preferential because officers recognize that the window of opportunity for facilitating treatment is a small one. This particular frustration is hardly unique to Vancouver's skid row police; as Plotkin and Narr (1997) note, inadequate resources for marginalized groups is an all too common condition generally in North America and one that is seen to make the process of providing assistance much more difficult for frontline officers.

Conclusion

In this chapter, I explored the policing of Vancouver's skid row district through an examination of the management style and frontline practices of members of the Vancouver Police Department. What was revealed through this analysis is an institution that shapes itself according to the demands of its political environment. This environment is, on various levels, an imperfect mixture of welfarism and American-style neo-liberalism, inclusion and exclusion. This meld is reflected in the development of a new order maintenance policing program which involves saturating the Downtown Eastside with police in order to create a stable environment for the purpose of facilitating a wider inclusionary project – the Four Pillars plan – aimed at ameliorating the conditions of Vancouver's skid row.

This order maintenance policing program is intended to support inclusionary goals. It has been embraced by many formerly excluded individuals and groups within the larger community because it fosters their inclusion, particularly through permitting them to enjoy access to public spaces. However, it has also had some exclusionary effects on the ground. Addicts and service providers cite the increased police presence as having deleterious effects on the community of addicts, both in terms of potential health consequences and of the cohesiveness of that group.

Although CET casts the police role primarily as that of a peacekeeper within an often unstable and violent environment, the organization itself utilizes each of the frameworks discussed – law enforcement, peacekeeping, social and knowledge work – as tools for creating and supporting their demand-negotiating strategies. We see, for example, a move toward the use of inter-institutional knowledge networks for social work purposes: attempts at using a combination of law enforcement strategies and data sharing as means of removing the vulnerable from the skids. These four frameworks are also articulated within the strategies that frontline officers use to perform their duties on the street. These strategies similarly reveal a mix of inclusionary and exclusionary means and ends.

8 Policing as the Art of Negotiating Demands

Q [attempting to summarize the views of two SFPD officers on 'negotiating demands' on skid row]: So you're thinking on your feet, with no rule book; what's the best way to make the most people happy within the boundaries of the law?

SFPD Officer #1: Exactly what you said. How do I make the most people happy within the boundaries of the law? That's pretty much what you spend your day doing. There are easy ones. You robbed a bank, that's an easy one: you rob a bank, you go to jail. But like the other day, the homeless lady peed in the parking lot. And then a guy got mad and came out after her screaming and yelling. Well OK, 'don't pee in his lot, don't attack her.'

Officer #2: It's like a catch-22. She said she had a bad bladder. Okay, well, 'you know you have a bad bladder so what were you drinking?' 'Well, I had three beers and a water and half a vodka.'

Officer #1: 'There's a public toilet down the street.' 'Oh well, people shoot heroin there.' But like you said, you're trying to make the most people happy within the boundaries of the law.

The conceptualization of police as 'demand negotiators' arose from my understanding of the political dimensions of policing, particularly within contested sites where police are called upon to respond to often contradictory sets of inclusionary-exclusionary demands from groups that define themselves as 'the community.' As a contested site, skid row became the primary focus for this study because it is here that we can often see this polarization most clearly with resident and business groups frequently demanding exclusion, skid row denizens and community groups issuing inclusionary counter-demands, and a range of city officials supporting public policies that fall along the continuum of exclusion–inclusion. Within this politicized environment, the role of the police is often to negotiate contradictory sets of demands as a means of keeping order. This task must be accomplished first in accordance with the law and the institution's mandate. It is also to be accomplished within a particular institutional environment that can be variously constraining or supportive of the positions that the police adopt in response to demands made. Just as the demands themselves are produced within a particular moral-economic context, so too are the institutions that are tasked with resolving these demands. Through examining some of the internal and external factors that support and/or constrain each organization's responses, as well as the ways in which they negotiate with other public and private institutions for support for their work, we can see aspects of both the larger political culture as well as the political character of each force.

The focus of the present chapter is to contextualize the style of response of each force to demands made of them in respect of their work on skid row through a closer examination of their institutional environments. This examination begins with a comparative assessment of the resources that each agency can bring to bear in its work on skid row in the form of police budgets and force strength. Assessment of these two factors reveals some of the political strategies that each agency employs in its quest to fulfill its organizational goals on the row. The issue of institutional supports and constraints on skid row policing is then explored through an analysis of two major social factors that impact not only the quality of life on the row but also the extent to which police are utilized to govern here: homelessness and addiction. This analysis reveals how each organization works within and through its unique political environment, employing those strategies that are likely to meet with local approval and bring success to the organization. The discussion then turns to a fuller exploration of the police as 'demand negotiators,' that is, as political actors responding to inclusionary-exclusionary demands within a political environment. The chapter ends with some final conclusions drawn on the data presented.

Institutional Resources: Budgets and Force Strength

In this section I discuss the institutional resources available to each force through an examination of two key indicators: police budget and force strength (see tables 8.1 and 8.2).

Table 8.1 Amount Spent on Policing Services per Resident
(2003–4) (in U.S. dollars)

Edinburgh	San Francisco	Vancouver
$204	$380	$174

Sources: Lothian and Borders Police press office 2004; City
of San Francisco 2003; City of Vancouver 2003.

Table 8.2 Ratio of Sworn Police Officers per 1000 Population

Edinburgh	San Francisco	Vancouver
2.7	2.6	1.8

Sources: Lothian and Borders 2003b; Office of the Controller
(San Francisco) 2002; Graham 2003.

As a significant portion of the police budget is allocated for staffing, it is impossible to discuss one set of figures without reference to the other; thus, they need to be read together for a clearer interpretation. On the surface, these numbers suggest that policing is a significant priority in San Francisco; we can see from the amount spent per resident each year that this city's residents pay a higher percentage of their tax dollars towards policing services than do Vancouver residents. The SFPD's staffing levels are also notably higher than those in Vancouver, although both forces claim to be significantly understaffed. With respect to Edinburgh, the amount spent on policing services is also higher than that of Vancouver, as is the staffing level, similarly indicating that policing is a higher-priority service item in Edinburgh and conversely a lower spending priority in Vancouver, a city of comparable size.

However, despite variations between funding and sworn staffing levels among the three forces, representatives of each organization have claimed, both in public forums as well as in private interviews for this research, that they are underfunded and understaffed for the tasks they are expected to undertake. Further, public criticism of police operations were held to be linked to critical staffing shortages and general budget constraints that have limited the ability of organizations to expand their staff rosters and to add new technologies and other resources. Each of the organizations studied has utilized different means of circumventing these apparent limitations, with varying degrees of success.

In Edinburgh, because of the nature of its cost-sharing arrangements, increases to the Lothian and Borders (L&B) force budget must be agreed upon by each of the contributing levels of government. As one police source indicated of attempts at securing budget increases, 'it's a fight every year.' This fight is because, as several police sources indicated in interviews, successive Councils have been unwilling to fund major increases to police budgets. However, an exception to this process lies in the fact that local Council can either directly fund officers for specialized details within the city or work with the force to seek such funding from the Scottish Executive. Under one such initiative, the L&B were able to secure funding for an additional thirty-six officers to work on estate housing to address local issues. Thus, by actively working with city officials at all levels – from local inspectors building relationships with individual Council members in their sectors to senior officials actively liaising with members of the Council's Police Committee – L&B management have been able to secure small resource increases at a time when most other policing jurisdictions are experiencing shrinking or frozen budgets. As a senior officer explained, 'My impression is that funding can be there at Council level and Scottish Executive, but it's really getting somebody who is really good at finding out what's out there and what we can turn to. And that's where this partnership working is definitely already making a difference.'

The willingness of local and national powers to supply extra funding to the police does not prevent L&B staff from utilizing 'lack of resources' as an excellent justification for refusing to engage in both policing and non-policing activities. As I have noted previously in relation to the second set of activities, the partnership working model is predicated, in part, on the belief that there is a system capacity limit to the number of tasks that police can take on, limits that are seen as existing outside the scope of traditional law enforcement. In relation to traditional policing activities, these same system capacity limits are frequently invoked. With respect to demands that police engage in aggressive policing of the homeless, street drinkers, and the like, a frontline supervisor advised that police tell complainants that 'we can't be the Cowgate police force or the Hunter Square police force. We just don't have the resources to do that.' However, discussions with senior officials reveal a much more likely reason why police on Edinburgh's skids refuse to engage in zero-tolerance policing: they believe that such methods do not address the root of the social problems underlying homelessness and addiction but rather perpetuate these problems as policing issues without hope or end.

In contrast to the situation in Edinburgh, San Francisco's policing services are funded solely by the city (with the exception of special services or programs funded at the state and/or the federal level, such as airport policing duties, federal narcotics programs, and state drug abuse programs). Further, whereas Edinburgh has seen small funding increases, in 2003 SFPD members were complaining of a lack of basic resources despite annual budget overruns. As may be recalled from chapter 5, police in San Francisco lack even the most basic of modern computer tools and/or communications systems. As a senior officer explained when asked if he had sufficient resources to carry out his department's 'community policing' mission in the Tenderloin, 'I'd like to say that we have enough resources; we do not.'

Faced with a massive $47 million budget deficit in 2003–4, San Francisco's City Council requested that the SFPD cut its budget by 5.5 per cent (see Hampton 2004). This was a remarkable request given the public perception that the SFPD and the San Francisco Fire Department hold 'sacred cow' status within the city's portfolio of services, a representation that was lent some weight when the SFPD subsequently overran its budget targets in 2003–4 despite the requested cut (ibid.). What is particularly interesting about this development is that the department's failure – while excoriated in the press by the head of the Council's budget committee, a notable critic of the police department – was otherwise largely unremarked upon by civic leaders, local businesses, and other groups that typically decry deficit budgets, potential fee increases, and tax hikes (ibid.). Further, with the exception of a couple of small social service groups whose funding had been cut, few complaints were publicly registered concerning the continued privileging of the police budget at the expense of organizations that support child welfare, health, homelessness, and other critical services.

Whereas senior police officials in Edinburgh have set out to cultivate extensive cooperative relations with City Council and its departments, this does not appear to be a tactic similarly utilized in San Francisco. This is not to suggest that the police and city officials do not work together; they do, but some relationships are clearly held at arm's length. One explanation underlying the difference between the L&B and SFPD approaches is that the latter force is part of a political system that is marked by opposing ideologies, a conservative–liberal split that is prevalent not only at City Council but throughout the city itself. As I discussed extensively in chapter 5, the predominant ideology of the SFPD is conservative, reactionary, and law-enforcement-oriented, and this is reflected in their practices. The city's liberal contingent, some of whom are represented at the Council level and throughout the current civic administration, deplore the emphasis placed on law enforcement as the solution to economic and social ills. As one civic leader stated of the SFPD's use of the broken windows model, 'It's not about solving crime because it's never about getting to the actual root causes of why people are out there. There aren't many people within the San Francisco police department, even in the upper ranks, that get this ... I'm an advocate for taking money out of the police department and putting it in the health department.' To the extent that police managers attempt to squeeze funds and other resources out of city officials who hold such views, the result is, according to one police manager, a set of 'fractured special interests' within the current administration. However, as long as the mainstream of San Francisco society continues to support the present style of policing, the SFPD's budget and staffing levels will continue to hold a privileged status and be treated accordingly by city officials.

In comparing the Vancouver Police Department (VPD) with that of San Francisco, we see that the former has been asked to police a city with approximately 200,000 fewer residents but at less than half the cost of services. The comparatively lower budget and staffing levels of the VPD can be attributed to years of repeated denials of increased police funds by the previous civic administration (requests that preceded years of annual police budget overruns). However, a small shift occurred following the election of the current administration, which gave the VPD a 6 per cent increase in its budget to increase staffing levels. I asked a senior officer if this shift was the result of Vancouver police managers working more effectively with city officials to facilitate funding, as occurs in Edinburgh. His view was that, despite the new administration, the VPD remained unable to shake money loose from the city's coffers: 'It's kind of funny, we've gone from the bean counters of the NPA[1] to the left-wing radicals. We can't win.' In short, the increased budget should not be interpreted as indicating either a new attitude towards the prioritizing of policing services by City Hall or as unqualified support for the current police administration.

As will be recalled, the cornerstone of the VPD's plan to 'restore order' to the Downtown Eastside (DTES) – the City-wide Enforcement Team (CET) project – is funded solely by the VPD out of its overtime budget, despite repeated requests for city funding. City Hall's reluctance to fund this project can be explained as a consequence of political concerns over a program that may have negative impacts on the DTES and outlying neighbourhoods. This reluctance can also be partially explained as a result of the VPD's decision to implement CET unilaterally –

a political decision with significant consequences for the city as a whole – with only limited prior discussion of the plan with city officials and other agencies (Bula and Fong 2003).[2] Although operational decisions fall within the discretionary authority of the police chief, this move, in conjunction with repeated requests for additional funding, angered some Council members and threatened to create a split among the Council's governing faction. In order to avoid such a split, as well as to avoid creating an open conflict between Council and the police department, the mayor stepped in to persuade police officials to withdraw a second funding request pending the results of a commissioned study to assess the impacts of CET (Bula 2003b; Garr 2003).[3]

The decision to implement the resource-intensive CET program occurred during a period in which the VPD is facing a significant personnel shortage. As one senior officer explained, 'our patrol divisions have carried about 20 per cent vacancy for some time.' Resource problems are compounded as a consequence of changes to the VPD's pension program, which have resulted in 150 experienced officers leaving the force on early retirement. When the VPD announced staffing decreases throughout the city, residents were angered over the potential loss of school liaison positions (McLellan 2003), although in none of the articles located on the subject did residents interviewed publicly decry the continuation of the CET program despite the impact elsewhere in the organization.

A cynical observer might interpret VPD pronouncements on significant staffing cuts to programs such as school liaison, the drug squad, and others as an attempt at forcing City Hall into supporting the CET program, thereby freeing up funds and resources for popular community programs. Such a cynic would have some support for this view: there is a history of Vancouver police playing budget politics in this fashion. This fact was referenced in an interview with a senior officer in relation to one of the current chief's predecessors: 'The last police chief that used to do ... he would just simply go [to City Council] and play poker. Well, I've got school liaison, I've got this and that; I need these extra 150 officers and they need to go here or they have to go there; otherwise I have to start cutting these services. You know generally you get those increases.' In relation to the current VPD administration, if it was their intention to 'play poker' using the school liaison positions as part of a bluff, they failed to achieve their goal; public outcry over the reduced number of liaison officers, coupled with a few publicized incidents of school violence, sparked police to find alternative means of filling those roles. Had they not done so, it is likely that public support for CET, which has been largely favourable given the public perception that order has been returned to the DTES, would have begun to erode.

The Institutional Environment: Working through Homelessness and Addiction

The police on skid row are part of a larger system of governance that includes both public and private organizations tasked with the surveillance, maintenance, and regulation of those who live there. As I stated in the first chapter, part of my purpose is to situate the public police as an institution within the context of a larger set of inter-institutional relations that constitute 'policing' on skid row. The work of these other agencies has a direct effect on the public policing of skid row: shrinking welfare cheques and decreasing low-income housing stocks push people into the streets to beg, deal, squat, steal, prostitute, or otherwise attempt to survive. The extent to which these survival activities are defined as requiring coercive state intervention to prevent them creates demands on the police as an institution. However, these same agencies can be utilized by police as a source of political support and resources. Thus, as we have seen throughout the present study, public police agencies work with other organizations to mobilize resources that bring order and discipline to the row.

Skid row can be defined as a physical and social space embodying a constellation of both significant and lesser social problems. Two of the most significant of these problems that affect both the quality of life on the row and the nature of policing are homelessness and addiction. Thus, these are my primary focuses in this section.

In order to contextualize the homelessness problem within each of the cities, it is important to look not only at rates of homelessness but also at the extent to which income aid, shelter, and other resources are available for those in need. As table 8.3 reveals, provision for assistance is substantially higher in Edinburgh, where the income assistance rate is exclusive of shelter, which is provided separately. In contrast, the rates provided for both San Francisco and Vancouver include shelter (San Francisco provides food stamps under a separate program).

Table 8.4 illustrates the general rates of homelessness within each city.[4] As these figures reveal, the rate of homelessness is remarkably low in Edinburgh, particularly in contrast to San Francisco, where homelessness averages between 1 and 2 per cent of the city's population. In Vancouver,

Table 8.3 Monthly Income Assistance Rates per Recipient (2003 rates) (in U.S. dollars)

Edinburgh	San Francisco	Vancouver
$356	$385	$374.50

Sources: Department for Work and Pensions (U.K.) (2004); City of San Francisco (2004); Ministry of Human Resources (BC) (2002).

Table 8.4 Ratio of Homeless per 1000 Population

Edinburgh	San Francisco (8024 estimate)	San Francisco (15,000 estimate)	Vancouver (1100 estimate)	Vancouver (1900 estimate)
.229	10.3	19.3	1.9	3.4

Sources: Rough Sleepers Initiative 2003; Office of the Controller (San Francisco) 2002; Graves 2004.

homelessness rates are lower than those of San Francisco, but lack of shelter continues to be a part of many people's daily reality. The variations among the figures cited above can be explained as a consequence of several factors, including differences in income assistance rates, rental market rates, the availability of low-income housing, employment rates, addiction treatment spaces, and mental health measures among others. Each of these factors must be understood as products of unique social-political-economic forces.

It may be recalled that Edinburgh has been fairly successful in tackling its homelessness problem through socially inclusive local and federal housing initiatives, as well as through citizen advice bureaus that assist individuals in need in effectively securing accommodations and other resources. This city's poor are also helped through income assistance provisions that appear generous[5] in comparison with those offered Vancouver residents by the province of British Columbia. It may also be recalled that, despite Canada's leftover reputation as something of a welfare state, the effect of provincial government policies in British Columbia, resting on American neo-liberal platforms, has been to steadily push people off the welfare roll while increasing poverty and hardship. The city of Vancouver has attempted to ameliorate the homelessness exacerbated by low provincial income aid rates and an expensive local rental market through slowly increasing its stock of low-income housing. San Francisco, in contrast, has insufficient low-income housing stock,

Table 8.5 Ratio of Shelter Beds per 100 Homeless Population

Edinburgh	San Francisco (8024 estimate)	San Francisco (15,000 estimate)	Vancouver (1100 estimate)	Vancouver (1900 estimate)
243	23.4	12.5	68	39

Sources: Rough Sleepers Initiative 2003; Office of the Controller (San Francisco) 2002; Graves 2004.

low rates of income assistance, and an unusually tight rental market, meaning that most of the city's poor are unable to find affordable accommodation. Unsurprisingly, San Francisco residents view homelessness as a significant social issue year after year.

Compounding the homelessness problem in both San Francisco and Vancouver is the fact that neither site has sufficient shelter beds to accommodate those in need. As table 8.5 reveals, in contrast to Edinburgh, which has approximately 2.4 beds available for every rough sleeper, individuals in San Francisco and Vancouver are significantly less likely to find a shelter bed. The rate of available beds for the homeless is particularly troubling with respect to San Francisco: at best, fewer than 24 per cent of those in need can find a bed; at worst, fewer than 13 per cent of the homeless population can be accommodated. With respect to Vancouver, the figures improve slightly: at best, 68 per cent of those in need can find a bed; at worst, the figure lowers to 39 per cent.

The issue of police officers assisting individuals in finding shelter never arose during interviews in Edinburgh. One might be tempted to assume that there are sufficient beds for the entire homeless population of the city and that therefore there are no individuals in need of shelter. Certainly, because of the accessibility of shelter beds in Edinburgh, rough sleepers are often publicly dismissed as being in the streets by their own choice rather than out of legitimate need (see Rose [1999] for a fuller discussion on rough sleeping as a 'lifestyle choice'). Thus, it is possible that officers do not routinely assist individuals here in securing accommodation for just this reason. If so, this is problematic because, as service providers report, there is a lack of integrated services available for the mentally ill and/or active addicts, who may be considered too unstable for basic forms of accommodation and shelter (see also Kennedy and Fitzpatrick 2001). In other words, when beds are available within the system, such individuals often need extensive co-services that are not always accessible. Further, many individuals deemed 'hard to house' by social workers have been barred from shelters because of active drug use and/or selling, or as a result of incidents of theft, harassment, or violence, whereas others require shelter but fear intimidation or harassment from other users. In short, the need for housing services remains critical.

There is another likely reason why Edinburgh's frontline police do not appear to spend much time in assisting the homeless in seeking shelter: the current policing system stresses partnership working as a means of shifting 'non-police' functions onto other agencies; thus, social work functions are to be performed by social workers. Further, it is significantly easier for the homeless to access social work services here: a social work advice centre sits in the middle of Grassmarket, as do several other facilities serving the area's poor.

In contrast, several officers interviewed in San Francisco spoke of police providing active assistance to the Tenderloin's homeless through attempts at locating shelter or other required resources. As one frontline supervisor stated, 'We've become more of a resource to these homeless people; it may be detox, taking them to a shelter when they become an annoyance with the business owners and even the people that live in this area.' The provision of assistance seems to occur as a result of a demand that 'something be done' about a 'troublesome' individual. As I noted in chapter 5, the informal policy of taking individuals to shelters is seen by Tenderloin police as marking a significant shift in the policing role from strict law enforcement to what one officer interviewed termed 'being a resource officer.' This sentiment was echoed by other officers who were more likely to view themselves as social workers because they were being asked to fill gaps in the provision of social services through which the city's homeless are falling. It was clear during several interviews that police members were uncomfortable with the new 'social service' role that they felt was thrust upon them. For this reason, it is hardly surprising that the SFPD has been so quick to embrace the broken windows model with its emphasis on police as law enforcers. However, reliance on this model, coupled with a perceived lack of willingness to work with other public and private agencies, has alienated social service agencies and local community groups, thus limiting the potential for police involvement in addressing some of the issues that they are called upon to face as frontline service providers. Interestingly, while SFPD members decried the difficulties they faced when attempting to provide assistance for area residents without adequate support from social service agencies, no officer interviewed recognized the role that their own agency's policies may play in limiting support for inter-institutional cooperation.

As is the case in San Francisco, police in Vancouver also provide assistance to those seeking temporary shelter. However, in line with developments in Edinburgh, greater emphasis has been placed at the institutional level on police participation in inter-agency initiatives that seek to improve the quality of longer-term housing available to area residents. For example, in order to tackle hotels and other businesses that have been defrauding income aid recipients in the DTES, the VPD established a collaborative enforcement project with provincial welfare, federal taxation, and other relevant government authorities to target 'problem businesses' that exploit skid rowers. However, as Edinburgh police similarly recognized with their partnership-working model, collaborative efforts are often fraught with difficulties. For the VPD, these difficulties often arise in trying to secure agreement and financial support for enforcement activities from other levels of government. As a senior officer explained, 'Some of the organizations, like Welfare, we've gone to and said, "We'd like to do a sting operation on [hotels] bilking welfare cheques." They said, "Who's going to pay the money for this enforcement project?"' What I find particularly interesting about such reticence on the part of provincial welfare authorities is that this is the same provincial department with a very apparent interest in reducing income assistance expenditures. It would seem that implementing policies that reduce the number of welfare recipients is acceptable practice but that paying for enforcement to reduce welfare scams that degrade the quality of conditions on the row is not. This situation is another example of the exclusionary treatment of row residents by a government embracing the punitive end of neoliberal ideology.

The police on skid row spend a great amount of their time dealing with the health, social, and criminal problems associated with addiction. Effective government spending on treatment, harm reduction, and integrated rehabilitative services that match addicts' needs not only can be seen as generally creating an inclusionary (or perhaps coercively inclusive) environment for those marginalized through addiction, but can also lead to the development of pro-social policing initiatives through effective inter-agency partnerships. For these reasons, I was interested in examining some of the facts surrounding each city's response to the problem of addiction.

Table 8.6 contains figures representing the number of residential treatment services (detox and/or short-term treatment beds) available in each of the cities studied. In looking at these figures, we see what appears to be an interesting shift. Edinburgh, which is comparatively

Table 8.6 Ratio of Residential Detox/Addiction Treatment Beds per 1000 Population

Edinburgh	San Francisco (all beds)	San Francisco (publicly funded beds)	Vancouver
.11	1.4	.64	.47

Sources: Scottish Executive 2004; Hampton 2003a; Vancouver Coastal Health Authority 2004.

generous in its treatment of those in need, has the lowest level of residential treatment beds available (forty-seven, all publicly funded).[6] This figure may be explained, in part, as a consequence of the fact that the city provides extensive outpatient services for addicts and alcoholics, most of whom are housed in Council housing. However, for homeless individuals the government's reliance on outpatient services presents difficulties as they must compete for beds in residential treatment facilities where waiting lists are, on average, of one to two weeks' duration.

In contrast, San Francisco has 1100 residential beds (500 of which are publicly funded). Although San Francisco has the highest rate of beds available for its population, these beds do not come close to fulfilling the demands for treatment (Office of the Controller 2002). City officials have acknowledged that 10,000 people annually are placed on waiting lists for substance abuse treatment in San Francisco, and an estimated 23,000 others do not seek treatment at all because of insufficient resources (Hoge 2001a). The problem of treatment delays is further compounded in cases involving individuals who are mentally ill and require addiction services, because there are fewer still programs that deal with dual-diagnosis clients (ibid.).

In Vancouver, where all of the 261 detox/treatment beds are publicly funded, waiting lists for detox services have been substantially decreased over the past few years. The Vancouver Health Authority advises that the average wait time is approximately two days, with a range of zero to five days (Skelton 2004). However, service providers and police both report problems due to ongoing delays in accessing treatment.

Aside from addiction treatment services, each city has other resources that assist the public police in the governance of the addicted skid row population. Edinburgh has recently adopted a more pragmatic approach towards the treatment of addiction, recognizing that harm reduction may assist social work goals more practicably than a simple punitive response. There is, for example, also a 'wet hostel' in Edinburgh's Grassmarket that caters exclusively to alcoholics who are continuing to use. Some discussions have also been held as to permitting alcoholics not only to live in Council-funded beds when under the influence but also to allow residents to use on the premises. Such a move would provide an alternative to street drinking, reducing demands for 'something to be done' about public drinking.

As noted in chapter 3, police routinely come into contact with the street drinkers found throughout the Cowgate and Grassmarket areas. As in the other two jurisdictions studied, L&B members arrest intoxicated individuals who have passed out or are found in situations in which they or others may come to harm. In Edinburgh the policy is to take such individuals to the city's major hospital so that they may sober up under medical care. In both Vancouver and San Francisco, such individuals are instead placed in cells in the local jail ('drunk tanks') for several hours until they are deemed sober enough to be turned loose.

With respect to drug addiction services, recently there has been a move in Scotland towards the implementation of drug courts, with two courts operating in Glasgow and Fife. In Edinburgh, there is no similar coercively inclusive scheme. Instead, efforts tend to be significantly more inclusionary: education and harm reduction are deemed a more appropriate focus of local efforts. For example, Council-funded information bureaus in the Cowgate and in other areas throughout the city provide information on accessing detox and treatment beds. Further, there have been recent efforts by health and social service providers, working with L&B officials, to adopt an education/harm reduction strategy in Edinburgh. As of this writing, discussions have taken place which are likely to lead to police working more closely with service providers at offering injection drug users information on both detox services and alternative methods of using heroin. Such a move is seen as being potentially effective in reducing the number of deaths that occur from injection drug use. The rationale behind the move towards an education/harm reduction strategy is clearly reflective of the partnership-working approach with its emphasis on multi-agency cooperatives utilizing pro-social approaches to crime and disorder. A senior officer in the L&B describes this force's motive:

> We can build any amount of prisons and we can have a huge drug squad and we can be as good as any agency in the world, but if you've still got a demand for drugs there, you'll have a supply. And how you must tackle that is, you must reduce the demand. And the only way you reduce the demand is by education and health. So, this is not a law enforcement problem, this is not

a drugs war; it's actually a social problem on a huge scale, the like of which we have not seen before. And we've got to tackle that as a social issue, because we don't have the answers.

The approach taken to the treatment of alcohol and drug addiction in San Francisco similarly mirrors the predominant ideology: middle- and upper-class addicts use their cash and/or insurance to buy treatment spots in private clinics, while the poor sit on waiting lists for weeks before treatment beds in the public system become available. In a scathing report on the city's homelessness strategy, the San Francisco Office of the Controller made clear the consequences that a significant lack of publicly funded substance abuse and mental health treatment beds, transitional housing, and available shelter have had on the treatment of the city's homeless. In an environment that utilizes law enforcement as a substitute for social services, the report's author noted:

For an undetermined number of homeless people who are mentally ill or substance abusers, the cycle of hospital to street to jail to street to hospital is, reportedly, fairly common. Cycling through institutions happens to all kinds of homeless people, but those whose behavior offends others are most likely to move between hospital and jail stays. (Office of the Controller 2002: 58)

In San Francisco, various pieces of legislation cast the police as an integral component of a coercively inclusive–exclusionary system for dealing with addiction. The police serve first as the agents of surveillance who identify, monitor, and track suspected substance abusers. Second, they effect the arrests that initiate the legal dynamics that follow. However, it is not the case that the nature of the police role, as defined within legislation, requires police to surveil and arrest indigent addicts. Rather this task is set by local police administrators according to their conception of appropriate institutional priorities. Indeed, with the exception of serious violent offences that typically generate a public outcry for service, this prioritizing is largely dependent on a combination of political and resource-related factors, such as the number of complaints received and the number of officers required to effect a solution. The organization's response, simply put, is to favour demands and solutions that privilege a law enforcement–oriented treatment of addicts. This response accords well with organizational culture and serves to satisfy a mainstream majority.

Police officials also develop organizational policies and programs, outside of a legislative framework, that they view as legitimate responses to demands from 'the community.' In San Francisco, one such initiative represented a local attempt at widening the net to capture more addicts within the city's coercively inclusive system. The program, also known as 'Three Drunks You're Out,' was intended to force street-based alcoholics into treatment under the threat of jail time. Unsurprisingly, this initiative subsequently failed as a consequence of the lack of available detox beds (Hoge 2001b).

Despite Vancouver's apparently progressive attitude towards the treatment of addiction, as evidenced by the opening of its first safe injection site and a city mandate to increase accessibility to treatment, the fact remains that too few dollars have been invested to date in treatment beds. As one frontline officer summed the situation in Vancouver's skid row:

> The problem is there's treatment available, but it takes about three weeks to get in. Which you might think is not that bad but the problem is that I work with these people and sometimes they come to their senses and they want to get clean. It lasts for about a half-hour.

Although, as I have noted above, the average wait time for a residential detox bed has been reduced to about two days, this officer's central point is not the length of the delay, but the fact that any delay is problematic when dealing with addiction. The preferred solution offered by those who are experienced with addiction, including the officer cited above, is treatment upon demand.

One avenue through which treatment is made available to Vancouver's addicts is the drug court system, which was implemented in 2001. The rationale behind this program is the same as for those found in San Francisco and elsewhere: that addicts require coercion to put them through the recovery process. However, where the Vancouver drug court program differs from others, including the San Francisco program, is in the fact that individuals processed through the system have been arrested primarily for non-status offences. They must be arrested for the commission of non-violent crimes attributed to their addiction (such as shoplifting or theft from autos) rather than for being intoxicated and/or in possession of controlled substances.

In contrast to the coercively inclusive/punitive approach towards street-based addiction found in San Francisco, Vancouver, like Edinburgh, has recently been favouring a less punitive and more pragmatic harm reduction–based treatment of addiction. For example, in San Francisco police not only are called upon to arrest individuals they come across who are under the influence of controlled substances, but moreover are routinely assigned the specific task of identifying and arresting addicts under the pretext of providing rehabilitation. In contrast, not only does the VPD not generally arrest intoxicated individuals, but it has also adopted an informal institutional policy of not arresting individuals for possession of personal use amounts of narcotics (Lee 2001). Testifying before a Canadian Senate committee on marijuana decriminalization, the former head of the VPD's Vice and Drug Section advised that officers 'tacitly ignore people who carry small amounts of drugs for their own use' (ibid.: A1). As one officer explained a common misconception, 'We don't charge because you've got a dirty needle. We don't charge because you've got heroin in your body. We don't charge people.' This use of discretion can perhaps be explained as a consequence of at least two critical factors. First, police here are aware of the lack of available treatment resources and other services for addicts; thus, they know that individuals arrested today are simply released tomorrow to resume their behaviour. Second, police operate within a political environment marked by increasingly relaxed social attitudes towards the use of narcotics and the treatment of addicts. Thus, willingness of VPD officers to exercise their discretion with respect to possession is also a partial reflection of the lack of political support for a 'war on drugs.'

Policing: Politics by Another Name

In *'Society Must Be Defended'* (2003), a collection of 1975–6 lectures delivered at the Collège de France, Michel Foucault charts the rise of disciplinary power in emerging Western liberal societies through an inversion of Clausewitz's famous aphorism 'War is a mere continuation of policy [politics] by other means.' What this inversion permits is the basis of a new understanding of power and its exercise through political relations and institutions (ibid.: 18). Power is not simply a repressive moment in history – exemplified by *a* war – but rather a 'relationship of force,' a continual warfare perpetually reinscribed in social institutions, finding expression in the acts of those institutions, in the inequalities they produce, in the rhetoric employed in support of those activities (e.g., the 'war on drugs'), and even in the means by which the state touches the bodies of individual citizens (e.g., through laws that permit the state to render certain forms of conduct problematic, necessitating state intervention into the very body of the individual, such as urine testing for addicts assigned to drug courts). As Foucault explains, 'politics, in other words, sanctions and reproduces the disequilibrium of forces manifested in war' (ibid.: 16). It does so in support of the goals and desires of the larger populace, who, despite the rise of models that push 'individual responsibilization,' clamour for ever-increasing forms of security, demanding that their safety and well-being be secured through the state.

The public police are central to this process. Their function is, after all, to support the relations of ruling in both war and peace or, perhaps more appropriately, through both war and peace. Thus, while policing has often been understood as political in the sense that the public police serve as an arm of the state, policing *is* inherently a form of politics, or, rather, it is better understood as politics by another name. This realization strikes at the centre of a longstanding debate on how to conceptualize the police: as an arm of the state (in support of elites) or as a part of the body politic (with the consent of the governed). Foucault's answer to this conundrum is unhelpful: he portrays the police as both a disciplinary and state apparatus but fails to offer any detailed analyses of the workings of this institution in support of his characterization (ibid.: 250).

I suggest that the 'arm of the state' conceptualization, which is largely seen to flow from Weber's (1947 [1919]) characterization of the modern state as a territorial entity defined by its use of legitimate force (and thus the police as one of the principal agents of coercion), is inadequate both analytically and descriptively. As an institution, the police are hardly unreflexive instruments of the state, nor can their role be easily reduced to that of a coercive tool of those in power. Rather, they serve as an integral component of an overall apparatus of civic governance aimed at fostering conditions that promote social order and prosperity (Foucault 1991, 1994; Neocleous 1998; Dean 1999). Further, as we have seen throughout the present study, their members are best understood as political actors who negotiate the demands made of them within a unique institutional environment, complete with a set of ideologically organized supports and constraints. In this section I want to address the political nature of this work more explicitly.

Early British police proponents recognized from the onset the need to acquire the 'consent of the governed' in order to ensure the success of this emerging technology of government (Reiner 1992; Silver 1992). As Silver explains, 'the replacement of intermittent military intervention in a largely unpoliced society by continuous professional bureaucratic policing meant that the benefits of police organization – continual perva-

sive moral display and lower long-term costs of official coercion for the
state and propertied classes – absolutely required the moral cooperation
of civil society' (ibid.: 66–7). Thus, much early Anglo police doctrine
emphasized the police function in society as tied to an institutional
imperative to seek and reaffirm the legitimacy of the police among the
general public. This continual process entails what I have termed the
task of negotiating demands: as a now integral part of the liberal-
democratic system of governance, the police must be seen as representing the will of the majority. This expression of will is evidenced largely
through the ways in which the institution responds to the political
demands made of it, and to the extent to which its members use their
unique position in society as an influential part of an inter-institutional
network of governance that can bring resources to bear on a variety of
social issues.

Some critics might counter that an emphasis on public legitimacy is
ridiculous, that the police institution, having long ago established its
need for existence in the public perception, is no longer concerned with
reaffirming its legitimacy. Nothing could be further from the truth. The
notion of public legitimacy was raised in several interviews I conducted
with both police and community group members in Edinburgh. Police
were quick to depict themselves as citizens whose only distinction lies in
the fact that their occupation renders them more, not less, accountable
to the public as a whole. This depiction is in keeping, as the police
official quoted below similarly notes, with a tradition that emphasizes
the police as a civil agency that is dependent on public support:

> There's a famous quote from a criminologist who said that the model of
> policing here was that the police are the public and the public are the
> police. This is very simplistic, but actually it captures this desire of ours to be
> interwoven and inter-community, and for the public to be our eyes and ears
> and part of us, and we part of them. And that's why we've got the traditional
> police uniforms. We're as far apart from the military as we could be, deliber-
> ately, so that even to the eye the police look different, civil. A civil police.

Reiner (1992: 61) explains this tradition of a 'civil police' – exemplified
by a cultivated image of the 'benign and dignified' police officer who
maintains a 'low-profile, legalistic stance' – as the result of deliberate
policies seeking to overcome political opposition to this new manifestation of power.

Today, this notion of a civil police in Edinburgh is supported by a political culture that encourages inclusionary policing while de-emphasizing aggressive, punitive approaches to social issues. Their use of a 'civil' approach results in this institution being viewed favourably as a source of and support for positive social change. This is no less true of police work on skid row, where, in contrast to other cities examined, they generate few complaints from the city's most marginalized groups.

Institutional legitimacy rests on popular support for the ways in which a public organization interprets and exercises its mandate. However, this process is relative. We see this in the development of policing systems in the United States. The 'freewheeling and aggressive style' found among U.S. police forces, Reiner explains, is a product of a different set of cultural concerns: in contrast to the situation facing English policing proponents who had to contend with overcoming opposition to their new forces, in the United States 'policing evolved not as a consequence of social divisions, but of the political integration of American society as something approaching a property-owning democracy' (ibid.: 61). Thus, 'popular participation in government meant confidence that control of the police could be entrusted to the political process rather than a tight framework of legal rules and regulations' (ibid.). However, while there is much in this account to explain the American style, what is missing is an important aspect of the unique character of American politics that gives rise to the coercively inclusive–exclusionary nature of its policing systems: its moral economy, which prescribes a harsher treatment of 'undeserving' populations.

Thus it is that despite years of allegations of mistreatment of ethnic minorities and other marginalized groups, and the openly abusive treatment of the human rights of the homeless, the SFPD finds popular support for their work among the mainstream of society and, for the most part, at City Hall. The police receive this support because a majority of the populace agree with the institution's conception of its primary social role as the 'thin blue line' protecting the law-abiding from the criminal population, the latter now an ever-widening group constituted not only of serious offenders, but also of beggars, homeless 'bums,' and other human signs of social and economic distress. The police have little reason to doubt this support given that this treatment is directly inscribed through laws delivered at local ballot boxes, tacit support of police practices by a civic majority that fails to support police reform initiatives, the continuing unwillingness of the public to challenge the lack of police accountability, and the privileged status of the department's budget.

The issue of police legitimacy is slightly more complex in the Canadian context. This is because Canadian policing is perhaps best understood as representing a combination of the two forms previously described. As McKenna (1998) notes, early Canadian police organizations such as the Northwest Mounted Police were similar to their U.S. counterparts in that they were tasked largely with maintaining law and order in an anarchic frontier environment, where stability was desperately required for the furtherance of economic development. However, these same police services were modelled on the British system, seen most notably in the rank structure of Canadian forces, which largely mirrored that of their British counterparts. Thus, we can say that some but not all of the aggressive aspects of frontier policing that we find in the United States have been tempered through the importation of British police custom with its emphasis on 'civil policing.' When this unique configuration of policing is assessed within a larger culture that similarly represents an uneasy mix of distinct political ideologies, one can see how the issue of maintaining public legitimacy for the institution might be both an important concern and a problematic one. After all, there is significantly less ideological unity here, particularly in comparison with the environments in which police operate in Edinburgh and San Francisco.

On Vancouver's skid row, the VPD attempt to chart a political course in a hyper-politicized space within a larger political environment that uneasily melds two different sets of political ideologies. As one officer contends of the politics of local policing, 'there is no consensus ... there is no consensus about how you want the policing done.' Within this confused space, the VPD has implemented CET, which utilizes a combination of strategies that more or less favour coercively inclusive to inclusionary measures (the notable exception is those exclusionary strategies aimed at pushing dealers and other illegal entrepreneurs out of the neighbourhood and/or into jail). Every step of the decision to implement CET is clearly linked to the need of the institution to reaffirm itself in light of ever-shifting public perceptions. A major catalyst for creating this program appears to have been the perceived need of the institution to maintain public legitimacy in the face of an increasing perception that police had abandoned the DTES, thereby threatening the rest of Vancouver with the possibility of a spillover of chaos and crime. Further, it is also apparent that CET was developed as a peacekeeping model largely for the purpose of garnering public support for the project itself. This point was articulated in an interview with a senior officer who explained the rationale underlying this model:

I look at this from the standpoint of we're on the right track in terms of focusing on behaviour versus the technical illegality of being in possession of a substance. That's not a bad thing because from a public standpoint that'll give us more support. When you think about it, people really hate technical applications of the law, but when you provide them a rationale that makes sense to their well-being, safety, and the safety of others, they accept it and will have you.

The police on skid row are clearly reflexive about both the political nature of the roles they assume and the demands that they face with respect to how they police the row and its inhabitants within a larger political system that variously supports and/or constrains their work. For example, a senior officer in San Francisco acknowledged the political negotiations that take place when he attends community meetings that are filled with individuals and groups making contradictory demands of him and his officers: 'You'll have groups that will advocate the violation of civil rights, to the groups that would say you're criminalizing the homeless and the poor.' As this officer further noted, community concerns must be weighed not only against each other but also in light of the law, available internal and external resources, as well as prevailing popular sentiments. The more politicized the area policed, the higher the stakes in determining an appropriate set of institutional responses. The tension of negotiating often-conflicting sets of demands is revealed in the following exchange with a senior Vancouver officer about criticisms by various community groups concerning the policing of skid row:

Q: How do you win?
A: You don't. You do actually. I shouldn't say that. I think it's always ... if we're doing it properly it's always going to be a situation where one side or the other, and we're usually talking the minority on one side or the other, is pointing the finger saying you're too close to the other side. My fear would be if only one side was doing it because then maybe we are too close. If both sides are pointing the finger then we're probably talking to everybody. And we're probably involved with everybody, and that's a good thing.

The observation that police are political would seem to contradict the image of police as law enforcers who merely *represent* the law, who are neutral as to its contents and workings. This is a representation that is particularly vaunted in Edinburgh, but also to lesser extents in Vancouver and San Francisco. I explored this subject with an experienced officer in

Scotland, and the following exchange is instructive as to how police actors reconcile their political work with a public image that stresses political neutrality:

> A: You cannot be political, you are not allowed to be a member of a political party, and you cannot be a member of a political party.
> Q: See, that's interesting because even though I had a senior inspector in Vancouver tell me that constables are not political, I had a constable tell me that in order to get things done on his beat he'll ask advocates in different groups to write political letters for him.
> A: That's entirely different. You have a community officer who really has suffering in his area and if you mean well, go to your local politicians of any party, of any party at all, to assist in making things work. It's not making it work for him, but for the community. I don't classify that as political ... that's just being politically astute.

Political work for the police officer is thus redefined as 'community work,' on the grounds that the individual officer, indeed the organization as a whole, is simply responding to the expressed demands of a given community. However, not all sets of demands have the same political weight for police. Outcomes of the weighing process as expressed through the setting of departmental priorities, resource allocations, and internal budgeting can be seen as a direct product of the social system in which police officers operate. While there is always room for the exercise of discretion by individual officers, at an institutional level the police remain largely bound within the existing political culture. For most organizations this is not problematic because the institution and its agents are drawn from the same social system that they police; thus the values and beliefs of the mainstream culture are shared and reproduced through their work. In spaces where the political climate is changing, police organizations must adapt accordingly or at least give some appearance of a willingness to change.

In the preceding chapters I utilized the four frameworks discussed – law enforcement, peacekeeping, social work, and knowledge work – in order to show how police officers make sense of their work. To the extent that these frameworks fall within the organizing principles of the police institution's mandate, they are also employed at an institutional level to justify police work to the public and to other institutions. As such, the linking of police policies or programs to a particular framework or set of frameworks has political utility for the institution.

Much has been written about how officers venerate law enforcement over other patrol-related functions. Kleinig (1993: 26) suggests that part of the appeal of the law enforcement response at the institutional level may lie in the fact that it provides the police 'with a manageably determinate role.' We see the utility of this frame with respect to the previously cited quote from a senior police manager in Edinburgh, who stated, 'We're a law enforcement agency, we do not have the answers to all of society's ills.' This invocation of the institution's law enforcement mandate provides the police with justifications for reducing the scope of services provided and for offloading responsibilities onto other agencies.

The law enforcement frame serves other political uses as well. As Kleinig notes, in the face of calls for harsher treatment of marginalized groups, the police may reassert their claim to political neutrality by falling back on the position that they simply enforce the law as it is (ibid.). For example, in negotiating conflicting sets of demands in Edinburgh centring on the removal of Cowgate and Grassmarket street residents from public areas, a frontline supervisor advised that 'you can't just go in and throw them out much as the residents want you to do that. It's not going to happen because we'd be acting ... [outside] of our powers. I wouldn't sanction that. And none of my cops would do that anyway.'

At face value, such a claim endorses a view of the police as merely neutral observers of the law; however, police organizations frequently lobby for increased powers, so the fact that the L&B chooses not to use such demands as an opportunity for garnering new and/or enhanced legal powers is indicative of a key aspect of the organizational culture. Further, the fact that the larger community is not – beyond small, localized calls for change – demanding an increase in those powers says much about the local political culture. This is similarly the case in Vancouver, where police acknowledge walking a tightrope between opposing constituencies in the DTES: beyond exclusionary demands from local businesses and some middle-class resident groups, who claim that they are 'the community,' we hear little from the larger community about the necessity of pushing street residents out of the DTES (and one presumes out of Vancouver entirely). The result is that beyond CET, which has largely been a peacekeeping operation, police only infrequently engage in forms of aggressive law enforcement. One of the rationales for this situation heard in interviews with senior officers is that they enforce the law 'as it is.'

Conversely, the political neutrality claim can also be used as a justification for police work that is seen by some to be discriminatory against skid row residents and other excluded groups. We see this use in the following quote from a police manager in San Francisco:

> I always tell [groups that view the police as criminalizing the homeless and the poor] that we do not enforce laws against homelessness; we only enforce criminal statute laws. Unfortunately some of those criminal statute laws are being violated by the homeless, but we're not targeting the homeless – we're just targeting crime that occurs within the district.

There is however a monumental untruth at the heart of this claim: aside from the fact that the SFPD operates as a lobby group when its powers are at stake, this institution sets organizational agendas that privilege some tasks over others. It has been widely reported that there are countless murders, assaults, rapes, and other forms of violence in the Tenderloin and throughout the city of San Francisco that are left uninvestigated each year as a consequence of departmental policies that place resources on the streets rather than in the Investigative Bureau (Parrish and Van Derbeken 2002; Van Derbeken and Parrish 2002; Van Derbeken and Wallace 2002). The decision to allocate resources into frontline policing, and to have frontline officers focus on 'broken windows' issues, is not politically neutral and cannot be justified by the claim that the police are simply following their mandate to enforce all laws.

For many organizations, peacekeeping is seen as a frame that accords with the police mandate to maintain order but is viewed as less socially divisive, and therefore less politically controversial. In Edinburgh, as in Vancouver, emphasis by senior managers on the police as peacekeepers as opposed to law enforcers plays to larger political concerns. This was articulated in a discussion with a high-level officer who noted that police organizations across the U.K. do not use uniforms and equipment that evoke militaristic images, as we see in the United States and Canada. The rationale is clear: 'We're not an army of occupation.' The peacekeeping approach – as exemplified in the statement by a high-ranking official in the L&B that 'we don't dress up in helmets and shields and parade about the streets' – permits the police to retain a public image of themselves as part of the civil society they police rather than as a force apart. Not only does this accord with social views as to the proper role of the police, but it also prevents and/or limits the potential for anti-police organizations to spring up and to make political points at the expense of the police institution. As was explained to me by a senior officer, '[We] keep it fairly low key. We'll try to make our police officers look as much like local police officers [peacekeepers rather than law enforcers], because Cop Watch[7] and those kinds of things are an absolute nightmare.'

Peacekeeping thus serves institutional political ends, particularly when a political climate is ambiguous or even hostile to aspects of the institution's policies or practices or where support for police practice is tenuous or conditional. The situation with respect to Vancouver's police force offers a case in point. The creation and subsequent 'selling' of CET to City Council and the public as a peacekeeping measure rather than as a law enforcement program was intended to provide police management with a way of charting a course of action within the DTES that would improve their chances of drawing both wider political support as well as increased financial support from the current civic regime. The politics underlying this strategy were revealed in an interview with a senior officer:

> The reality is that if you look [outside of] Vancouver, the police get to go and do enforcement because they know that the Mayor and Council is basically supporting them. Whereas in this political environment, we don't have that. And we've been placed in this dilemma many, many times of basically feeling that we're going to be out there on our own if we do this, because this is a political decision.

Recognizing that aggressive policing of lower-level offences is itself a political act, and one that would not be supported within the current civic political environment, police management in Vancouver have shied away from some of the tactics utilized in San Francisco, where such activities draw popular support.

The social worker response permits the police to function within the skid row community and is born partly out of role expectations and partly out of political considerations. With respect to the former, the public expects that police officers will provide assistance to those in need. They also expect that police will facilitate orderly conditions, a feat often best accomplished on skid row through the provision of assistance to residents there. In relation to political considerations, increased community activism on the row may place demands upon the police to respond to skid rowers as members of a community to whom the police must be responsive and accountable. In Vancouver, a general emphasis on community policing presents interesting challenges for both the individual officer and the institution because of the fractured, politically charged nature of the DTES. As an officer explains: 'On the one hand you've got groups of citizens that say police aren't banging heads enough down here for us, because we're the functional community and we're the ones that the police should be defending ... [however] you could make the case that the community down there is drug-addicted, and that's the community that you should serve.'

In San Francisco, there is no similar ambiguity over the question of which community receives the bulk of police social work services. It is clearly the community of the morally deserving: seniors, youth, and upright citizens who receive crime prevention education, police activity leagues, and support for public-based surveillance patrols. Occasionally, however, the social work frame is also cynically used to justify police actions centred on the morally undeserving, such as when the institution portrays the process of arresting addicts for being under the influence as a beneficial social work function on the grounds that arrest can facilitate acceptance of treatment options.

As we saw in the preceding chapter, the VPD has directed some of its energies at implementing programs and policies that assist the most marginalized within the community. The decision on whether to call this a form of social work appears to be largely context-dependent. When dealing with groups in the DTES who represent marginalized communities, and to a certain extent within City Hall as well, police describe such efforts using social work terms. However, within the organization and when dealing with business groups, such efforts are often characterized as being peacekeeping initiatives or as creating departmental efficiencies by reducing calls for police service. Avoiding descriptions of such projects as social work in the latter situations allows police to sell initiatives more easily to audiences (internal and external) that might otherwise be hostile. Police in Edinburgh avoid this problem altogether by recasting social work as knowledge work. Compassionate ends are seen as more readily justified through the use of terms such as efficiency and productivity.

As a political response, the knowledge worker approach is one that is particularly useful for the police institution. This response permits the institution to counter demands for services through redirecting social problems to other institutions. The police facilitate this transfer through brokering information. Indeed, they often frame the data they provide into formats that, in a sense, force other institutions to respond. Delinquent youth become 'youth at risk' who must be treated under the social services umbrella rather than as a police problem. The same frequently holds true for cases involving other special groups, such as the mentally ill and occasionally addicts.

There are also numerous examples of how the knowledge worker response is used in the face of increased demands for law enforcement. Because law enforcement consumes police resources and offers low returns in the form of convictions, police broker information to other institutions that also serve order maintenance ends. An excellent example can be found in the relationship that exists between public and private police in some cities. In Vancouver, as elsewhere, police actively network with private security both within and outside the row (Huey, Ericson, and Haggerty 2005). Inside the DTES, relations between police and private security consist of routine, informal information-sharing on identified targets and joint crime concerns (ibid.). The police there provide private security with both information and training, with the expectation not only that the guards will serve as unofficial information-gatherers for the police but also that the guards' active presence there will displace certain 'problem' inhabitants, thus satisfying demands that 'something be done' (ibid.). In the nearby downtown core, police and private security have entered into a more formalized set of relations characterized by, among other things, computer-networked data sharing on criminal and disorderly activities, routine meetings between private security interests and police, police training of security, and joint cooperation on anti-theft programs (ibid.).

Conclusion

The primary focus of this chapter has been the politics of skid row policing. In order to contextualize the responses of each force to the inclusionary-exclusionary demands made of them with respect to each city's skid row district, I explored their respective institutional environments. This was done first through looking at the resources that police are able to command (budgets and personnel), as well as the means they utilize to acquire these resources. Through this examination we saw some of the ways in which police function politically in order to meet their organizational goals and institutional mandates. I then looked at two significant aspects of the inter-institutional environment that shapes skid row and its policing: homelessness and addiction. What this analysis revealed was not only the ways in which the larger political environment variously supports and/or constrains certain forms of skid row policing but moreover the political methods police utilize to effect inter-institutional solutions.

The section that followed dealt with the claim that police are essentially political actors. This claim rests not simply on their status as 'an arm of the state' but also on the fact that police operate within and through a political system, using political means to achieve political ends. Integral to the institution's work is the need to reaffirm its legitimacy in the eyes of the public. Thus, I explored some of the ways in which each of the forces studied attempt to maintain public support for their work, both generally and in relation to skid row. In Edinburgh, police follow a historical tradition that is widely supported within the local population. The L&B are a 'civil' police force; this is reflected in visible but largely non-aggressive policing within and outside of the row. In San Francisco, police similarly find support by following both tradition and popular dictates: in this case through the utilization of aggressive law and order policing directed principally at the regulation of skid rowers and other marginalized groups. Policing in Vancouver also accords with both its historic roots and popular dictates: the style is a unique combination that incorporates many elements of the highly democratized British policing traditions with some of the more aggressive elements of the frontier system developed south of the border. In short, in each city we find a policing style that represents an attempt at garnering maximal public support.

Finally, I explored the political nature of police work through the four theoretical frames employed throughout. Through integrating these perspectives and placing their use within their respective civic moral-political economies, I argued that we come to a new conception of the police function on skid row. They are not simply agents of exclusion who execute measures intended to further a punitive drive, but rather political actors who negotiate often conflicting sets of demands placed upon their institution with reference both to their own mandate and to the larger political environment. The frames discussed serve as justifications for determinations as to which demands will be privileged by the institution and for subsequent police action in response to privileged demands and, conversely, for lack of police action with respect to those demands viewed as less meritorious.

9 'A Community Gets the Policing That It Wants'

I decided a long time ago that the most important lesson that I took from the SFPD is that a community gets the policing that it wants. So you may as well work with the community to do it their way, because if you do it their way, you'll meet success. (former SFPD officer)

In the previous pages I explored how conflicting demands shape the nature of policing of skid row communities. In doing so, I advanced three claims. The first claim was that contrary to recent critiques of neo-liberalism, exclusion and inclusion are twin strategies for enforcing group solidarity and thus are social facts found to varying degrees within all societies. I rested this claim on empirical data drawn from three examples of one of the most excluded of communities – skid row districts – where demands are routinely generated of and within these sites across different civic environments. My second claim was that the political economy of crime – what I term 'moral economy' – shapes demands upon the policing institution that range from increased exclusion to increased inclusion of marginalized groups. To support the claim that police function within the local moral economy as 'demand negotiators,' I drew upon field data collected on policing practices within three of these sites – the Cowgate and Grassmarket, the Tenderloin, and the Downtown Eastside. What was revealed was that demands placed on the police translate into administrative policies and frontline practices that accord largely with those interests perceived as politically popular within the local 'moral economy.' The final contention that framed this book was that police, both the institution and its individual officers, are keenly aware of their role as political actors and are reflexive about both the nature of the roles they assume and the range of inclusive-exclusive demands that they face from the public.

My intention in this closing chapter is not simply to review these arguments but to consider the larger social implications of the research findings offered here. I have titled this chapter 'A Community Gets the Policing That It Wants' in order to draw attention to what is perhaps the most important conclusion that I took away from this research: the idea that communities articulate their values through their policing practices. In the final section of this chapter, I consider the implications of this insight.

Moral Economy in the City: The Inclusive, Exclusive, and Coercively Inclusive

I began this book with a central concern: much of the contemporary theorizing on the subject of political economy within the social sciences has, of late, focused nearly exclusively on state structures or international processes, producing theoretical insights that are often of limited use for exploring local phenomenon. Through my research on one of the most highly contested of marginalized communities, I have attempted to break from this pattern by examining the processes by which political economies at local levels are shaped through unique combinations of factors. In doing so, I have sought to refine our understanding of political economy by directing our attention to its expression in civic forms as 'moral economies.' This notion of 'moral economy' retains the concern with recognizing the uniqueness of local political economies while simultaneously drawing our attention to the ways in which elements of the moral underpinnings of political ideologies are retained and expressed through local politics.

Policing of the skid row districts of Vancouver, Edinburgh, and San Francisco was thus examined as a means of providing a more subtle and complex picture of the expression of exclusivity 'on the ground.' Each of the sites studied embodies different elements and degrees of exclusion, inclusion, and coercive inclusion. Differences in the relative strength or weakness of inclusive-exclusive tendencies within each of these cities is explained as a cultural effect, shaped by historical, political, social, and economic factors that ultimately find expression in the acceptance and promotion of social attitudes that loosely fall under the umbrella of what may be termed 'American-style neo-liberalism,' 'ordoliberalism,' or 'third-way variants.'

What my work thus reveals is that there has been no singular uniform move towards increased exclusivity as a consequence of a rise of U.S.-style neo-liberalism. Further, mythical examples of peace, love, and brother- and sisterhood cannot obscure the fact that outsiders have always been excluded or subject to coercive inclusionary tactics under discourses of 'reform' and 'rehabilitation.' Today not only is exclusion present in public policies and attitudes, but inclusivity of the coercive and ultimately self-defeating kind also remains a fundamental feature of contemporary public discourse on the treatment of crime and deviancy. And, perhaps most importantly, this work also draws attention to the fact that even in the most marginalized of communities, we find to varying extents countering inclusionary discourse in the form of demands for greater social acceptance, demands that frequently hold the potential for significant local political change.

Institutional Environments, Public Demands, and Police Responses

As I stated in the Introduction, because of their exceptional powers, the exercise of which is often said to occur to an extraordinary degree within excluded spaces, it is easy to view the police solely as agents of exclusion tasked with ensuring that those who might otherwise 'plague' or offend society are kept in contained geographical and social locations. However, such a view is too simplistic and does not take into account the diversity of forms of policing that we see – ranging from the more or less inclusive to the outright exclusive. Nor does it take into account the politics of policing, which is shaped in myriad ways by the socio-politico-economic dimensions of the larger civic economy.

Institutions are directly influenced by social, political, and economic conditions within their institutional environments. For example, at a practical level, budgets, personnel, and the ability to access or acquire resources either directly or through other institutions are all contingent upon the ability of police command staff to garner both public and extra-institutional support for their work. Such support is predicated upon the ability of the police to effectively negotiate the demands placed upon their institution. Some of these demands legitimately fall within the police mandate. Others arise from the failures of other civic or state bodies. Gaps in resources for the homeless, the mentally ill, and the addicted place people in the streets to beg, openly use drugs and alcohol, urinate publicly, and engage in a variety of other behaviours deemed offensive to members of the general public. Although not properly considered police business, if such social issues inflame public sentiments enough, they shortly become police matters as a consequence of vehement public demands for 'something to be done' that are articulated in civic policy and/or legislation.

The ability of the police to cope with the demands generated of them is constrained by the nature of the public discourse that frames a given issue. This is the case for three reasons. First, and at the risk of being repetitive, police budgets clearly depend on public support for institutional activities. Second, the police themselves are products of the social environment that generates these demands; thus their responses will necessarily be tailored according to the social system in which they live and work. A third extra-institutional factor that is variously constraining or supportive of particular police responses is the willingness of the public to support funding for social problems that are not, in and of themselves, policing matters. The clearest example of the relationship between social funding and policing practices can be found in San Francisco, which has cut social service expenditures in the face of a homeless crisis but maintains a large police budget while its citizens continue voting for anti-homelessness ordinances. One of the most direct results of the creation of this environment is that individual police officers, should they choose to, have few resources to call upon when attempting to help the homeless, the mentally ill, the addicted, or others; nor is there political support for such individual pro-social policing efforts.

Reflexive Actors: The Police and Political Agency

As the words, policies, and practices of the agencies examined reveal, the police are reflexive political actors who understand that in order to achieve the public legitimacy necessary to the functioning of their institution, they must carefully negotiate political demands both locally and within the larger political system. Police negotiate these demands by forming alliances with politicians and public and private organizations, currying favours from other agencies, manipulating through the selective presentation of facts in public media, and sometimes through bluffing. They also utilize another method: they carefully select and utilize specific frames in order to negotiate demands made of them. These frames include law enforcement, peacekeeping, social work, and knowledge work. The selection of a frame coincides with a particular desired outcome. Police may become knowledge workers when they want to acquire resources and/or support from other institutions. The law enforcement role may be invoked when police want to delimit their involvement with a problem or issue or absolve themselves from responsibility for following a particular course of action – 'we're only following the law.' As I have detailed extensively in preceding chapters, each of these frameworks can be used to support exclusionary, inclusionary, or coercively inclusive responses by the police institution.

Much of the literature on policing has ignored the fact that frontline practitioners not only are part of the larger political process as instruments of the institutions they serve but also operate as reflexive political actors in their own right. The reality of skid row policing is that it is inherently political work at all levels of the organization. Decisions made as to how to approach particular issues or problems on the frontlines are shaped within organizational cultures that are, in turn, influenced by civic politics. While there is always room for deviation on the ground – indeed police and community groups alike were clear to state that a 'good' skid row police officer is one who adopts a flexible, contingent approach to his or her craft in response to the exigencies of the street – frontline policing styles in each of the cities often accord with those institutional policing frames privileged by their respective organizations.

Each of the frames that police utilize on skid row permit the individual officer a means of negotiating institutional and situational demands. Resort to law enforcement in arresting an area addict for possession can be justified through the expedient of stating that she is just 'enforcing the law as it is.' Through framing this action in light of the 'law enforcement imperative,' the officer attempts to distance herself from the political nature of her work. This is similarly true for decisions made utilizing other frames that may also lead to exclusionary, inclusionary, or coercively inclusive outcomes. The privileging of a particular framework is again frequently a product of the larger civic environment.

The Police Are Us: Reframing the Police–Public Relationship

The style of policing on skid row reflects the values and beliefs of the larger civic culture. The more punitive and/or exclusive the culture towards those deemed morally unregenerate or otherwise outcast, the harsher the style of policing we see directed at those individuals and groups. Conversely, the more open and tolerant of difference a community is, the more generally inclusive the style of policing manifested there. However, to the extent that all societies have the capacity for inclusive, coercively inclusive, and exclusive treatment of those within their midst who are deemed 'other,' we see variations reflecting these forms of treatment in policing policies and practices not only across different police organizations but also to a lesser extent incorporated within different programs within the same institution.

In making this argument, both in writing and in discussion, I am occasionally surprised by interpretations of my work that gloss over the rather complex, nuanced findings that I report here. For example, one friend observed of the San Francisco Police Department that 'they sound like bullies.' This is not an entirely accurate representation of either the entire SFPD or of my own work. In relation to the former, I note that, as described in the fourth chapter, several of the members of the SFPD interviewed spoke of trying, on an individual level, to help the citizens of the Tenderloin when and where they could, and in the face of a serious lack of both internal support for pro-social policing measures and access to external resources. With respect to the misrepresentation of one of the central points in this book, I cannot state clearly enough that strands of inclusion, exclusion, and coercive inclusion are found to varying degrees within the programs, policies, and practices of each of the institutions and in the work of their individual officers. These strands are carefully tied to the larger civic environment that both directly and indirectly shapes the police institution.

To make this point more forcefully: the public is their police. Thus, to the extent that we might find certain policing practices objectionable, we need to turn our attention to the larger civic culture that creates and sustains those practices. There is an unfortunate tendency to reify the police and to do so in a manner that constructs this institution as both separate from and above the public as a whole. This is a convenient fallacy. What my research supports is a view of the public as implicated in the practices of their police forces. While this influence may not always be direct, or even intentional in some circumstances, we create the demands that the police must negotiate, influence their prioritization, and set the conditions that shape the responses available to police agencies. To make this point even clearer: as we can see with respect to the three cities studied, the fewer the resources available to address in meaningful ways issues of mental illness, addiction, poverty, and homelessness, the more likely we will see greater numbers of individuals with these conditions, thus increasing the potential for the public to seek to use the police and other criminal justice agencies in response.

In conceptualizing police decision making as 'negotiating demands,' I

am essentially outlining not a deterministic model, but rather a form of
ceteris paribus. The police as a political institution rank-order demands
made in light of a variety of factors, including laws, coherence with other
institutionally defined mandates, available resources, funding, extra-
institutional support, and potential outcomes. They perform this task
not only within a context that is culturally defined but also as members
of that culture or, in the case of senior administration brought in from
elsewhere, certainly with the knowledge that what will be defined as
'success' is largely determined by the civic culture within which they are
operating. Thus, the leaders of this institution are aware that attempts to
stand either separate from or above the public as a whole will impair
ongoing attempts at affirming the legitimacy of the institution. As good
political actors, they must cultivate extensive positive relations with various segments of the public – or rather 'publics' – especially those publics
aligned with dominant civic interests. This view of the politics of policing, as may be recalled, was captured in the comment of a Vancouver
community group member who wryly noted, 'the police picks their
community.'

The flexible interpretation of the structure and practices of the police
that I am offering here runs counter to the largely deterministic, instrumentalist view of this institution frequently held by many scholars as well
as by community activists and some citizens. Understandably, such an
interpretation, particularly one that locates members of the public in
police practices, may engender a resistance to wanting to treat the
police, particularly those agencies that have been implicated in harsh,
punitive practices, as the agents of community will. And yet it seems
readily apparent enough that if we truly want to influence policing in
positive ways, then we must attend to those cultural values, beliefs, and
attitudes that support and sustain both objectionable as well as pro-social
policing forms. Finally, I add that to the extent that the police are us, and
we them, the seeds of potential change can be found in both.

Appendix: Research Methods

Collection of the data used in this study took place between January 2000 and December 2003. Data-gathering methods included interviews, direct observation, and document analysis. Eighty-six interviews were conducted with 101 subjects (see table A1). Some subjects were identified through a preliminary study of textual materials and contacted directly. Others were identified through the use of snowball sampling.

One of the limitations of previous studies of skid row policing has been that field researchers have focused almost exclusively on understanding policing practices from the perspective of frontline police officers. To address this deficiency within the literature, the present study utilized interviews collected from police personnel of varying ranks and positions within each force. These ranks represented both the frontlines (officers and their immediate supervisors) and police managers. Aside from general questions about the selected organization or research site, police managers were asked about departmental policies and practices. In particular, I was keen to know about the politics of policing and the ways in which organizations attempt to broker demands from other institutions and various segments of the population. Managers were also asked about social inclusionary policing practices and at what levels within the organization they believed the potential for change existed. Frontline officers were asked about their perceptions of the politics of skid row policing, as well as about the roles they perform on skid row, constraints and challenges of the jobs, and whether they felt they could make a difference at the local level.

Also missing from many of the earlier accounts of skid row policing are the experiences and perceptions of those policed. Residents were interviewed in order to provide a street-based perspective on skid row

Table A1 Interviews

Subject Category	Edinburgh	San Francisco	Vancouver	Totals by Category
Police personnel	8	9	12	29
Community groups/ service providers	9	9	12	30
Area residents	14	11	7	32
Local businesses	1	1	2	4
City representatives	2	2	2	6
Totals per city	34	32	35	101

policing. Their views offer a crucial lens through which to understand both the effects of practice and policy and the nature of demands concerning the use of police services. Residents were asked general questions about the neighbourhood and their perceptions as to local levels of crime and violence. They were also asked to discuss their feelings and/or experiences with the local police and whether they noted any changes in policing styles over time.

One of the major difficulties in studying homeless and/or transient populations is the question of access. Usual contact measures – letters, phone calls, or even e-mails – do not apply to those without fixed abodes or access to modes of communication that most of us take for granted. Further, life on the street is a hard one, and many of the individuals I encountered were naturally suspicious of an apparently middle-class white woman wanting to speak to them about their views and experiences of police activities. I was able to overcome this problem with the help of a community activist group that facilitated access to some of their members. Similar difficulties in Edinburgh and San Francisco were also smoothed over with the cooperation of community groups.

The views of service providers have been largely ignored within the skid row policing literature. Their exclusion is unfortunate given that they are uniquely placed to assist in representing the views of those policed: service providers who work with groups of clients are more likely to see and understand the nature of patterns over time; thus they were asked to speak to past or emergent trends on the row. Further, to the extent that many of these agencies work with police in providing conditions necessary to survival on skid row, community workers also offered insights into policing policies and practices at institutional and individual levels.

The category of city representatives encompasses both local elected and civic officials. Their inclusion assists in understanding the politics of policing, from police budgets and resources to public demands for police services. Aside from questions concerning the politics and economics of a given site, interviewees within this category were asked about the provision of local policing services, their interactions with police representatives, and the nature of policing demands from different constituencies.

I also sought to interview business associations, owners, and/or managers who operate within the selected skid row districts. I had hoped to learn more about the nature of demands for police service that local businesses generate. Those who did agree to participate were asked general questions about the crime in their neighbourhood, the quality and level of police services, as well as any direct experiences they had had with the police. Unfortunately, the bulk of businesses and business groups contacted failed to respond to requests for interviews. As those who were contacted through the mail failed to respond either to an initial letter or to follow-up requests, I can only speculate as to their reasons. I have attempted to partially overcome this limitation through the collection of published interviews with business agents in local newspapers.

The interview format used with all participants was open-focused: interviews were not conducted with a set of pre-prepared questions but rather relied upon a set of general concerns that subjects addressed. With such an open and loose interview style, subjects were able to raise issues that had not been previously considered. The nature of the questions necessarily changed from participant to participant in order to capture the beliefs, thoughts, and experiences of differently situated subjects more fully. Open-focused interviews also facilitated discussions that were conversation-like and thus permitted a greater degree of flexibility in the questions asked.

All interviews were taped with the subject?s consent. All subjects were guaranteed confidentiality. To facilitate this ethical requirement, identifying information was removed during the transcription process, and the identified gender of some subjects was modified in the final text. Where quoted, subjects are further identified as belonging to one of the generic categories noted above (e.g., resident, police) or are listed as an unnamed 'subject,' 'respondent,' or 'individual.' Some exceptions have been made where extra description does not compromise the identity of the subject.

To supplement the interview data, I conducted observational research for a period of approximately one month in each of the research sites. Fieldwork was conducted two to three days per week, for two- to six-hour periods during both day and nighttimes. Efforts were made to capture observations in each of the sites at various points during the day and on different days of the week. Time spent in the field was roughly equivalent for each of the spaces. Where appropriate, notes and photographs were taken to assist in documenting physical and social characteristics of a particular environment. Some of these photographs have been placed throughout the text.

I also attended various public and private meetings and other events. In Vancouver, I observed several Police Board and City Council meetings, attended board meetings of selected community groups, and made several visits to a homeless encampment in the DTES. Previously I had received two guided police tours of sites within the DTES, including local bars, various street hangouts, and a single-resident occupancy hotel. These visits informed aspects of the present study. In Edinburgh, I observed a local community development meeting for the City Centre, at which city councillors, police, and residents were present. On one occasion I also volunteered at an area mission, handing out food. I also toured the Cowgate/Grassmarket site separately with a senior police official and a local outreach worker. In San Francisco I spent two mornings at a community centre in the Tenderloin talking with volunteers and drop-in clients, attended a lecture at the SFPD's Citizens' Police Academy, and observed a planning meeting for a local community event.

Primary and secondary documents were gathered and analysed in order to provide an understanding of some aspects of the social, political, economic, and geographical nature of each of the cities' downtown environs. Document sources varied and included both hard-copy text and Web-based materials: city reports, news articles, community reports, and materials of non-governmental organizations and relevant legislation and regulations. During interviews, I was sometimes given copies of police forms and organizational reports that were subsequently used to inform the analysis offered here. News articles were obtained as follows. For stories on Vancouver, searches of the Canadian newsdisc database were performed for the years 1997 to 2003, using the keywords 'police' and 'Downtown Eastside.' These searches yielded articles that supplemented other news stories and commentary that I had been collecting from local papers not found in the database. Relevant news stories on

Edinburgh were obtained through searches of the archives of online editions of the *Edinburgh Evening News*, *The Scotsman*, and *Scotland on Sunday* from 1999 to 2003. Similarly, news articles were obtained through searching the online archives of the *San Francisco Chronicle* from 1999 to 2003 and from reading online editions of *The San Francisco Examiner*.

Notes

Chapter 1. Inclusion, Exclusion, and the Policing of the Skids

1 For example, excepting the Nixon regime, U.S. governments tended to avoid the creation of public corporations and wage and price controls (Yergin and Stanislaw 2002).

2 One of the manifestations of inclusivity in the United States that supporters of the 'golden age hypothesis' point to is U.S. President Lyndon Johnson's War on Poverty, which attempted to bring African-Americans into the formal economy through affirmative action programs and other inclusionary policies. However, as Weir (1996) details extensively, the War on Poverty was ultimately a failure, in part because of white resistance (white Americans tended to view Johnson's policies as conferring benefits based solely on race – that is, as conferring benefits that they would not be entitled to). The result was a backlash that saw many affirmative action programs rolled back during the Reagan era (ibid.). I note this because one of the potential supports for the 'golden age hypothesis' is actually an excellent example of how inclusivity and exclusivity are parallel and overlapping phenomena.

3 An exception to the lack of general societal attention paid to skid row noted during the 'golden age' of welfarism was in the form of newspaper coverage. One particular pictorial spread illustrates the nature of news coverage of this space: it is a series of pictures of 'hobos' drinking homemade alcohol from jars (Young 1951).

4 I think that Robert Kaplan (1997) makes a very good point when he states that crime is often a function of underemployment – or unmet expectations – rather than of unemployment.

5 The term skid row is derived from 'skid road,' the latter more commonly used in North America's Pacific Northwest region, and incorporates in its name a

history bound with labour – these were spaces attached to areas where log-
ging skids carried lumber to be processed at local mills (Spradley 1970). In
their first incarnation, as sites to temporarily house labourers, they were
primarily a North American phenomenon. Later, they became a more general urban condition associated with moral decay and physical and mental
downward slide – 'skid rows.'

Chapter 2. Alkies, Smackheads, and *Ordos*: Skid Row under Ordoliberalism

1 It is not a coincidence that twelve to sixteen of the purported victims of the
notorious serial killers Burke and Hare lived in Cowgate (Edinburgh Evening
News 2002).
2 I use the term slum here in keeping with the site's historical use. From
Stevenson's description, it appears that while the Cowgate and Grassmarket
were infamous as a warehouse for the city's poor, the neighbourhood was not
at that time synonymous with moral delinquency.
3 Rose (1999) suggests that the term 'rough sleeper' used in Britain is morally
freighted, used to indicate someone whose lack of home is the result of
personal pathology and/or lifestyle choice.
4 To be accurate, Piss Alley actually extends from the Cowgate up the
Grassmarket, which also holds beer gardens, pubs, and hotel bars, to the strip
and lap dancing bars at the top of West Port (e.g., the strangely named
Western Bar and the Burke and Hare).
5 A few months prior to my visit, the narcotics squad raided a space that provides a number of services for the homeless and other street-entrenched. This
raid was considered unsurprising by both service providers and street people,
who made it clear to me that the service provider's site had become a well-
known spot for buying drugs.
6 In their study of Edinburgh's homeless population, Kennedy and Fitzpatrick's
(2001) subjects report similar experiences of victimization by drunken youth.
7 In 1997, a referendum on devolution from the United Kingdom (central
government) model was held in Scotland. The result was an overwhelming
majority (74 per cent) voted in favour of the creation of a largely independent Scottish Parliament. In 1999, following passage of the Scotland Act
1998, the Scottish Executive and Parliament came into existence. Under the
terms of the devolution, the Scottish Parliament can enact legislation relating
to: health and social work; education and training; local government and
housing; justice and police; agriculture, forestry, and fisheries; the environment; tourism, sport, and heritage; and economic development and internal
transport (Scotland Office 2002). The United Kingdom, however, retains

legislative and policy-making authority with respect to employment, fiscal and monetary policy, taxation, social security, and social benefits and pensions (ibid.). These are referred to as 'reserved powers.'

8 The new act has clearly had an immediate effect: figures released in 2003 show that the number of homeless households (individuals, families, and groups) put into temporary accommodation by Edinburgh's local council increased by 42 per cent in 2002 (Mooney 2003).

9 The U.K. government fixes income support rates annually.

10 Using national survey data from both Scotland and England, Paterson et al. (2001: 121) note 'that the striking feature of the 1980s and early 1990s was in fact that England remained left of centre even while it was electing the governments of Margaret Thatcher and John Major.'

11 The authors describe this link as being between support for devolution and 'broadly left-of-centre politics' (ibid.: 200). The latter term is somewhat vague. In examining further what the authors mean by 'left-of-centre,' I would presume that they are discussing support for redistributive policies and programs, such as the National Health Service, education, and social welfare. Thus, I have chosen to use the term 'welfarist' instead.

12 Following the Second World War, Britain implemented the recommendations of the Beveridge Report, which led to the creation of the first major welfare state.

Chapter 4. Junkies, Drunks, and the American Dream: Neo-liberal Skid Row

1 Some perpetrators physically restrain victims by throwing them in a head-lock in order to forcibly remove valuables.

2 In order to provide assistance to those who are ineligible for the federal TANF (Temporary Assistance to Needy Families) program – adults without dependent children, including the elderly, the disabled, and those with mental health problems or addictions – counties in California operate programs that are variously known as General Assistance (GA) or General Relief (GR).

3 A report by San Francisco's Office of the Controller (2002: 5) acknowledges this fact: 'in January 1996, Mayor Willie Brown ended the Matrix program but vowed to continue enforcing the laws it covered.'

4 In 2003, however, Californians face an estimated budget deficit of $38 billion (Werner 2003). This deficit can be explained, in part, as a consequence of the state's energy crisis and the need by Californians to purchase large amounts of electricity from other U.S. states and from British Columbia.

5 San Francisco SOS is a civic lobby group founded by U.S. Senator Dianne Feinstein, investment banker Warren Hellman, and GAP founder Donald Fisher (Hua 2003).

Chapter 5. Enforcing the Law with Broken Windows

1 Section 4.127 of the City of San Francisco's Charter mandates a minimum staffing level of 1971 full-duty sworn officers. From 1994 onwards, the Charter also requires that all new full-duty officers be dedicated to neighbourhood community policing, patrol, and investigations.
2 Central, Southern, Bayview, Mission, Northern, Park, Richmond, Ingleside, Taraval, Tenderloin, and Treasure Island police stations.
3 This captain left the district, as most do, because of the department's policy of three-year rotations for captains. However, one community group member noted another reason for captains departing districts: 'There's a scandal ... there's been a couple scandals in the police department in this last year. I just think this police department's not as, I don't know, progressive.'
4 51.50 is a provision in the California legal code that allows the state to detain someone for psychiatric observation. Under this section, the police have the authority to arrest someone who appears to be a danger to themselves or others and transport them to the county hospital for observation.

Chapter 6. Crazies, Crack Addicts, and the 'Middle Way'

1 The injection site was set up as a pilot program in partnership between the Vancouver Coastal Health Authority, the city of Vancouver, the Vancouver Police Department, and the Portland Hotel Society (Luba 2003).
2 In 2001, the provincial Liberal government held a referendum on the issue of treaty-making with First Nations. Both First Nations peoples and many within the larger public viewed the referendum as a cynical attempt by the government to use 'neopopulism' as a means of rolling back gains made by Aboriginals through the treaty process and various court decisions. The attempt backfired: large sections of the general population refused to send in ballots or returned spoiled ballots.
3 At the time of writing there is speculation that one of the province's largest public companies, BC Hydro, will be sold off in whole or in part.
4 COPE won eight out of ten seats; members of the Non Partisan Association (NPA) hold the two remaining seats.
5 Education is provincially funded, with the provincial government supplying funds to local school boards.

6 For example, in previous elections Vancouver voters elected a right-wing mayor, Gordon Campbell, the current premier of the province and leader of the provincial Liberal party, at the same time that the province had a left-wing government under Mike Harcourt and the New Democratic Party. When former mayor Mike Harcourt was still in city government, the province had a radically conservative government under Premier Bill Vander Zalm.

7 Canadians' national passenger rail service, VIA Rail, offers an excellent example in support of the contention that, federally, Canada's politics can be best described as representing a political compromise between the neo-liberal and welfarist agendas. In an era of privatization, the rail service continues to be federally funded because the provision of transport service to such a vast nation is crucial, particularly for communities that are geographically isolated. Brown (2002: 35) makes this same point: 'Canadian governments have had to be more proactive in areas such as transportation and communication with a host of economic and political tools to overcome [Canada's] geographic legacy and keep together a sparse east-west chain of provincial communities and regional economies.'

Chapter 7. Peacekeeping through Saturation

1 This figure represents approximately 19 per cent of total city expenditures (Klein 2003; Spencer 2003). I note that the 2003 police budget represents a 4 per cent increase over 2002 (Klein 2003).

2 While the original sixty officers included officers from other areas who were 'conscripted' into service in this neighbourhood, the forty-eight who remain elected to stay.

3 It was reported that prior to the reduction of CPC services, there were some seven hundred volunteers working out of the seventeen centres (Lee and Goddard 2003).

4 Van Maanen (1978b: 223) defines an 'asshole' as an individual who does 'not accept the police definition of the situation' (such as an argumentative speeder). This officer's use of the term is different; he is using 'asshole' as a derogatory term for a 'bad guy' – an evil or morally corrupt person whose behaviour is viewed as worthy of punishment (Herbert 1996) – rather than as an individual who is unwilling to accept the police definition of a given situation.

5 This is the police term for stranding 'problem' individuals in outlying areas of the city.

6 Officers interviewed believed that some of the use-of-force complaints lodged were the result of a lack of understanding of the dynamics of drug dealing.

When the police arrest a dealer that they have been watching, it can appear to spectators that they have attacked someone who was simply standing and minding his or her own business. This appearance is the result of the fact that dealers use 'runners' (individuals who carry and sell the drug for the dealer).

7 City Council refused to fund the Youth at Risk Database.

8 The Woodwards building is a vacant site in the DTES that formerly housed the Woodwards department store. It was occupied in September 2002 by squatters protesting the lack of social housing in the community. The encampment was raided by police in December 2002. Squatters were offered accommodations elsewhere by city officials.

Chapter 8. Policing as the Art of Negotiating Demands

1 As may be recalled from chapter 7, the Non-Partisan Association, or NPA, was the party formerly in power in City Hall.

2 Although the plan for CET had supposedly been developed six months prior to its implementation, the first mention of CET in the Police Board minutes appears in the minutes of the 26 March 2003 meeting. The minutes state that, at that time, police were in the process of organizing meetings with DTES stakeholders (Vancouver Police Board 2003).

3 At the time of writing, several months after its commission, the study has still not been released, and there have been no public announcements as to the long-term viability of the program.

4 Several difficulties were encountered in my attempts to gather population statistics specific to each skid row site. I was unable to secure data for either Edinburgh's Cowgate/Grassmarket or for San Francisco's Tenderloin homeless populations. Thus, the population estimates offered here are with respect to the general homeless problem in each city, and these figures represent, at best, approximations. Further, estimates based on city counts versus those offered by service providers varied so significantly in San Francisco that table 8.4 includes both figures. For Vancouver, I have also listed two separate estimates of homelessness provided by the city. These figures represent high and low ends of the range of perceived homelessness in the city.

5 Even so, as Fitzpatrick and Kennedy (2001) note, income assistance cheques seldom stretch far enough to meet all the expenses of life on Edinburgh's streets.

6 Kennedy and Fitzpatrick (2001: 2012), in their analysis of begging and rough sleeping in Scotland (Edinburgh and Glasgow), note that 'there is not only a widely acknowledged shortage of detoxification and rehabilitation services

for drug and alcohol misusers, but such facilities as do exist are particularly difficult for homeless people to gain access to.'

7 Cop Watch is a program found in the United States, Canada, and parts of Britain, organized by anti-police activists who conduct surveillance of police activities in order to prevent police abuse of citizens' rights and to effect a greater degree of police accountability. Cop Watch programs operate in both Vancouver and San Francisco but not in Edinburgh.

References

Statutes and Regulations

Police Act, Revised Statutes of British Columbia 1996, Chapter 367.
San Francisco City Charter, 1996 (Revised).
Vancouver Incorporation Act, Statutes of BC 1886. Chapter 32.

Books and Articles

Adilman, Steve, and Gordon Kliewer. 2000. 'Pain and Wasting on Main and Hastings: A Perspective from the Vancouver Native Health Society Medical Clinic.' *BC Medical Journal* 42(9): 422–5.

Allen, Tom C. 2000. *Someone to Talk To: Care and Control of the Homeless.* Halifax, NS: Fernwood.

Anderson, Simon, Richard Kinsey, Ian Loader, and Connie Smith. 1994. *Cautionary Tales: Young People and Policing in Edinburgh.* Aldershot: Avebury.

Baldassare, Mark. 2002. *A California State of Mind: The Conflicted Voter in a Changing World.* Los Angeles: University of California Press.

Banton, Michael. 1964. *The Policeman in the Community.* London: Tavistock.

Bauman, Zygmunt. 1997. *Postmodernity and Its Discontents.* Cambridge: Polity Press.

Bauman, Zygmunt. 1999. 'The Burning of Popular Fear.' *New Internationalist* 310: 20–4.

Bauman, Zygmunt. 2000. 'What It Means "To Be Excluded": Living to Stay Apart – or Together.' In Peter Askonas and Angus Steward (eds), *Social Inclusion: Possibilities and Tensions*, 73–88. London: St Martin's Press.

Bermingham, John. 2004. 'Welfare Cheques Put Demand on Injection Site.' *The Vancouver Province*, 19 August, A26.

Bittner, Egon. 1967. 'The Police on Skid-Row: A Study of Peace Keeping.' *American Sociological Review* 32(5): 699–715.

Bittner, Egon. 1990 [1970]. *Aspects of Police Work.* Ann Arbor, MI: Northeastern University Press.

Black, Donald J. 1980. *The Manners and Customs of the Police.* New York: Academic Press.

Blomley, Nicholas. 1998. 'Landscapes of Property.' *Law and Society Review* 32(3): 567–613.

Blumberg, Leonard U., Thomas E. Shipley, Jr, and Stephen F. Barsky. 1978. *Liquor and Poverty: Skid Row as a Human Condition.* New Brunswick, NJ: Journal of Studies on Alcohol.

Blumberg, Leonard, Thomas E. Shipley, Jr, and Irving W. Shandler. 1973. *Skid Row and Its Alternatives: Research and Recommendations from Philadelphia.* Philadelphia: Temple University Press.

Bradford, Neil. 1999. 'The Policy Influence of Economic Ideas: Interests, Institutions and Innovation in Canada.' *Studies in Political Economy* 59 (Summer): 17–60.

Brown, Douglas M. 2002. *Market Rules: Economic Union Reform and Intergovernmental Policy-Making in Australia and Canada.* Montreal: McGill–Queen's University Press.

Brown, Michael K. 1981. *Working the Street: Police Discretion and the Dilemmas of Reform.* New York: Russell Sage.

Buchan, Bruce. 2002. 'Zero Tolerance, Mandatory Sentencing and Early Liberal Arguments for Penal Reform.' *International Journal of the Sociology of Law* 30(3): 201–18.

Bula, Frances. 2001. '700 Sign Up to Speak against Centres for Drug Users: Chinatown Merchants Vow to Fight Health Board Initiatives for the Downtown Eastside.' *The Vancouver Sun,* 17 February, B4.

Bula, Frances. 2003a. 'Homeless Top Issue for Vancouver Voters.' *The Vancouver Sun,* 28 November, B5.

Bula, Frances. 2003b. 'Mayor Takes Flack for Police Deficit Plan.' *The Vancouver Sun,* 11 July, A1.

Bula, Frances, and Petti Fong. 2003. 'Police Drug Plan was Six Months in the Making.' *The Vancouver Sun,* 11 April, A1.

California State Attorney General's Office. 2003. http://caag.state.ca.us/ (accessed 6 June 2003).

Castel, Robert. 1991. 'From Dangerousness to Risk.' In Graham Burchell, Graham, Colin Gordon, and Peter Miller (eds), *The Foucault Effect: Studies in Governmentality,* 281–98. Chicago: University of Chicago Press.

Chan, Janet B.L., Chris Devery, and Sally Doran. 2003. *Fair Cop: Learning the Art of Policing.* Toronto: University of Toronto Press.

City of Edinburgh. 2003. 'City Of Edinburgh Council: Key Facts And Figures 2003–2004.' http://www.edinburgh.gov.uk (accessed 15 April 2004).

City of Edinburgh. 2004. http://www.edinburgh.gov.uk (accessed 15 April 2004).

City of San Francisco. 2003. 'Consolidated Budget and Annual Appropriate Allowance for Fiscal Year Ending June 20, 2004.' http://www.sfgov.org/ (accessed 29 April 2004).

City of San Francisco. 2004. http://www.sfgov.org (accessed 19 May 2004).

City of Vancouver. 2000. *Downtown Eastside Community Monitoring Report.* Vancouver: City of Vancouver.

City of Vancouver. 2001. *Downtown Eastside Community Monitoring Report.* Vancouver: City of Vancouver.

City of Vancouver. 2003. http://www.city.vancouver.bc.ca (accessed 16 January 2003).

Clarke, P.H. 2000. 'Adam Smith, Stoicism and Religion in the 18th Century.' *History of the Human Sciences* 13(4): 49–72.

Coalition on Homelessness (San Francisco). 2003. http://www.sf-homeless-coalition.org (accessed 30 June 2003).

Daiches, David. 1978. *Edinburgh.* London: Hamish Hamilton.

Davidson, Lynn, and Brian Ferguson. 2003. 'First Step in Rebirth of Fire-Hit Old Town.' *Edinburgh Evening News*, online edition. http://news.scotsman .com (accessed 3 April 2003).

Davis, Mike. 1992. *City of Quartz: Excavating the Future in Los Angeles.* New York: Vintage Books.

Dean, Mitchell. 1999. *Governmentality: Power and Rule in Modern Society.* London: Sage.

Decker, John. 2002. *Covington's Homeless.* http://www.intac.com/~jdeck/ Covdex2. html (accessed 12 March 2002).

Denholm, Andrew. 2004. 'Funding Fears Grow over Anti-social Behaviour Bill.' *Edinburgh Evening News*, online edition. http://news.scotsman.com (accessed 14 April 2004).

Denver, David, James Mitchell, Charles Pattie, and Hugh Bochel. 2000. *Scotland Decides: The Devolution Issue and the 1997 Referendum.* London: Frank Cass.

Department for Work and Pensions (United Kingdom government). 2004. www.jobcentreplus.gov.uk (accessed 19 May 2004).

Dick, Sandra. 2003. 'Building a Picture of the Past.' *Edinburgh Evening News*, online edition. http://news.scotsman.com (accessed 3 April 2003).

Directors of Central Area Planning and Legal Services. 1996. *Policy Report to Vancouver City Council*, 9 April 1996. Department file no.: VAI.

Duneier, Mitchell. 1999. *Sidewalk.* New York: Farrar Strauss and Giroux.

Edinburgh Evening News. 2002. 'More than 500 Years of History Goes up in Smoke.' *Edinburgh Evening News*, online edition. http://news.scotsman.com (accessed 3 April 2003).

Edinburgh Evening News. 2003a. 'Division of the Capital's Resources.' *Edinburgh Evening News*, online edition. http://news.scotsman.com (accessed 17 June 2003).

Edinburgh Evening News. 2003b. '103 People Sleeping Rough on City Streets.' *Edinburgh Evening News*, online edition. http://news.scotsman.com (accessed 27 April 2004).

Edinburgh Old Town website. 2003. http://www.edinburgholdtown.org.uk (accessed 6 May 2003).

Edmondson, Richard. 2000. *Rising Up: Class Warfare in America from the Streets to the Airwaves.* San Francisco: Librad Press.

Ellickson, Robert C. 1996. 'Controlling Chronic Misconduct in City Spaces: Of Panhandlers, Skid Rows, and Public-Space Zoning.' *The Yale Law Journal* 105(5): 1165–1248.

Ericson, Richard V. 1982. *Reproducing Order: A Study of Police Patrol Work.* Toronto: University of Toronto Press.

Ericson, Richard. 1994. 'The Division of Expert Knowledge in Policing and Security.' *British Journal of Sociology* 45(2): 149–75.

Ericson, Richard, Dean Barry, and Aaron Doyle. 2000. 'The Moral Hazards of Neo-liberalism: Lessons from the Private Insurance Industry.' *Economy and Society* 29(4): 532–58.

Ericson, Richard V., and Kevin D. Haggerty. 1997. *Policing the Risk Society.* Toronto: University of Toronto Press.

Fagan, Ronald W. 2002. 'Homelessness.' In Charles F. Hohm and James A. Glynn (eds), *California's Social Problems*, 2nd ed., 15–30. Thousand Oaks, CA: Pine Forge Press.

Ferguson, Brian. 2003a. 'Council Tax Rises by 4%.' *Edinburgh Evening News*, online edition. http://news.scotsman.com (accessed 3 April 2003).

Ferguson, Brian. 2003b. 'Cairns Declares War on Capital Beggars.' *Edinburgh Evening News*, online edition. http://news.scotsman.com (accessed 21 April 2004).

Ferguson, Brian. 2003c. 'Homeless Training for Shop Staff.' *Edinburgh Evening News*, online edition. http://news.scotsman.com (accessed 22 April 2004).

Fielding, Nigel G. 2002. 'Theorizing Community Policing,' *British Journal of Criminology* 42: 147–63.

Fitzpatrick, Suzanne, and Catherine Kennedy. 2001. 'The Links between Begging and Rough Sleeping: A Question of Legitimacy?' *Urban Housing Studies* 16(5): 549–68.

Forbes, Elaine, and Emily Gumper. 2002. 'Processing "Quality of Life" Violations.' *Legislative Analyst Report.* City of San Francisco. 15 May.

Foucault, Michel. 1979. *Discipline and Punish: The Birth of the Prison.* Translated by Alan Sheriden. New York: Vintage Books.

Foucault, Michel. 1991. 'Governmentality.' In Graham Burchell, Colin Gordon, and Peter Miller (eds), *The Foucault Effect: Studies in Governmentality,* 87–104. Chicago: University of Chicago Press.

Foucault, Michel. 1994. 'Omnes et Singulatim: Towards a Critique of Political Reason.' In Paul Rabinow and Nicholas Rose (eds), *The Essential Foucault,* 180–201. New York: The New Press.

Foucault, Michel. 1995 [1977]. *Discipline and Punish: The Birth of the Prison.* Translated by Alan Sheridan. New York: Vintage Books.

Foucault, Michel. 2003. *'Society Must Be Defended': Lectures at the Collège de France, 1975–1976.* Edited by Mauro Bertani and Allessandro Fontana. Translated by David Macey. New York: Picador.

Gammadge, Allen X., David L. Jorgensen, and Eleanor M. Jorgenson. 1972. *Alcoholism, Skid Row and the Police.* Springfield, IL: Charles C. Thomas Publishers.

Gardner, Anthony, and Peter Lindstrom. 1997. 'Police on the Homelessness Front Line: A Postmortem of San Francisco's Matrix Program.' In Martin L. Forst (ed.), *The Police and the Homeless: Creating a Partnership between Law Enforcement and Social Service Agencies in the Development of Effective Policies and Programs,* 98–117. Springfield, IL: Charles C. Thomas.

Garland, David. 1996. 'The Limits of the Sovereign State: Strategies of Crime Control in Contemporary Society.' *The British Journal of Criminology* 26: 445–67.

Garr, Allen. 2003. 'New Police Chief Alienating Longtime Allies.' *The Vancouver Courier,* 4 May, 10.

Giamo, Benedict. 1989. *On the Bowery: Confronting Homelessness in American Society.* Iowa City: University of Iowa Press.

Giddens, Anthony. 1994. *Beyond Left and Right: The Future of Radical Politics.* Stanford, CA: Stanford University Press.

Giddens, Anthony. 1998. *The Third Way: The Renewal of Social Democracy.* Cambridge: Polity.

Giffen, P.J. 1966. 'The Revolving Door: A Functional Interpretation.' *Canadian Review of Sociology and Anthropology* 3(3): 343–54.

Gitlin, Todd. 1995. *The Twilight of Common Dreams: Why America Is Wracked by Culture Wars.* New York: Henry Holt.

Gordon, Rachel. 2002. 'Census Data Yields Surprises about San Francisco Districts.' *The San Francisco Chronicle*, online edition. http://www.sfgate.com (accessed 15 January 2003).

Gordon, Rachel. 2003. 'S.F. Budget Plan Avoids Deep Cuts, Big Layoffs: City's Businesses, Residents, Visitors Will Share the Pain.' *The San Francisco Chronicle*, online edition. http://www.sfgate.com (accessed 15 April 2004).

Graham, Jamie H. 2003. 'Revised Community Policing Centre Model.' *Report to Vancouver Police Board* (#03-24), 27 April.

Graves, Judy. 2004. 'Shelterless in Vancouver, 2004.' *Administrative Report to Vancouver City Council*, 10 February. CC File no. 4659.

Gray, John. 1999. *False Dawn: The Delusions of Global Capitalism*. London: Granta.

Greene, Jack R. 1998. 'Evaluating Planned Change Strategies in Modern Law Enforcement: Implementing Community-Based Policing.' In Jean-Paul Brodeur (ed), *How to Recognize Good Policing: Problems and Issues*, 141–60. Thousand Oaks, CA: Sage.

Hamilton, Jane. 2003. 'Capital Police Costs Hitting Beat Bobbies' *Edinburgh Evening News*, online edition. http://news.scotsman.com (accessed 24 September 2003).

Hamilton, Jane, and Miranda Fettes. 2003. 'Is Masterplan a Criminal Failure?' *Edinburgh Evening News*, online edition. http://news.scotsman.com (accessed 17 June 2003).

Hampton, Adriel. 2003a. 'Judge Spikes Voters' Plan for Homelessness.' *The San Francisco Examiner*, online edition. http://www.sfexaminer.com (accessed 15 May 2003).

Hampton, Adriel. 2003b. 'With Newsom in Mexico, Supes Pass CnC Rival Bill.' *The San Francisco Examiner*, online edition. http://www.sfexaminer.com (accessed 9 July 2003).

Hampton, Adriel. 2004. 'Daly: Stop Babying the Police Budget.' *The San Francisco Examiner*, online edition. http://www.sfexaminer.com (accessed 15 May 2004).

Harcourt, Bernard. E. 1998. 'Reflecting on the Subject: A Critique of the Social Influence Conception of Deterrence, the Broken Windows theory, and Order-Maintenance Policing New York Style.' *Michigan Law Review* 97(2): 291–390.

Harcourt, Bernard E. 2001. *Illusion of Order: The False Promise of Broken Windows Policing*. Cambridge, MA: Harvard University Press.

Harris, Richard N. 1978. 'The Police Academy and the Professional Self-Image.' In P. Manning and J. Van Maanen (eds), *Policing: A View from the Street*, 273–91. Santa Monica, CA: Goodyear Publishing.

Hayek, Friedrich A. 1969 [1944]. *The Road to Serfdom*. Chicago: University of Chicago Press.

Hearn, Jonathan. 2002. 'Identity, Class and Civil Society in Scotland's Neonationalism.' *Nations and Nationalism* 8(1): 15–30.

Heath, Joseph. 2001. *The Efficient Society: Why Canada Is as Close to Utopia as It Gets*. Toronto: Penguin.

Herbert, Steve. 1996. 'Morality in Law Enforcement: Chasing "Bad Guys" with the Los Angeles Police Department.' *Law and Society Review* 30(4): 799–817.

Herbert, Steve. 2001a. 'Policing the Contemporary City: Fixing Broken Windows or Shoring Up Neo-liberalism?' *Theoretical Criminology* 5(4): 445–66.

Herbert, Steve. 2001b. '"Hard Charger" or "Station Queen?" Policing and the Masculinist State.' *Gender, Place and Culture: A Journal of Feminist Geography* 8(1): 55–72.

Hoge, Patrick. 2001a. 'Squalor in the Streets: S.F. Turning Blind Eye to Homeless Addicts Tenderloin Drug Busts Underway.' *The San Francisco Chronicle*, online edition. http://www.sfgate.com (accessed 15 January 2003).

Hoge, Patrick. 2001b. 'Call for Action on Street Drunks.' *The San Francisco Chronicle*, online edition. http://www.sfgate.com (accessed 16 May 2003).

Howell, Mike. 2003a. 'Police Crackdown Having an Effect.' *The Vancouver Courier*, 7 May 2003, 7.

Howell, Mike. 2003b. 'Police Form Task Force to Tackle Problem Crime Areas.' *The Vancouver Courier*, 5 March, 7.

Hua, Vanessa. 2003. 'Business Community Disappointed: S.F. Merchants Had Backed Proposition N.' *The San Francisco Chronicle*, online edition. http://www.sfgate.com (accessed 29 April 2004).

Huey, Laura, Richard V. Ericson, and Kevin D. Haggerty. 2005. 'Policing Fantasy City.' In D Coolley (ed.), *Reimagining Policing*, 140–208. Toronto: University of Toronto Press.

Hughes, Everett C. 1951. 'Work and the Self.' In J.H. Rohrer and M. Sherif (eds), *Social Psychology at the Crossroads: The University of Oklahoma Lectures in Social Psychology*, 313–23. New York: Harper and Brothers.

Jeffrey, Brooke. 1999. *Hard Right Turn: The New Face of Neo-conservatism in Canada*. Toronto: HarperCollins.

Johnson, Pat. 2002. 'Vancouver Voters Usually Give the Boot to Victoria's Toadies.' *The Vancouver Sun*, 15 February, A15.

Jordan, Bill. 1996. *A Theory of Poverty and Social Exclusion*. Cambridge: Polity Press.

Kaplan, Robert D. 1997. *The Ends of the Earth: A Journey to the Frontiers of Anarchy*. New York: Vintage Books.

Kelling, George L., and Catherine M. Coles. 1996. *Fixing Broken Windows : Restoring Order and Reducing Crime in Our Communities.* New York: Martin Kessler Books.

Kennedy, Catherine, and Suzanne Fitzpatrick. 2001. 'Begging, Rough Sleeping and Social Exclusion: Implications for Social Policy.' *Urban Studies* 38(11): 2001–16.

Keynes, John Maynard. 1927. *The End of Laissez-Faire.* London: Hogarth Press.

Klein, Annette. 2003. *Operating Budget – Final Estimates.* City of Vancouver Administrative Report, CC File no. 1605, 22 April 2003.

Kleinig, John. 1993. 'Policing the Homeless: An Ethical Dilemma.' *Journal of Social Distress and the Homeless* 2(4): 293–309.

Lee, Jeff. 2001. 'Police "Not Pursuing" Arrests for Possession of Hard Drugs: Vancouver Inspector Makes Revelation at Senate Hearing.' *The Vancouver Sun*, 19 November, B1.

Lee, Jeff. 2002. 'Landslide Trigger: West-Side Swing Vote: District of Both the Premier and Mayor-Elect Mirrors Outcome.' *The Vancouver Sun*, 19 November, B1.

Lee, Mario, and Bill Goddard. 2003. 'New Community Policing Centres Model.' *Vancouver City Council Administrative Report*, RTS no. 3466, C.C. File no. 3703, 18 June 2003.

Lelchuk, Ilene. 2002. 'Campaign 2002: S.F. Homeless Crisis Spills onto Ballot.' *The San Francisco Chronicle*, online edition. http://www.sfgate.com (accessed 15 January 2003).

Lelchuk, Ilene. 2003. 'Homeless Protest S.F. Fingerprinting Plan.' *The San Francisco Chronicle*, online edition. http://www.sfgate.com (accessed 18 March 2003).

Lelchuk, Ilene, and Julian Guthrie. 2002. 'S.F. Board OKs Ban on Public Urination: Unanimous Vote "Demonstrates We Live in a Civilized Society."' *The San Francisco Chronicle*, online edition. http://www.sfgate.com (accessed 15 January 2003).

Lloyd, Mike. 2001. 'Rough Sleepers Come in from the Cold.' BBC News online. http://www.bbc.com (accessed 31 March 2003).

Loader, Ian. 1999. 'Consumer Culture and the Commodification of Policing and Security.' *Sociology* 33(2): 373–92.

Lothian and Borders Police. 2001. *Lothian and Borders Police Strategic Aims 2001– 2004.* Internal report of the force.

Lothian and Borders Police. 2003a. Operation Capital website. http://www.operationcapital. com (accessed 27 July 2003) (now defunct).

Lothian and Borders Police. 2003b. *The Record, Public Performance Report 2002– 2003.* http://www.lbp.police.uk (accessed 29 October 2002).

Lothian and Borders Police press office. 2004. Personal communication to author.

Lothian and Borders Police website. 2003c. http://www.lbp.police.uk (accessed 29 October 2002; 19 September 2003).

Luba, Frank. 2003. 'Vancouver Given Green Light to Open First Safe-injection Site in North America.' *The Vancouver Province*, 25 June, A4.

Lyons, William. 1999. *The Politics of Community Policing: Rearranging the Power to Punish*. Ann Arbor: University of Michigan Press.

Macallair, Dan, and Khaled Taqi-Eddin. 1999. *Shattering 'Broken Windows': An Analysis of San Francisco's Alternative Crime Policies*. San Francisco: The Justice Policy Institute.

MacPherson, Donald. 2001. *A Framework for Action: A Four Pillar Approach to Drug Problems in Vancouver*. City of Vancouver report.

Maleshefski, Tiffany. 2003. 'Park Officials Hope to Stave Off Deep Cuts.' *The San Francisco Examiner*, online edition. http://www.sfexaminer.com (accessed 20 May 2003).

Manning, Peter. 1977. *Police Work: The Social Organization of Policing*. Cambridge, MA: MIT Press.

Manning, Peter. 1978. 'The Police: Mandate, Strategies, and Appearances.' In P. Manning and J. Van Maanen (eds), *Policing: A View from the Street*, 7–31. Santa Monica, CA: Goodyear Publishing.

Manning, Peter K. 2003. *Policing Contingencies*. Chicago: University of Chicago Press.

Marx, Karl. 1966 [1844]. *The Economic and Philosophic Manuscripts*. Edited by Dirk J. Struik. Translated by Martin Milligan. New York: International Publishers.

Mather, Adrian. 2003. 'Old Town Shops Call for Blitz on Drunks.' *Edinburgh Evening News*, online edition. http://news.scotsman.com (accessed 7 June 2003).

Mattier, Phillip, and Andrew Ross. 2002. 'S.F. Billboards Slap Handouts for Feeding Panhandlers' Vices: Hotel Council Says Giving to Beggars Fuels Drug Use, Venereal Disease.' *The San Francisco Chronicle*, online edition. http://www.sfgate.com (accessed 1 May 2004).

Mayor's Office on Homelessness (San Francisco). 2002. *2002 Homeless Count Report*. http://www.sfgov.ca.us (accessed 17 April 2004).

McDougall, Dan. 2002. 'Handouts to Heartbreak.' *Scotland on Sunday*. http://www.scotsman. com (accessed 31 March 2003).

McInnes, Craig. 2002. 'Fewer People Get Welfare: About 29,000 Have Gone off the Rolls in 12 Months.' *The Vancouver Sun*, 25 July, B7.

McKenna, Paul F. 1998. *Foundations of Policing in Canada*. Toronto: Prentice Hall.

McLaughlin, Eugene, and Karim Murji. 2001. 'Lost Connections and New

Directions: Neo-Liberalism, New Public Managerialism and the "Moderniza-
tion" of the British Police.' In K. Stenson and R. Sullivan (eds), *Crime, Risk
and Justice: The Politics of Crime Control in Liberal Democracies*, 104–22. Portland,
OR: Willan Publishing.

McLellan, Wendy. 2003. 'Parents, Trustees Want School Police Back to Full
Strength.' *The Vancouver Province*, 4 November, A11.

McNulty, Jim. 2002. 'Campbell Cuts Put Harris, Klein to Shame.' *The Vancouver
Province*, 20 January, A27.

McSheehy, William. 1979. *Skid Row*. Boston, MA: G.K. Hall and Co.

Miller, Ronald J. 1982. *The Demolition of Skid Row*. Lexington, MA: Lexington
Books.

Ministry of Human Resources (BC). 2002. *A New Era Update: 2001/02 Annual
Report.*

Ministry of Human Resources (BC) website. 2003. http://www.mhr.bc.gov.bc.ca
(accessed 24 January 2004).

Monaghan, Bernadette. 1997. 'Crime Prevention in Scotland.' *International
Journal of the Sociology of Law* 25(2): 21–44.

Mooney, Chris. 2003. 'More Homeless Given Roof over Their Heads.' *Edinburgh
Evening News*, online edition. http://news.scotsman.com (accessed 7 June
2003).

Morton, Brian. 2002. 'Chinatown Merchants Blast Addict Centre: Area Is Scary,
One Shop Owner Says.' *The Vancouver Sun*, 17 January, B7.

Murray, Charles. 1999. 'And Now for the Bad News.' *Society* 37(1): 12–16.

National Centre for Social Research. 1999. *Scottish Parliamentary Election Study*
(Scottish Social Attitudes Survey, 1999). Colchester, Essex: UK Data Archive.
June 2001. SN 4636.

Neocleous, Mark. 1998. 'Policing and Pin-Making: Adam Smith, Police and the
State of Prosperity.' *Policing and Society* 8(4): 425–49.

Nordberg, Maya. 2002. 'Jails Not Homes: Quality of Life on the Streets of San
Francisco.' *Hasting's Women's Law Journal* 13 (Summer): 261–315.

Obe, Don. 1960. 'Skid Road Aid Picks Pockets of Taxpayers, Expert Says.' *The
Vancouver Sun*, 2 December, 1, 2.

O'Connor, Brendan. 2002. 'Policies, Principles, and Polls: Bill Clinton's Third
Way Welfare Politics 1992–1996.' *Australian Journal of Politics and History* 48(3):
396–411.

Office of the Controller, City of San Francisco. 2002. 'Homeless Services: The
City Lacks Commonly Accepted Goals and an Effective Plan for Its Homeless
Services.' http://www.sfgov.org (accessed 29 April 2004).

Office of the Controller, City of San Francisco. 2003.'Police Department Budget
2002–03.' http://www.sfgov.org (accessed 22 May 2003).

O'Malley, Pat. 1992. 'Risk, Power and Crime Prevention.' *Economy and Society* 21(3): 252–75.

O'Malley, Pat, and Darren Palmer. 1996. 'Post-Keynesian Policing.' *Economy and Society* 25(2): 137–55.

One City (Edinburgh City Council). 2003. http://www.edinburgh.gov.uk (accessed 9 June 2003).

Parrish, David. 2002. 'Outdated Technology Compounds Cops' Woes: New Software Could Help S.F. Crime-Solving Record.' *The San Francisco Chronicle*, online edition. http://www.sfgate.com (accessed 1 May 2003).

Parrish, David, and Jaxon Van Derbeken. 2002. SFPD Dead Last at Solving Violent Crime.' *The San Francisco Chronicle*, online edition. http://www.sfgate .com (accessed 4 December 2003).

Passaro, Joanne. 1996. *The Unequal Homeless: Men on the Streets, Women in Their Place.* New York: Routledge.

Paterson, Lindsay, Alice Brown, John Curtice, Kerstin Hinds, David McCrone, Alison Park, Kerry Sproston, and Paula Surridge. 2001. *New Scotland, New Politics?* Edinburgh: Polygon.

Plotkin, Martha R., and Tony Narr. 1997. 'Police: The Forgotten Service Provider.' In Martin L. Forst (ed.), *The Police and the Homeless: Creating a Partnership between Law Enforcement and Social Service Agencies in the Development of Effective Policies and Programs*, 58–86. Springfield, IL: Charles C. Thomas.

Punch, Maurice. 1979. *Policing the Inner City: A Study of Amsterdam's Warmoesstraat.* London: Macmillan Press.

Reiner, Robert. 1992. *The Politics of the Police*, 2nd ed. Toronto: University of Toronto Press.

Rich, B., and D. LePard. 2003. '2003 Police Sworn Staffing Funding Request for the Downtown Eastside.' *Vancouver City Council Administrative Report*, RTS no. 03482, C.C. File no. 1376/8104, 27 June.

Roberts, Dorothy E. 1999. 'Foreword: Race, Vagueness, and the Social Meaning of Order-Maintenance Policing.' *Journal of Criminal Law and Criminology* 89(3): 775–837.

Robinson, Tony. 1995. 'Gentrification and Grassroots Resistance in San Francisco's Tenderloin.' *Urban Affairs Review* 30(4): 483–514.

Ropke, Wilhelm. 1987. *The Problem of Economic Order, Welfare Freedom and Inflation.* Edited by Johannes Overbeek. New York: University Press of America.

Rose, Nicholas. 1999. *Powers of Freedom: Reframing Political Thought.* Cambridge: Polity.

Rossi, Peter H. 1989. *Down and Out in America: The Origins of Homelessness.* Chicago: University of Chicago Press.

Rough Sleepers Initiative. 2003. *Monitoring the Target of Ending the Need to Sleep*

Rough by 2003. Report of the Scottish Executive. http://www.scotland.gov.uk (accessed 31 March 2004).

Rubenstein, Jonathan. 1978. 'Controlling People.' In P. Manning and J. Van Maanen (eds), *Policing: A View from the Street*, 255–65. Santa Monica, CA: Goodyear Publishing.

Ruddick, Sue. 2002. 'Metamorphosis Revisited: Restricting Discourses of Citizenship.' In Joe Hermer and Janet Mosher (eds), *Disorderly People: Law and the Politics of Exclusion*, 55–64. Halifax, NS: Fernwood Publishing.

Rustow, Alexander. 1980. *Freedom and Domination: A Historical Critique of Civilization*. Edited by Kankwart A. Rustow. Translated by Salvator Attanasio. Princeton, NJ: Princeton University Press.

Safety Awareness for Everyone (SAFE). Undated. 'How to Organize a SAFE Neighbourhood.' Brochure.

San Francisco Police Activities League (SFPAL). Undated. 'San Francisco Police Activities League.' Brochure.

San Francisco Police Department (SFPD) website. 2003. http://www.sfgov.org/police (accessed 15 May 2003).

San Francisco Police Officers Association (SFPOA). 2001. http://www.sfpoa.org (accessesd 1 November 2003).

San Francisco Rescue Mission. 2003. http://www.sf911.com (accessed 15 June 2003).

San Francisco SOS website. 2003. http://www.sfsos.org (accessed 10 June 2003).

Saskatoon Star-Phoenix. 2003. 'Most Junkies Too Paranoid to Use Safe Injection Site.' *Saskatoon Star-Phoenix*, 26 December, C5.

Saunders, Ralph. H. 1999. 'The Politics and Practice of Community Policing in Boston.' *Urban Geography* 20(5): 461–82.

Schrag, Peter. 1998. *Paradise Lost: California's Experience, America's Future*. New York: The New Press.

Scotland Office. 2002. Website of the Scottish Secretary (United Kingdom government). http://www.scottishsecretary.gov.uk (accessed 29 October 2002).

Scottish Advisory Committee on Drug Misuse. 2003. 'Mind the Gaps: Meeting the Needs of People with Co-occurring Substance Misuse and Mental Health Problems.' A Report of the Scottish Executive. http://www.scotland.gov.uk (accessed 21 March 2004).

Scottish Executive. 1999. 'Major Cash Boost for Rough Sleepers.' Press release. http://www.scotland.gov.uk (accessed 31 March 2003).

Scottish Executive. 2000. *The Way Forward: Framework for Economic Development in Scotland*. Edinburgh: Scottish Executive.

Scottish Executive. 2004. 'Corporate Action Plans.' Drug Misuse in Scotland website. http://drugmisuse.isdscotland.org (accessed 29 May 2004).

Scull, Andrew T. 1977. *Decarceration: Community Treatment and the Deviant – A Radical View.* Englewood Cliffs, NJ: Prentice Hall.

Shearing, Clifford D., and Philip C. Stenning. 1984. 'From the Panopticon to Disney World: The Development of Discipline.' In Anthony Doob and Edward Greenspan (eds), *Perspectives in Criminal Law.* Aurora, ON: Canada Law Book. Pp. 413–22.

Shearing, Clifford D., and Jeffrey S. Leon. 1992. 'Reconsidering the Police Role.' In Kevin R.E. McCormick and Livy A. Visano (eds), *Understanding Policing,* 209–28. Toronto: Canadian Scholars' Press.

Silver, Allan. 1992. 'The Demand for Order in Civil Society.' In Kevin R.E. McCormick and Livy Visano (eds), *Understanding Policing,* 57–82. Toronto: Canadian Scholars' Press.

Simmel, Georg. 1971 [1903]. 'Metropolis and Mental Life.' In D. Levine (ed.), *Georg Simmel on Individuality and Social Forms,* 324–39. Chicago: University of Chicago Press.

Skelton, Chad. 2004. 'B.C. Detox Bed Shortage Helps Spread HIV, Study Suggests: Addicts Who Try to Get Treatment and Fail Are More Likely to Share Needles.' *The Vancouver Sun,* 26 May, A1.

Skogan, Wesley G. 1990. *Disorder and Decline: Crime and the Spiral of Decay in American Neighborhoods.* New York: Free Press.

Skolnick, Jerome H. 1999. 'On Democratic Policing.' *Ideas in American Policing.* Police Foundation paper. August.

Smith, Adam. 1986 [1759]. 'The Theory of Moral Sentiments.' In Robert L. Heilbroner (ed.), *The Essential Adam Smith,* 57–148. New York: W.W. Norton.

Smith, Adam. 1986 [1766]. 'Lectures on Jurisprudence.' In Robert L. Heilbroner (ed.), *The Essential Adam Smith,* 37–56. New York: W.W. Norton.

Smith, Adam. 1986 [1776]. 'The Wealth of Nations.' In Robert L. Heilbroner (ed.), *The Essential Adam Smith,* 149–320. New York: W.W. Norton.

Smyth, Michael. 2001. 'Welfare No Longer a Free Ride, Coell Warns.' *The Vancouver Province,* 7 October, A3.

Smyth, Michael. 2003. 'Gordon Campbell's Liberals Continue to Lead a Charmed Life.' *The Vancouver Province,* 29 May, A6.

Special Joint Committee on 'Skid Road.' 1966. Meeting minutes, 22 August 1966. City of Vancouver archives, City Clerk files (series 20). Locn.: 79-C-5 (file 3).

Spencer, Kent. 2003. 'Taxes Hit Wallets Hard.' *The Vancouver Province,* 19 May, A3.

Spitzer, Steven. 1975. 'Towards a Marxian Theory of Deviance.' *Social Problems* 22: 641–75.

Spradley, James P. 1970. *You Owe Yourself a Drunk: An Ethnography of Urban Nomads*. Boston: Little, Brown.

Stein, Janice Gross. 2001. *The Cult of Efficiency*. Toronto: Anansi.

Stewart, Kennedy. 2003. 'Storming the Tower.' Vancouver's Voice (COPE) newsletter (Winter/Spring): 4–5.

Takser, Anne. 1992. *Profile of the Downtown Eastside: The People and the Place*. Report of the Downtown Eastside Economic Development Society.

Toch, Hans, and J. Douglas Grant. 1991. *Police as Problem Solvers*. New York: Plenum.

Trojanowicz, Robert, Victor E. Kappeler, Larry K. Gaines, and Bonnie Bucqueroux. 1998. *Community Policing: A Contemporary Perspective*, 2nd ed. Cincinnati, OH: Anderson Publishing.

Tryon, Pat. 1953. 'Salvation Army's "Harbour Light" Brings New Hope to Outcasts.' *The Vancouver Province*, 28 October, 13.

Turvey, John. 2000. 'Our Street, Monday Morning: An Insider's View from Vancouver's Downtown Eastside.' *The Vancouver Sun*, 19 September 2000, A13.

Vancouver Coastal Health Authority website. 2004. http://www.vch.ca (accessed 24 November 2004).

Vancouver Police Board. 2003. *Meeting Minutes*, 26 March.

Vancouver Police Department. 1977. *Annual Report*. City of Vancouver archives, Police Department fonds (PDS25).

Vancouver Police Department. 2003. *Annual Statistical Report 2002*. Vancouver: VPD.

Vancouver Province. 2003. 'What B.C.'s Budget Means to You.' *The Vancouver Province*, 19 February, A4.

Van Derbeken, Jaxon. 2003. 'Shakeup of S.F. Police Investigators: Teams Join Night Shift at District Stations.' *The San Francisco Chronicle*, online edition. http://www.sfgate.com (accessed 4 December 2003).

Van Derbeken, Jaxon, and David Parrish. 2002. '"A Wake-up Call": S.F. Police Chief Promises Changes after Report that Department Solves Only 28% of Violent Crime.' *The San Francisco Chronicle*, online edition. http://www.sfgate.com (accessed 9 May 2004).

Van Derbeken, Jaxon, and Bill Wallace. 2002. 'SFPD Still Lags in Solving Violent Crimes: Dismal Record Unchanged Despite Embarrassing Reports.' *The San Francisco Chronicle*, online edition. http://www.sfgate.com (accessed 4 December 2003).

Van de Water, Adam, Jesse Martinez, Gabriel Cabrera, Elaine Forbes, and Emily Gumper. 2002. 'Summary of 2000 City and County Census Data.' *Legislative Analyst Report*. File no. 012214. City of San Francisco, 26 February.

Van Maanen, John. 1978a. 'Kinsmen in Repose: Occupational Perspectives of Patrolmen.' In P. Manning and J. Van Maanen (eds), *Policing: A View from the Street*, 115–40. Santa Monica, CA: Goodyear Publishing.

Van Maanen, John. 1978b. 'The Asshole.' In P. Manning and J. Van Maanen (eds), *Policing: A View from the Street*, 221–37. Santa Monica, CA: Goodyear Publishing.

Wacquant, Loic. 2002. 'From Slavery to Mass Incarceration: Rethinking the "Race Question" in the U.S.' *New Left Review* 13 (January–February): 23–40.

Wacquant, Loic. 2003. 'Ghetto.' In Neil J. Smelser and Paul B. Baltes (eds), *International Encyclopedia of the Social and Behavioral Sciences*, 129–47. London: Pergamon Press.

Waddington, P.A.J. 1993. *Calling the Police Interpretation of, and Response to, Calls for Assistance from the Police*. Aldershot: Avebury.

Wallace, Samuel E. 1965. *Skid Row as a Way of Life*. New Jersey: Bedminster Press.

Ward, Doug. 2002. 'COPE Win Gives Liberals an Opposition.' *The Vancouver Sun*, 18 November, A7.

Wardhaugh, Julia. 1996. '"Homeless in Chinatown": Deviance and Social Control in Cardboard City.' *Sociology* 30(4): 701–16.

Waters, Rob, and Wade Hudson. 1998. 'The Tenderloin: What Makes a Neighborhood.' In James Brook, Chris Carlsson, and Nancy J. Peters (eds), *Reclaiming San Francisco: History, Politics, Culture*, 301–16. San Francisco: City Lights Books.

Weber, Max. 1991 [1904]. *The Protestant Ethic and the Spirit of Capitalism*. Translated by Talcott Parsons. London: Harper Collins.

Weber, Max. 1947 [1919]. *Theory of Social and Economic Organization*. Edited by Talcott Parsons. New York: Free Press.

Websdale, Neil. 2001. *Policing the Poor: From Slave Plantation to Public Housing*. Boston: Northeastern University Press.

Weir, Margaret. 1996. 'From Equal Opportunity to "The New Social Contract": Race and the Politics of the American "Underclass."' In Malcolm Cross and Michael Keith's (eds), *Racism: The City and the State*, 93–107. New York: Routledge.

Werner, Erica. 2003. 'Recall Could Be an Example for Nation.' *San Francisco Examiner*, online edition. http://www.sfexaminer.com (accessed 9 July 2003).

Wilson, James Q. 1968. *Varieties of Police Behavior: The Management of Law and Order in Eight Communities*. Cambridge, MA: Harvard University Press.

Wilson, James Q., and George L. Kelling. 1982. 'Broken Windows: The Police and Neighborhood Safety.' *Atlantic Monthly*, March, 29–38.

Wilson, William Julius. 1996. *When Work Disappears: The World of the New Urban Poor*. New York: Alfred A. Knopf.

Winokur, Scott. 1999. 'Thugs, Drugs and Shrugs.' *The San Francisco Chronicle*, online edition. http://www.sfgate.com (accessed 15 January 2003).

Wiseman, Jacqueline P. 1970. *Stations of the Lost: The Treatment of Skid Row Alcoholics*. Englewood Cliffs, NJ: Prentice Hall.

Yergin, Daniel, and Joseph Stanislaw. 2002. *The Commanding Heights: The Battle for the World Economy*. New York: Simon and Schuster.

Young, Cy. 1951. 'Skid Road.' *The Vancouver Sun Weekend Picture Magazine*, 1 December, 7–11.

Young, Jock. 1999. *The Exclusive Society: Social Exclusion, Crime and Difference in Late Modernity*. London: Sage.

Zoellner, Tom. 2000. 'Tough Duty: Gritty Tenderloin Force Will Soon Move Out of Basement Quarters.' *The San Francisco Chronicle*, online edition. http://www.sfgate.com (accessed 15 January 2003).

Zweig, Konrad. 1979. 'The Origins of the German Market Economy: The Leadings Ideas and Their Intellectual Roots.' *Paper of the Adam Smith Institute*. http://www.adamsmith.org (accessed 21 January 2004).

Index